CALLAS

As They Saw Her

CALLAS

 *As They Saw Her*

EDITED BY DAVID A. LOWE

The Ungar Publishing Company

New York

Design by Kay Lee

Library of Congress Cataloging-in-Publication Data

Callas, as they saw her.

Bibliography: p.
Discography: p.
1. Callas, Maria, 1923–1977—Criticism and interpretation. 2. Singers—Biography. I. Lowe, David Allan, 1948–
ML420.C18C35   1986   782.1'092'4   86-6898
ISBN 0-8044-5636-4

For the legions of admirers, present and future

Acknowledgments

The publisher and editor are grateful to the following individuals, periodicals, newspapers, and book publishers for permission to include selections from copyrighted material, as well as to owners of letters never before published. Every effort has been made to trace and acknowledge all copyright owners. If any acknowledgment has been inadvertently omitted, the necessary correction will be made in the next printing.

ABC (Madrid). From articles by Antonio Fernández-Cid in March 25, 1958, and May 3, 1959, issues.

Mrs. Thomas Howe Akin. From letters by Francis Robinson in the Francis Robinson Archives, Vanderbilt University.

American Record Guide (a publication of the Helen Dwight Reid Educational Foundation). From review by George Louis Mayer on *Medea* in August 1959 issue.

Atlanta Constitution. From review by Richard F. Gray in October 15, 1958, issue.

L'Avant-scène. From special issue on Callas, October 1982 (including photographs). Copyright © 1982 by *L'Avant-scène.*

Chicago Tribune. From "On the Aisle" by Claudia Cassidy in August 4, 1952, November 2, 16, 1954, November 12, 1955, July 9, November 26, December 4, 1956, January 15, May 3, 1957, January 23, 1958, issues; reviews by Thomas Willis in March 3, 1974, issue and Seymour Raven in November 9, 1954, issue.

Il Corriere della Sera. From reviews by F. Abbiati in June 10, 1951, April 3, July 20, December 8–9, December 27, 1952, December 11, 1953, January 10, April 13, December 8, 1954, January 20, February 17, May 22, 1956, May 20, 1958, December 12, 1961, issues.

Dallas Morning News. From reviews by John Rosenfield in November 7, 1958, November 1, November 7, 1959, issues.

Detroit Free Press. From review by Dorsey Callaghan in November 18, 1958, issue.

Doubleday & Co., Inc. From *My Life* by Tito Gobbi. Copyright © 1979 by Tito Gobbi and Ida Cook. Reprinted by permission of Doubleday & Co., Inc.

Madeleine Fagandini. Translation of "The Callas Debate" in September–October 1970 issue of *Opera.*

The Guardian. From review by Philip Hope-Wallace in January 22, 1964, issue.

High Fidelity. From reviews by Ronald Eyer in November 15, 1954, November 15, December 1, 1956, issues; by Solomon Kahan in September 1952 issue; by Martin Mayer in September 1954 issue; by Newell Jenkins in July, August 1951, March, May 1952 issues; by Robert Sabin in January 1, 1957, issue; by Howard Talley in November 15, 1955, issue of *Musical America.* All rights reserved.

Hutchinson Publishing Group (Australia). From *La Stupenda: A Biography of Joan Sutherland* by Brian Adams.

Kölnische Rundschau. From review by E. in July 6, 1957, issue.

Little, Brown and Company. From *The Noel Coward Diaries,* edited by Graham Payne and Sheridan Morley.

Stewart R. Manville. From review in January 1956 issue of Opera.

McDonald & Jane's. From *My Life* by Tito Gobbi.

Natalie Dauer Murray. From "Letter from Paris" by Genet (Janet Flanner) in June 13, 1964, issue of *The New Yorker.*

Music and Musicians. From review by Peter Hoffer in January 1953 issue.

Musical Times. From review by Andrew Porter in July 1964 issue.

The Nation. From review by Richard Dyer in March 23, 1974, issue.

The New York Times. From reviews by Peter Heyworth, Harold Schonberg, Howard Taubman. Copyright © 1951, 1955, 1956, 1957, 1959, 1965 by The New York Times Company. Reprinted by permission.

The New Yorker. From reviews by Winthrop Sargeant. Reprinted by permission. Copyright © 1956 and 1958, copyright duly renewed, The New Yorker Magazine, Inc.

Newsweek. From article in February 17, 1958, issue. Copyright © 1958 by Newsweek, Inc. All rights reserved.

The Observer. From reviews by Noel Goodwin in December 16, 1960, issue; by Peter Heyworth in June 22, 1968, issue; interview by Kenneth Harris in February 8 and February 15, 1970, issues.

Opera. From numerous reviews (see individual critics).

Opera News. From reviews by Fedele d'Amico in March 4, 1961, issue; G. F. in September 29, 1962, issue; John Freeman in March 16, 1953, issue; Trudy Goth in October 28, 1961, February 7, 1962 issues; Frank Granville Barker in March 11, 1957, October 3, 1959, issues; Robert Jacobson in December 4, 1982, issue; Cynthia Jolly in April 5, 1954, issue; Robert Lawrence in October 27, 1952, issue; Mary Ellis Peltz in September 26, 1964, issue; Signe Scanzoni in January

26, 1953, issue; Desmond Shawe-Taylor in March 21, 1964, issue; Ernest de Weerth in January 6, 1958; unsigned reviews in September 29, 1958, April 4, 1970, issues.

Andrew Porter. From reviews in July 1964 issue of *Musical Times*; July 1952 issue of *Opera*.

Giuseppe Pugliese. From review in August 1951 issue of *Opera*.

La Prensa (Buenos Aires). From reviews in May 2, June 18, 1949, issues. Seymour Raven. From review in *Chicago Tribune*.

Harold Rosenthal. From reviews in August 1958, February 1961, July 1963, March 1964, August 1964 issues of *Opera*; July 1964 issue of *Musical Times*.

St. Louis Post-Dispatch. From review by Thomas B. Sherman in January 12, 1959, issue.

San Francisco Examiner. From review by Alexander Fried in November 28, 1958, issue.

Saturday Review. From reviews by Everett Helm in January 17, 1959, issue; Irving Kolodin in November 13, 1954, November 10, December 1, December 22, 1956, February 22, March 15, 1958, February 14, July 11, 1959, issues. Copyright © 1954, 1956, 1958, 1959 by Saturday Review Magazine. Reprinted by permission.

Desmond Shawe-Taylor. From reviews in December 1955, April 1958 issues of *Opera*.

Scoop. From interview by Marlyse Schaeffer in *Elle*, No. 1219, April 28, 1969.

Le Soir. From review by L. V. in July 16, 1956, issue.

Der Tagesspiegel (Berlin). From articles by Werner Oehlmann in October 1, 1955, May 19, 1963, issues.

Time. From reviews in November 15, 1954, November 11, 1955, November 26, 1956, December 2, 1957, March 26, 1965 issues. Copyright © 1954, 1955, 1956, 1957, 1965 by Time, Inc. All rights reserved. Reprinted by permission from *Time*.

The Times Newspapers Limited. From reviews in June 5, June 16, June 27, 1953, February 4, August 7, 1957, June 11, 1958, July 15, 1959, November 27, 1973, issues of *The Times* (London). Copyright © 1953, 1957, 1958, 1959, 1973 by The Times Newspapers Limited.

John Warrack. From review in April 1962 issue of *Opera*.

Henry Wisneski. From translations of numerous reviews first published in *My Wife Maria Callas* by Giovanni Battista Meneghini, and in *Maria Callas: The Art behind the Legend* by Henry Wisneski.

Contents

≡ ⋇ ≡ ⋇ ≡ ⋇ ≡ ⋇ ≡ ⋇ ≡ ⋇ ≡

Preface

Callas: As They Saw Her owes its existence to Leonard Klein, a former editor at Ungar who invited me to use the special Callas issue of L'Avant-scène (October 1982) as the starting point for a similar collection of materials in English. The resulting volume in fact reproduces several of the essays and most of the photographs in the French publication, but I have added reviews, interviews, memoirs, and other documents, many of which have never before been available in English. The overall compositional principle is that of a mosaic, and although I am a nearly fanatical admirer of Callas's art, I have taken no special pains to suppress materials that do not flatter the great soprano. Nonetheless, I certainly hope that Callas: As They Saw Her leaves readers with the conviction that whatever her warts, Callas was one of the greatest operatic artists in history. Anyone who comes away with any other impression has not seen the forest for the trees.

Essays other than my own were originally published in L'Avant-scène, and unless otherwise indicated, translations from French and Italian are mine. Many individuals have contributed advice and support in the preparation of the book, but I owe a special debt of gratitude to Helena Goscilo, Brittain Smith, Ronald Meyer, the staff of Special Collections at the Jean and Alexander Heard Library (Vanderbilt University), and Leonard Klein, Edith Friedlander, and Rita Stein of The Ungar Publishing Company.

David A. Lowe
Vanderbilt University

Diva Assoluta: Life, Art, Legacy

≡∷≡∷≡∷≡∷≡∷≡ ∷≡∷≡∷≡

by David A. Lowe

The mystery of her art, the memory of her superb presence on stage, these are what remain—will always remain—of the life of Maria Callas. Others may probe the private Callas, ascribe the intensity of her performances to her early life in war-torn Greece, or link her mastery of the tragic mode to her abortive affair with Aristotle Onassis. The facts show that by the time she became involved with him her most compelling performances were already history. As an artist, Callas remains supreme. The secret of her art cannot be revealed by sifting through her private life.

Callas's life, nevertheless, exerts considerable fascination. A world-famous and wealthy diva suggests that her mother jump out the window if she cannot provide for herself. The most celebrated Norma of the second half of the century withdraws from a performance of the role after the first act, thereby creating an incident that acquires first national and then international dimensions. After ten years of marriage a seemingly devoted wife walks out on her husband and enters into a liaison with one of the wealthiest men in the world, only to have him abandon her and marry the widow of the thirty-fifth President of the United States. At the height of her powers, the most illustrious soprano of her time experiences a rapid vocal decline: within five years the voice is hardly recognizable, within a few more, utterly unusable. No one would deny the potency of this brew, and naturally the world devoured it all, and continues to do so.

A sober analysis of the existing published documents about Maria Callas's life—newspaper and magazine articles, interviews, tributes, memoirs, biographies—leads, however, to unexpected and paradoxical conclusions. The first is that a persuasive and revelatory intimate biography of Callas not only has not yet appeared, but is in fact an impossibility. The path taking us to the "real" Maria Callas, "the woman behind the legend," is essentially a pitch-dark tunnel clogged with immovable obstacles and ending in a cul-de-sac. Of the several biographers who pretend to lead their readers along that path, only Pierre-Jean Rémy comes close to admitting that, by comparison, Plato's cave is awash in brilliant sunlight.

Several reasons underlie the difficulties with a biography of Callas. The primary one is that the woman herself was ultimately inaccessible. People who thought they knew her well were always subject to rude awakenings, as her ex-husband's memoirs testify in their ineptly eloquent way. At best, Callas's friends and colleagues came to know certain aspects of her personality, but the total picture emerges as a jigsaw puzzle that can never be assembled because too many pieces were missing from the very beginning.

Callas's personality and private thoughts and actions are not the only puzzle here. Her life itself begins and ends in controversy. The very date of her birth is open to dispute. The circumstances surrounding her death, especially the identity of the person responsible for the funeral arrangements and the incident involving the temporary disappearance of the funeral urn, continue to fuel rumor and speculation.

The most noteworthy area of mystery lies in Callas's relations with people who at one time or another stood at the center of her existence: her mother, her husband, and Aristotle Onassis. When it comes to the whys and wherefores in any of these private dramas, the biographer can at best offer conjectures. Callas developed a monumental grudge against her mother and treated her in what certainly looks like a cruel fashion, but no psychological explanation for this attitude will ever be forthcoming. To judge by Meneghini's memoirs and what others have written about him, the man thoroughly lacked charm, taste, and intelligence. Yet Callas married him, and her letters to him demonstrate a genuine sense of attachment. A biographer with any degree of conscience would have to admit being perplexed. As for the topic "Callas and Onassis," it is sheer quicksand for anyone who would seek to understand what really happened there, on any level.

Callas thought of herself as a fighter (if not, indeed, a martyr) and additionally as someone for whom privacy was essential. To her horror and amazement, from the mid-1950s on, she found that she had to fight for her privacy. Although doubts may arise about whether certain of Callas's battles were fought anywhere other than in her imagination, the war she waged to maintain her privacy was excruciatingly and exhaustingly real. The debris on the battlefield—all those lethal headlines, poisonous gossip columns, and pestilential paperbacks—shows that, appearances to the contrary notwithstanding, Callas was stunningly victorious. Her privacy is largely intact—for all time.

Now, however, comes the second paradoxical conclusion about biographical studies of Callas. While much about her personality and private life eludes our grasping curiosity, there is still adequate evidence to show that the media created an image of Callas that relied more on fantasy than on fact. But it would be only a partial truth to claim that Callas was exclusively a victim of the media's maniacal attentions. After all, her status as a celebrity eventually created the conditions that allowed her to practice her art, largely on her own terms, at the end with considerably diminished resources, and often for record fees. On the last point Callas reportedly was quite firm: she really did not care about money as such, but it had to be more than anyone else received. From one point of view, then, Callas's reputation, as fabricated by the media and bought by the public, sold tickets, especially in the late 1950s and early 1960s, when people who could not distinguish Rossini from linguine rushed to the box office when appearances by Callas were announced. This side effect of the media's publicity was not exactly to Callas's disadvantage.

On a less mercenary plane, the media's version of Callas, which was both distorted and unflattering, did her a colossal disservice. Moreover, that image proved to be so potent and so enduring that even today it is a useful exercise to test the popular perception of the artist against the information that the press chose to ignore or play down. Results show that Callas's reputation outside the opera house had two primary sources: fairy tales and very trashy fiction.

The fairy tale that wandered from column to column, article to article, and book to book is "The Ugly Duckling." In this redaction, a fat, awkward, homely girl from New York waddled her way through life until 1954, when, as the consequence of a miraculous diet, she emerged a transformed creature—slim, chic, and beautiful. Some sources even produce "before" and "after" photos. The truth of the matter is more complex and considerably more interesting. Certainly the mature Callas recalled her younger and heavier self with dismay, and of course there is that infamous review of an *Aida* wherein the critic claimed not to be able to tell the soprano's legs from the elephant's. Other early reviews, however, note Callas's regal bearing, captivating presence, and yes, even visual allure. Meneghini found Callas an attractive woman from the very beginning. And Luchino Visconti, a much more reliable judge of such aesthetic matters, also thought her remarkably beautiful, at least on stage, even in her Junoesque period. The full story, however, is to be found in the photographs.

The myriad photographs of Callas argue that throughout her life she was capable of looking strikingly handsome or stunningly awful. Her Mediterranean features were volatile, as even her earliest baby picture suggests. The fact that Callas tended to photograph better after the weight loss had more to do with clothing, hair style, and makeup than with her figure. Clearly, Callas's own taste in areas outside music was questionable. Her teacher, Elvira de Hidalgo, at times despaired over her pupil's lame attempts to be stylish. At least one visitor to the Meneghini home, the interior decoration for which was Callas's work, found the place a little suggestive of a cheap bordello with pretensions to class. Some of the publicity photos from the mid-1950s show Callas burdened by a variety of ghastly earrings, all of them resembling bunches of crystallized bananas. Milanese who saw Callas on the street in the early 1950s recall pizzeria-waitress hair styles and vulgar, rhinestone-studded glasses.

At her best, however, and apparently only when she relied on the advice of others, Maria Callas manifested a dramatic beauty, and especially as she aged or, rather, defied age. The photographs of Callas as Norma in Paris (1964–65) are breathtaking, and the audiences at the concerts in 1973 and 1974 saw a woman whose looks and bearing would do credit to a goddess. There may well have been artifice there, but it was artifice yielding sublime results.

So much for "The Ugly Duckling" aspect of the Callas image. The rest of the media's portrayal was the stuff of low-brow novels about high society. In their so-called reporting on Callas the singer, the press and television treated the public to a fiery diva who chewed up colleagues along with the scenery, canceled performances out of malicious caprice, and made of herself a pariah in the leading opera houses of the world. Once again, the media's version was far from the truth. The facts are especially contradictory with regard to the cancellations and their consequences. In the case of the Rome *Norma* of 1957, the administration of the Rome Opera clearly acted irrationally in revoking Callas's contract after her refusal to continue beyond the first act in the first performance of what was to be a run of the opera. An artist was vocally indisposed on a single occasion, and *therefore* the administration refused to permit any subsequent appearances by her. Only if the Mad Hatter were in charge of things would this make any semblance of sense.

The press loved the uproar, naturally, and Callas made headlines all over the world. Such were the effects of this hurricane in a thimble that the San Francisco Opera, already prepared psychologically for another example of Callas's "scandalous behavior," not only balked at her request for a change in the provisions of her contract and performance schedule, but promptly called off the performances and then wanted to take Callas to court. In calm retrospect, then, with both Rome and San Francisco Callas hardly looks like an irresponsible artist. After Rome and San Francisco came the "Edinburgh affair," where a quite innocent Callas was virtually crucified for fulfilling her contractual obligations to the letter—in spite of poor physical and vocal health—but declining to take on an additional performance. As reported to the public, Callas's conduct had been unworthy of an artist but quite to be expected of an imperious and fickle prima donna.

The story involving the Metropolitan Opera, crucial details of which have only recently come to light, casts Callas in a much less blameless role. By the time that Rudolf Bing severed the Met's connections with Callas, the atmosphere in the press was so thick that everyone took sides. Some commentators felt that Callas's fussing over parts and dates would deprive any mortal of his last half-ounce of patience and that Bing's action was justified. Other voices howled for Bing's decapitation: Callas may have been impossible, they said, but she was also Callas, and the Met should have been willing to prostrate itself in order to retain her services.

Meneghini's memoirs show that those who would have sacrificed Bing to the tigress were morally in the wrong. Callas and her husband, more than satisfied with a very remunerative upcoming North American concert tour, wanted to escape Callas's contractual obligations at the Met; they achieved their goal by consciously writing Bing letters that they knew must sooner or later lead to Callas's dismissal. Meneghini's tone in relating this episode with the Met never so much as hints that he and Callas had any ethical qualms about what they were doing.

The incident with the Met, then, is a serious blemish on Callas's professional life, as is the whole ugly Bagarozy case. In 1947 she had signed a contract with the would-be impresario Edward Bagarozy, appointing him her sole agent for a period of ten years and granting him ten percent of all her fees. Callas then promptly voided the agreement in her own mind and, together with her husband, managed her own career. When Bagarozy later sued, Callas tried to paint herself a rosy, innocent pink, when in fact she had been caught red-handed in violation of a contract that she had signed of her own volition. The protracted wrangling with Bagarozy, however, did not involve the cancellation of any performances. Between 1965 and 1973 Callas withdrew from a number of announced projects, but on the whole she was extraordinarily conscientious about appearances. In Edinburgh and Paris she even went on the stage in contravention of her doctors' advice. Compared with some other operatic superstars of today and yesterday, Callas was the very model of reliability and professionalism. That the media could have portrayed her in any other light now seems utterly fantastic.

The press inflated Callas's few nonappearances out of all proportion, just as it did her tiffs with colleagues. The feud between Callas and Tebaldi was real enough, but the press only added fuel to the flames and largely ignored Tebaldi's own contributions to the conflagration. Di Stefano walked out on the Visconti-Giulini production of *Traviata*, vowing never to sing with Callas again. What led him to do that, however, was his unwillingness to take the production as seriously as Callas did and to invest the spirit and rehearsal time in it that she did. Di Stefano kept his inane vow for precisely four months, although the press did not rush to report that fact. Finally, there was Enzo Sordello, the baritone who attempted to upstage Callas at the Met by holding his high G longer than Callas did hers. He soon found himself on a plane back to Italy, never to be reengaged at the Met. The media wasted no time in making a martyr of him, but in fact, he had irritated a number of his colleagues, not just Callas.

In general, reviews, memoirs, and interviews describe Callas as a gracious colleague. Certainly her generosity was never put to a harder test than in the Paris *Normas* with Cossotto, who went out of her way to show up Callas's vocal deficiencies. Callas not only swallowed her pride but at curtain calls urged the audience on in its ovations for the Adalgisa. More importantly, and a fact to which no one has ever taken exception, Callas was a workhorse who asked only that colleagues bring as much dedication to rehearsals and performances as she did. Her fellow artists recall with a sort of awe the energy and preparation that Callas demonstrated at rehearsals, her willingness to repeat passages over and over—in full voice—and her indifference to clocks and appetites. She impressed de Hidalgo very early with her fanatical diligence, and she retained her highly disciplined work habits in the opera house through-out her life.

The media took no interest in reporting the high degree of profes-sionalism that Callas brought to the operatic stage and to her relations with colleagues. Instead, newspeople focused on a jet-setting, party-going diva with a scandalous love life. If one has any sympathy for Callas and gratitude for her art, one can only regret that the party with Onassis was so brief and the hangover so crushing. A woman who had intoxicated as many audiences as she did certainly deserved some cham-pagne herself. No one in the media really seemed to think or care about that.

By and large, the press and television made of Callas a figure of legend, but for all the wrong reasons. Reading through newspaper and magazine articles about Callas, not to mention certain memoirs and biographies, can be a disheartening experience on many counts. What is particularly infuriating, however, is that in the accumulated mass of verbiage it only occasionally emerges—and then often only between the lines—that the person under discussion was an artist of a supremacy that defies an adequate epithet. That is the ultimate insult to Callas in her media image: it invited people to forget that in the end, when the subject is Maria Callas, the only thing really worth talking about is her immortal art.

.   .   .

Any discussion of Maria Callas's artistry must begin with her voice. The standard bromide, which turns up in everything from tributes to encyclopedia entries, holds that the Callas voice was never truly beautiful in and of itself, but that Callas made of it an exquisitely expressive instrument. This commonplace, like the notion that Callas suddenly turned into a beautiful woman in 1954, demands scrutiny. It is incomprehensible, for instance, how one could describe the voice heard in the Mexico City *Aidas* or the Berlin *Lucia* as anything other than ravishing. The critics who wrote about those performances confirm that impression. There is also Tito Gobbi, who declares in his memoirs that in the 1951 São Paulo *Traviata* he heard Callas produce sounds of a lushness such as one hears only once in a lifetime. Or one might point to Richard Bonynge, who in an interview included in the present volume exults over the dark splendor of Callas's voice in the early London *Normas*.

No one would claim that Callas's voice was consistently velvety. Throughout most of her career it displayed unsettling fluctuations in tone, size, and security. By the 1960s Callas regularly produced sounds in the upper register that would make even the most steadfast admirer cringe. As for the 1973–74 tour, well, Callas was guilty of the kind of wailing that can give opera a bad name. Attempts to analyze the causes of the deterioration are pointless, however. There are as many theories on the origins of the universe as there are on the mechanics of the singing voice.

Callas's voice invites comparison with her looks. In both cases examples of great beauty can be pointed out at almost any stage in Callas's adult life. The relationship is, however, one of inverse proportion. Callas herself aged well, but her voice, alas, did not. At its best it had an opulence that would understandably cause a Scarpia to forget God, even while other listeners might be moved, conversely, to light candles.

Nature endowed Callas with a voice, but the technique that embellished it was the product of years of arduous study and labor. Many reviewers and commentators have argued that the technique was somewhat faulty from the very beginning. The most widespread reproach in this regard concerns the uneven registers, Callas's "three voices." People forget, however, that the much-vaunted ideal of equalized registers is a fairly recent one. Many of the sopranos and mezzos from opera's so-called Golden Age, i.e., those who were documented by the newly born recording industry, shift vocal gears so emphatically that Swiss yodeling comes to mind. Even as late as the 1940s, mezzo stars of the Metropolitan Opera swooped hootily into and out of the chest register—such was the style of the age. In retrospect, then, Callas's way of handling her registers, as with so many other aspects of her art, represents an anachronism, but a grand one, and one that does not violate any immutable criteria of vocal taste, because there are none.

Callas in fact made a virtue of her distinct registers, especially the chest voice, the likes of which had not been heard in a soprano since Rosa Ponselle. In role after role and aria after aria Callas was able to work wonders with phrases that lie too low for most sopranos to make any impression with. And even Rosa Ponselle could not produce the pitch-black coloration in Gioconda's "Suicidio" with which Callas stuns the listener.

The question of register equalization aside, the splendor of Callas's technique—when she was in peak form—is there for all to hear. The range was enormous, from low F-sharp to E in alt. Early reviews and some reference works even mention top F, but there is no evidence that she went above E in performance—not that this is a crucial matter, in any event. Throughout that extensive range Callas was capable of every sort of modulation. Admirers still swoon over the sheer decibel count of the E-flat that Callas interpolated in the Mexico City Aïdas, while a review of the 1950 performances of Il Turco in Italia describes the same note, this time sung pianissimo. As for diminuendo, Callas used that technical resource in Norma's "Son io" and elsewhere to break listeners' hearts.

The most obviously impressive side to Callas's technique was the agility. Recordings of Rossini's Armida, Proch's "Variations," and individual arias such as "Ombre légère" or "The Bell Song" testify that in matters of trills, staccati, chromatic scales, and rapid passage-work of all sorts, other singers might equal Callas, but they could not better her. The agility was all the more dramatic because of the size of Callas's voice. Here was a veritable foghorn producing effects normally associated only with flutes and piccolos. The initial shock that audiences received was akin to what certain male ballet dancers provoke: astonishment that such size and power can be combined with grace and nimbleness. Callas regularly performed similar miracles.

Ultimately, the most remarkable aspect of Callas's technical proficiency was her legato. Even though she lacked the sort of pianissimi granted to Milanov or Caballé, thanks to her legato Callas was able to spin phrases that seem oblivious to the law of gravity. "Deh ti placa" in *Lucia* recalls the delicacy of a butterfly, and the soprano's verse of "Verrano a te" from the same opera rises and falls with the effortlessness and otherworldliness of a free-floating astronaut. What especially distinguished Callas's legato was the sense of tenuousness that accompanied it, the fear that Callas was walking a tightrope without a net beneath, the disbelief that the line could long be maintained. Callas's legato singing was not of the sort that could ever lull one; on the contrary, it kept one at the edge of his seat. As recordings show, because of her sublime legato, Callas could still work her special magic even when the top notes turned sour and coloratura passages fizzled. By the time of the last concert tour, however, Callas no longer commanded legato singing, the foundation of her art, and at that point Callas's vocal resources were definitely spent.

To a beautiful, expressive voice enhanced by a phenomenal technique Callas brought a superior musical intelligence that was grounded in knowledge. She was an excellent pianist. Moreover, Giulini alleges that Callas knew the score of *Traviata* better than he did. Since she was a first-class musician, she understood the importance of rhythmic accuracy, for instance, one of the hallmarks of her art that even today is not always recognized. A brilliant example of the effects that such accuracy can produce occurs in the studio recording of *Trovatore*. There, in the last-act exchange with an indignant Manrico, Callas emits Leonora's excited interjections with a fierce rhythmic precision that highlights a passage which in most performances seem but an opportunity for the tenor to rest.

Allied to Callas's musical intelligence was her instinct. Her ability to sing with accuracy of rhythm and intonation was no doubt learned, but the source of her uncanny way with phrasing and rubato evades any rational explanation. The interplay between intelligence and instinct, training and talent, often led to phrasing that may haunt the memory forever. As Callas sang Violetta's "Dite alla giovine," for instance, she always made an infinitesimal pause before the word "pura," because of its emotional associations for the courtesan. The result is subtle rubato within an overall pattern of strict rhythmic precision, a Dionysian moment within an Apollonian framework. Intelligence and training can lay the necessary groundwork for that sort of musicianship, but without instinct and intuition Callas could not have scaled the heights that she did.

Callas's resources, obviously, were considerable: a beautiful voice, marvelous technique, superior musicianship, and acute instincts. The uniqueness of her art, though, lies in how she applied those resources to the interpretation of words and music. Indeed, with Callas it is impossible to divorce the words she sang from the way she sang them. Because interpretation for Callas was such an all-embracing concept, she was able—in her best moments—to make everything she sang sound new and fresh. The effect of Callas's artistry was surprise, but the kind of surprise that in hindsight acquires a certain inevitability. A single note and a single word—Lucia's despairing "Ah!" after she reads the forged letter—could take on a significance that in the pre-Callas era would have seemed impossible. It was not just notes and phrases that Callas cast into a seemingly new light, however, but entire roles, along with the composers responsible for them. Thanks to Callas, for instance, Donizetti's position in the history of opera had to be reevaluated, and Bellini emerged an even greater master than many had supposed.

Finally, of course, with Callas there was that very special something for which no adequate term exists, but for which "intensity" will have to do. Something leaps out at the listener when Callas performs, demanding one-hundred-percent attention. The voice takes on its own presence, an explicitly dramatic one. In fact, as stupendous as Callas's acting was, as evocative as the photographs are, they only confirm what is already implicit in her singing. Multitudes of Callas's admirers no doubt regret—achingly, bitterly—that they did not have the chance to see her on the operatic stage, but in a very real sense that regret is needless, because Callas's singing—again, at its best—conveys exactly what must have or would have transpired on stage.

How did she do it? That is perhaps the greatest of the Callas enigmas. Katia Ricciarelli once remarked, incidentally, that sopranos who claim not to listen to Callas's recording are not to be believed. All sopranos, said Ricciarelli, get up in the morning, pour the orange juice and coffee, and then settle down to listen to Callas's recordings and try to learn from them. And in the end, that is all one can do—listen and *try* to understand the "how" of Callas's art, because as with all geniuses, the ultimate secret of her magic remains inexplicable.

Callas's legacy is multifaceted. Among other things, her talents and her status as a celebrity combined to resurrect the epithet and figure of the diva. Not since the nineteenth century, the age of Malibran, Pasta, and Viardot, had an opera singer acquired a renown that extended far beyond a relatively small circle of opera aficionados. Probably even against her own wishes, Callas made the diva a larger-than-life personage whose acclaim permeated all levels of society and culture. In so doing, Callas elevated the status of all opera singers.

She also created a new esteem for opera itself, especially Italian opera. It is easy to forget the general contempt with which arbiters of taste held Bellini, Donizetti, Rossini, and even—or perhaps especially—Verdi in the pre-Callas era. Francis Toye's admirable study of Verdi, for instance, is essentially an apology for his art. The London *Times* critic who reviewed Callas's early *Normas* at Covent Garden suggested that it was worth rehearing Bellini from time to time in order to be reminded of how banal his music was. True, the Germans had initiated a Verdi revival in the 1930s, but not until the 1950s—the peak of Callas's career—did a general and favorable reevaluation of Verdi and his most gifted Italian predecessors get under way. If the pleiad of Italian operatic composers of the nineteenth century earns hosannas in even the most desiccated academic circles today, Callas had something to do with that.

It would be a mistake, however, to claim—as many do—that Callas revived an entire repertory. In fact, none of the long-dormant operas mounted specifically for her has become anything like a standard offering in the world's lyric theaters. What she did resuscitate, or more accurately, provoke, was serious curiosity about forgotten works of the nineteenth and eighteenth centuries, in that order. That curiosity has led to concert performances, recordings, and sometimes even fully staged productions of what the twentieth century perceives as rarities: operas by Donizetti, Rossini, Bellini, Verdi, and many others. By now, conductors, singers, and stage directors are happily excavating scores not just from the Golden Age of Italian opera, but from all periods and all national schools. Callas paved the way for such explorations, and all operaphiles are in her debt.

In the area of performance per se, Callas raised standards by raising the audience's expectations. She was hardly the first singer, of course, to prove that opera and drama were not mutually exclusive categories. Earlier in the century Fyodor Chaliapin and Mary Garden had thrilled audiences with the power of their dramatic art as well as or even in spite of their vocal endowments. Throughout the history of human thought and activity, however, it has often fallen to a genius to remind people of the obvious. Such was the case with Callas. She forced people to reconsider the very nature of opera as one of the performing arts. Unfortunately, it cannot be claimed that the operatic stage has never been the same since Callas trod its boards. No, placid cows and oxen still sometimes wander on to graze in between and even during arias, but by and large, few of today's singers are content to ignore the dramatic side of the whole operation. If no one quite achieves Callas's synthesis of stagecraft and bel canto, that is because Callas was Callas, after all. Still, the number of genuine singing actors and actresses seems to be growing, and once again, this is in part Callas's doing.

Callas also forced the operatic world to alter its thinking about vocal categories for the female voice. That Callas simply erased them, as many commentators argue, is rather an oversimplification. No one expects a small-voiced soprano who excels, say, as Susanna, to board the ship carrying Tristan and Isolde to Cornwall, unless the prospect of watching the soprano suffer the fate of the *Titanic* is for some perverse reason attractive. Callas did not prove that sopranos can sing anything written for the female voice. What she in fact demonstrated was that a large soprano voice can develop impressive agility and a bold extension in the upper range and as a consequence can adapt itself to virtually any part. That was Callas's real lesson, one that happily was not lost on Joan Sutherland. At the outset, of course, some listeners found the combination of size, agility, and adaptability odd and even unpleasant. Here one is reminded of the example of Katharine Hepburn, after whose film debut people wondered why on earth she talked the way she did. Before long, though, people were asking why everyone didn't talk the way Hepburn did. The situation with Callas was similar, and in short time audiences were having difficulty erasing Callas's voice from their memories when they heard other sopranos essay "her" roles.

Along the way Callas made herself immortal, and thanks to her recorded legacy—her lasting gift to music lovers—Callas's fame continues to grow, and her art continues to attract worshipers. In this regard it is worth taking the example of the Soviet Union, where Callas never performed and where only very recently have a precious few of her recordings been offered on the open market. Yet not only is her name one of the first to arise in any discussion with Moscow's opera lovers, but all her recordings, including the pirated ones, circulate from hand to hand and are privately tape recorded. The video tapes are there, too. One would almost think that magic were involved here, and at bottom, in fact, it is—the Callas magic, that spellbinding artistry that, thank God, has been preserved on recordings and will continue to challenge conventional assumptions and to captivate listeners for generations to come.

Callas's Career in Reviews, 1938–1974

≡≡×≡×≡×≡×≡×≡×≡×≡×≡×≡×≡ ×≡×≡×≡

EDITOR'S NOTE: *The performance annals forming the core of this section were compiled by Sergio Segalini and originally published in his* Callas: Les images d'une voix *(Paris, 1979). They have been updated, however, to reflect recent discoveries documented in Polyvios Marchand's* Maria Callas *(Athens, 1983) and discussed in detail by John Ardoin in "Callas: The Early Years,"* The Opera Quarterly, *III, 2 (1985), pp. 6–13. All translations are by the editor unless otherwise indicated.*

1938

Student Concert, Parnassos Hall, Athens; 11 April. Program: "Leise, leise," *Der Freischütz*; aria from *La Reine de Saba* (Gounod); song, "Two Nights," by John Psaroudas; duet from *Tosca*, with Zanni Kambani.

1939

Cavalleria Rusticana, Olympia Theater, Athens; 2 April.
Student Concert; 22 May. Program: "Barcarolle," *Les Contes d'Hoffmann*, with Anita Bourdakou; "Ocean, Thou Mighty Monster," *Oberon*; "Ritorna vincitor," *Aida*; song, "I Will Not Forget You," by Psaroudas; "O terra addio," *Aida*, with Zanni Kambani.
Student Concert, 23 May. Program: "Ocean, Thou Mighty Monster," *Oberon*; "Dis-moi que je suis belle," *Thaïs*.

Student Concert, 25 June. Program: excerpts from *Un Ballo in Maschera*, Act 3; excerpts from *Cavalleria Rusticana*.

1940
Concert, 23 February. Program: "Mira, o Norma," *Norma*, with Arda Mandikian.

Concert, Athens Radio; 3 April. Duets from *Norma*, *Aida*, *La Gioconda*, with Arda Mandikian.

Concert, Athens Conservatory; 30 June. Program: *Suor Angelica*.

1941
Boccaccio, Royal Theater; 21 January. Also 3 July.

1942
Tosca, Royal Theater, Athens; 27 August, 8 September; Vasilakis; Delenda, Kalogeras/Xirellis.

All the mistakes, all the weaknesses of the stage direction are forgotten when Maria Kalogeropoulos appears, a young girl, still nearly a child. . . . She not only sustains the role without failings and sings it correctly, but she is capable at the same time of performing it with a conviction that in many places overwhelms the audience. The voice is full, over the entire range of the long register. No matter what the value of the training that she has received, it seems to me that she has something else too: the musical instinct in the highest degree and the dramatic sense are gifts that could not have been given to her in the classroom, and especially not at her age: she was born with them. It is not at all surprising, then, that she was able to transport the audience in that way!

Alexandra Lalaouni, *Vradyni*

Concert, Salonika; October.

1943
The Master Builder (Kalomiras), Royal Theater, Athens; 19 February.

Charity Benefit Concert; Athens; 28 February.

Concert; Athens Radio; 22 April. Program: *Stabat Mater* (Pergolesi), with Arda Mandikian.

Tosca, Royal Theater; 17 July.

Concert, Kosta Moussouri Theater, Athens; 21 July. Program: "Care selve," *Atalanta* (Handel); "Nacqui all'affanno," *Cenerentola*; arias from *Adriana Lecouvreur* and *Trovatore*; song, "They Are Marrying Off My Love" (Lavda); song, "Kimitri" (Palantio).

Solo Recital, Salonika; September. Program: songs by Schubert and Brahms; "Salce," *Otello* (Rossini); "Inflammatus," *Stabat Mater* (Rossini).

Concert, Olympia Theater; 26 September. Program: "Abscheulicher!" from *Fidelio*; "Dis-moi que je suis belle," *Thaïs*; "Ritorna vincitor," *Aida*; "Et incarnatus est," Mozart's Mass in C Minor; song, "Canzone spagnola" (Turina); song, "They Are Marrying Off My Love" (Lavda).

Benefit Concert, Athens; 12 December. Program: "Abscheulicher!" from *Fidelio*; "Bel raggio," *Semiramide*; aria from *Trovatore*; song by Turina.

1944

Tiefland, Olympia Theater, Athens; 22, 23, 30 April, 4, 7, 10 May; Doras; Delenda, Mangliveras.

Maria Kalogeropoulos was a Martha of earthy naturalness. What other singers must learn, she possesses by nature: the dramatic instinct, the intensity of her acting, and the freedom of her interpretation. Her voice at the top displays a penetrating metallic power and in quiet moments she knows how to reveal all the colors of her precious youthful and innately musical soprano voice.

Friedrich W. Herzog,
Deutsche Nachrichten in Griechenland,
translated by Henry Wisneski

Cavalleria Rusticana, Olympia Theater, Athens; May; Karalivanos; Delenda, Tsoumbris.

Maria Kalogeropoulos was a Santuzza of impulsive temperament. Her dramatic soprano voice showed itself to be both effortless and sensitive in a broad, sweeping operatic manner in which the "tears in the voice" were also not lacking.

Friedrich W. Herzog,
Deutsche Nachrichten in Griechenland,
translated by Henry Wisneski

Benefit Concert, Olympia Theater, Athens; 21 May. Program: "Casta diva," *Norma*.

The Master Builder, Herodes Atticus, Athens; 29, 30 July; Kalomiras; Remoundos, Mangliveras.

Fidelio, Herodes Atticus, Athens; 14, 19 August; Hörner; Delenda, Mangliveras, Moulas, Kokolios.

Recital, Salonika; October.

1945

Tiefland, Royal Theater, Athens; 14 March.

Concert, Athens; 20 March. Program: "Dido's Lament," *Dido and Aeneas*; song cycle *On Wenlock Edge* (Vaughan Williams); songs "Willow-Willow" (anon.), "Love, I Have Won You" (Ronald), "Think Not Strange" (Nimey and Jornay).

Concert, Athens; 3 August. Program: "Bel raggio," *Semiramide*; aria from *Don Giovanni*; arias from *Aida* and *Trovatore*; "Ocean, Thou Mighty Monster," *Oberon*; Spanish and Greek songs.

Der Bettelstudent (Millöcker), Royal Theater, Athens; 5 September.

1947

La Gioconda, Arena, Verona; 2, 5, 10, 14, 17 August; Serafin; Nicolai, Canali, Tucker, Tagliabue, Rossi-Lemeni.

The two American singers who performed the two leading roles, soprano Maria Callas and tenor Richard Tucker, showed themselves the possessors of excellent vocal means and were much applauded. . . .

Corriere della Sera

Tristan und Isolde, La Fenice, Venice; 30 December, 3, 8, 11 January; Serafin; Barbieri, Tasso, Torres, Christoff.

1948

Turandot, La Fenice, Venice; 29, 31 January, 3, 8, 10 February; Sanzogno; Rizzieri, Soler, Carmassi.

Turandot, Teatro Puccini, Udine; 11, 14 March; de Fabritiis; Ottani, Soler, Maionica.

La Forza del Destino, Politeama Rossetti, Trieste; 17, 20, 21, 25 April; Serpo; Canali, Vertecchi, Franci, Siepi, Parenti.

Maria Callas has a penetrating voice, not always of the loveliest timbre, but noteworthy for its security and power.

La Voce Libera, translated by Henry Wisneski

Maria Callas proved herself to be a first-rate actress, thoroughly prepared and secure in her top register.

Il Lavoratore, translated by Henry Wisneski

Tristan und Isolde, Grattacielo, Genoa; 12, 14, 16 May; Serafin; Nicolai, Lorenz, Torres, Rossi-Lemeni.

Noble, almost solemn, superb queen and passionate lover, her Isolde was one of the great interpretations. Her magnificent figure brought to the part an added appeal and irresistible grandeur. But the greatest fascination, the most moving quality was that projected by her voice, a majestic, splendid instrument, vibrant and warm, smooth and equalized in every register—the ideal voice for an Isolde.

Beppe Broselli, Corriere del Popolo, translated by Henry Wisneski

Turandot, Baths of Caracalla, Rome; 4, 6, 11 July; De Fabritiis; Montanari, Masini, Flamini.

[Maria Callas] has a large, penetrating voice, well schooled and expressive, at least as far as one can judge in the inhuman part of Turandot. She has excellent diction and a most remarkable dramatic sense. She embodied the cruel Chinese princess with a sensibility, art, and intelligence truly out of the ordinary.

Il Messaggero, translated by Henry Wisneski

Turandot, Arena, Verona; 27 July, 1, 5, 9 August; Votto; Rizzieri/ Tognoli/De Cecco, Salvarezza, Rossi-Lemeni.

Turandot, Carlo Felice, Genoa; 11, 14 August; Questa; Montanari, del Monaco, Salvarezza, Maionica.

Aida, Lirico, Turin; 18, 19, 23, 25 September; Serafin; Nicolai/Colasanti, Turrini, de Falchi.

Aida, Sociale, Rovigo; 19, 21, 24 October; Berretoni; Pirazzini, Turrini, Viaro.

Turandot, Pisa; between 13 and 21 November; de Ruggero; Campagno.

Norma, Comunale, Florence; 30 November, 5 December; Serafin; Barbieri, Picchi, Siepi.

Maria Callas found in the title role the fulfillment of her significant dramatico-musical gifts. She persuaded one with her considerable intelligence and impressive display of her vocal ability, which is especially evident in the gracefulness and harmonious balance of the melodic phrases. This young artist is already versed in the most demanding traditions of Italian bel canto.

Virgilio Doplicher, Il Nuovo Corriere,
translated by Henry Wisneski

Maria Callas was new to us, but after her entrance in the first act, we were immediately aware of finding ourselves in the presence of a soprano of truly significant ability. She has a powerful voice, one that is steady and attractive in timbre, penetrating in loud passages, and sweet in the more delicate moments. Her technique is secure and perfectly controlled. Her voice has an unusual color, and her schooling—although rather different from what we are accustomed to hearing—has its undeniable merits. Callas has created an interpretation rich in subtle and touching accents of femininity. She offers in *Norma*, besides the implacable priestess of the last act, the woman in love and then betrayed, the mother, and the friend.

Gualtiero Frangini, La Nazione,
translated by Henry Wisneski

1949

Die Walküre, Fenice, Venice; 8, 12, 14, 16 January; Serafin; Magnoni, Pini, Voyer, Torres, Dominici.

Maria Callas was a Brünnhilde of genuine Wagnerian spirit, forceful and touching, simple and incisive, with a splendid voice and power in the high passages and in the declamation. Visually she was superb.

Giuseppe Pugliese, Il Gazzettino, translated by Henry Wisneski

Callas was perfect: it is unlikely that one will soon hear a comparable Brünnhilde.

Vardanega, Gazzettino-Sera,
translated by Henry Wisneski

I Puritani, Fenice, Venice; 19, 22, 23 January; Serafin; Pirino, Savarese, Christoff.

But the most surprising triumph was that of Callas, who offered an unforgettable Elvira. From the heavy roles of Turandot and Brünnhilde burst forth an agile creature, sensitive, vital in every note, who breathes melody filtered through a superior intelligence.

Vardanega, Gazzettino-Sera,
translated by Henry Wisneski

A few days ago many were startled to read that our magnificent Brünnhilde, Isolde, and Turandot would interpret Elvira. Last evening everyone had an opportunity to hear her Elvira. Even the most skeptical—aware from the first notes that she was not the standard light soprano of tradition—had to acknowledge the miracle that Maria Callas accomplished, in large part due to the rigors of her early vocal studies with de Hidalgo (perhaps the greatest Rosina and Elvira of her time), the flexibility of her limpid, beautifully poised voice, and her splendid high notes. Her interpretation also has a humanity, warmth, and expressiveness that one would search for in vain in the fragile, pellucid coldness of other Elviras.

Mario Nordio, translated by Henry Wisneski

Die Walküre, Massimo, Palermo; 28 January, 10 February; Molinari-Pradelli; Magnoni, Sani, Voyer, Neri, Carmassi.

Turandot, San Carlo, Naples; 12, 16, 18, 20 February; Perlea; Montanari, Gigli, Petri.

Maria Callas is a most unusual singer. In softer passages her voice is beautiful and insinuating, yet her high notes are metallic and piercing. She has a nightmarish upper extension—awesome, sinister, inexorable.

Mario Baccaro, Roma, translated by Henry Wisneski

Parsifal, Opera, Rome; 26 February, 2, 5, 8 March; Serafin; Beirer, Cortis, Siepi.

Maria Callas, in fact, in a part among the most difficult whether from the vocal point of view or from that of stagecraft, revealed a strong and vivid temperament and a voice that triumphed over all difficulties.

F. L. Lunghi, Il Giornale d'Italia

Maria Callas was a magnificent Kundry. She seemed to us today a more polished singer. This soprano, who has security of vocal production, marvellous equalization of registers, and a fine upper extension, victoriously overcame every difficulty. She also knows how to personify most effectively the fascinating and tormented figure of Kundry, the sinner longing for redemption.

Adriano Bellin, Il Quotidiano,
translated by Henry Wisneski

Concert, RAI, Turin; 7 March; Molinari-Pradelli. Program: "Liebestod," *Tristan und Isolde*; "Casta diva," *Norma*; "Qui la voce," *I Puritani*; "O patria mia," *Aïda.*

Turandot, Colón, Buenos Aires; 20, 29 May, 11, 22 June; Serafin; Arizmendi, del Monaco, Zanin/Rossi-Lemini.

The role of the protagonist was taken by a singer new to our public, the Greek soprano Maria Callas, who as an actress made an expressive Turandot and who sang her part, one of extreme difficulty, with a voice that we shall evaluate on another occasion because the nervousness of a performance and a slight vocal indisposition did not permit one to hear her in the fullness of her means, although one could appreciate her middle voice and the facility of her upper register.

La Prensa

Norma, Colón, Buenos Aires; 17, 19, 25, 29 June; Serafin; Barbieri, Vela, Rossi-Lemeni.

The soprano Maria Callas undertook the role of Norma, much more in accordance with her vocal endowment than that of the protagonist of Turandot, in which she was presented before our public. As an actress she achieved a vigorous and human dramatic interpretation, and from the point of view of her voice she stood out in "Casta diva," which she sang with a delicacy and fine musical sense and had skillful moments in the rest of her part.

La Prensa

Aïda, Colón, Buenos Aires; 2 July; Serafin; Barbieri, Vela, Damiani, Rossi-Lemeni.

Concert, Colón, Buenos Aires; 9 July; Serafin. Program: "Casta diva," *Norma*; Act III of *Turandot*, with Arizmendi, del Monaco, Rossi-Lemeni.

San Giovanni Battista (oratorio by Alessandro Stradella); Church of San
   Pietro, Perugia; 18 September; Santini; Corsi, Pirazzini, Berdini,
   Siepi.
Concert, Verona; 31 October. Program: "Casta diva," *Norma*; "Lie-
   bestod," *Tristan und Isolde*; "Qui la voce," *Puritani*; "Shadow Song,"
   Dinorah; "Ah! fors'è lui," *La Traviata*.
Nabucco; San Carlo, Naples; 20, 22, 27 December; Gui; Pini, Sinim-
   berghi, Bechi, Neroni.

Maria Callas, considered to be one of the most highly gifted dramatic sopranos today, interpreted the difficult role of Abigaille with
impressive mobility of accent. The dramatic situation, besides offering
a display of vocal fireworks, was also revealed through the force and
incisiveness of her temperament. Her splendid voice, smoothly produced
throughout its wide range, was equal to all of the requirements of the
part, including the most difficult florid passages.

Alfredo Parente, *Il Risorgimento*,
translated by Henry Wisneski

Maria Callas once again impressed us with her vocal gifts, developed through vigorous training, and displayed in Act III and in Abigaille's death scene an uncommon dramatic flair. She astonished with
both the size and the range of her voice, which combines the power of
a dramatic soprano and the high notes of a light soprano.

A. Procida, *Il Giornale*,
translated by Henry Wisneski

Concert, RAI, 24 November. Program: *Tosca*, Act 2; *Manon Lescaut*,
   Act 4; with Campagnano; Baroni conducting.

1950

Norma, Fenice, Venice; 13, 15, 19 January; Votto; Nicolai, Penno,
   Pasero.

Callas knew how to project the complex, intimate drama of the
protagonist with passion and an extraordinary musical abandon. Norma's lofty pride, fiery indignation, and pangs of love were captured by
her in moments of the greatest musical beauty. She lavished her voice
upon that wealth of trills, phrases, and melodies with a prodigiousness

that is extraordinarily rare, and she achieved excellent results at the same time.

Giuseppe Pugliese, Il Gazzettino,
translated by Henry Wisneski

Aida, Teatro Grande, Brescia; 2, 7, February; Erede; Pini, del Monaco, Protti.

Tristan und Isolde, Opera, Rome; 6, 9, 19, 25, 28 February; Serafin; Nicolai, Seider, Franci, Neri/Nerone.

Certainly they are artists, wholly or almost wholly admirable and admired, beginning with Callas, who has recently exhibited in *Puritani* and *Norma* the artistry of a very intelligent singer, capable of giving a risky breadth and height to her voice. She is an Isolde who sometimes, by virtue of a doubtlessly laudable restraint, pauses in statuesque attitudes, in classical (or neoclassical) gestures, but who feels and who at times makes us feel the enchantment of the most memorable parts of the opera.

Vice, Il Giornale d'Italia

Norma, Opera, Rome; 23, 26 February, 2, 4, 7 March; Serafin; Stignani, Massini, Neri/Cassinelli.

Many times we have praised the particular and unlimited vocal possibilities of Maria Callas, especially in the upper register, and her expressive temperament: it does not seem to us, however, that such a voice and such a character suit the stylistic needs of *Norma*, which especially in its recitatives requires a vocal consistency at the center that the intelligent and excited accentuation of the word cannot supply.

I. F. I., Il Giornale d'Italia

Concert, RAI, Turin; 13 March; Simonetto. Program: "Ocean! Thou mighty monster," *Oberon*; "Ah, fors'è lui," *La Traviata*; "D'amor sull'ali rosee," *Il Trovatore*; "Ombra leggera," *Dinorah*.

Norma, Massimo Bellini, Catania; 16, 19, 22, 25 March; Berrettoni; Gardino, Picchi, Stefanoni.

Aida, La Scala, Milan; 2, 5, 18 April; Capuana; Barbieri, del Monaco, de Falchi/Protti.

On stage the title role was sung by Maria Meneghini Callas, whom we were hearing for the first time, and whom we admired very much for the dark timbre and intensity of her voice, her most uncommon musicality, her always alert stage presence, and the nobility of her phrasing.

Il Tempo di Milano, translated by Henry Wisneski

I did not care for Maria Callas, who although she has been singing for a while, is new to La Scala. She obviously possesses temperament and a fine musicality, but her scale is uneven. She seems to improvise differently, from note to note, the method and technique of her vocal production. She does not have clear diction and she also forces her high notes, thereby jeopardizing the security of her intonation.

Corriere Lombardo, translated by Henry Wisneski

Aida, San Carlo, Naples; 27, 30 April, 2, 4 May; Serafin; Stignani, Picchi, Savarese.
Norma, Palacio de Bellas Artes, Mexico City; 23, 27 May; Picco; Simionato, Baum, Moscona.

Maria Callas, the dramatic soprano who made her first appearance in Mexico in the principal role, did not leave the public with the impression they hoped for. She is without a doubt a good actress, she has an imposing presence, and her school of singing is one that can easily cope with the greatest difficulties. But the timbre of her voice is very uneven and does not always fulfill to the requirements of profound delight.

H. F. Sánchez, *El Universal*, translated by David Herren

Maria Callas is undoubtedly an extraordinary singer. The public has not even had time to evaluate her, and nonetheless, the feeling of being confronted with such an exceptional voice was in the air.

It has been a long time—we believe since Raisa—since a soprano in such a class has been heard in Mexico; and in Maria Callas we meet not only her remarkable extended range, but also the special color, the perfect agility, and the volume necessary for enabling us to say that in the Greek soprano there exists the quality of pure gold.

Mariano Paes, *Excelsior*, translated by David Herren

Maria Meneghini Callas is, as a matter of fact, a supreme soprano who sings the very high notes, and even staccatos, of a coloratura, as well as very low notes appropriate not even to a mezzo, but to an authentic contralto. What an admirable extension of the voice. We were enchanted, and if anything saddened us at the conclusion of such a glorious performance, it was that we would never again hear another such *Norma* in our life.

Junius, *Excelsior*

Aida, Palacio de Bellas Artes, Mexico City; 30 May, 3, 15 June; Picco; Simionato, Baum/Filippeschi, Weede.

Don Antonio Caraza Campos, who has been directing the National Opera with such success for five years, tells us that while he was examining the score with Maria Callas, he told her that the high E-flat had not been heard here since the distant times of the great Angela Peralta . . . and according to him he heard Maestro Guichenné suggest to Callas that she perform the heroic deed. She resisted doing it, but finally agreed to do it during Saturday's performance. In the heat of the moment, at the conclusion of the great "concertante," this woman's vocal organ rose to the most glorious heights, leaving us literally "knocked out." Nevertheless, I do not think that all her merit lies in virtuosity of that class; she played her role with such authority, such refinement, such feeling, such musicality, that whatever objections certain critics have made about her middle register disappear before her more important merits. Clearly no voice without defects exists (perfection is not of this world); but in the case of Callas, that same strange quality helped us to capture better the exotic sense of the Ethiopian slave.

Mariano Paes, *Excelsior,* translated by David Herren

In *Aida*, as in *Norma*, her triumph was complete—even greater. From her first aria, "Ritorna vincitor," the audience was moved. It followed her through the whole aria until the final limpid, brilliant point; initially she adopted the attitude of submissive slavery, but when she started to sing she began to grow and to move, as if she were remembering that she was also a princess of her court in Ethiopia (just as she is the queen of singers). The first applause exploded, enthusiastic and prolonged. The audience came to understand that it had found a rara avis among singers, one of exceptional qualities that merit calling her . . . a "soprano assoluta"—such were the ovations.

J. L. Tapia, El Universal, translated by David Herren

Tosca, Palacio de Bellas Artes, Mexico City; 8, 10 June; Mugnai; Filippeschi, Weede.

Il Trovatore, Palacio de Bellas Artes, Mexico City; 20, 24, 27 June; Picco; Simionato, Baum, Warren/Petroff, Moscona.

Tosca, Teatro Nuovo, Salsomaggiore; 22 September; Questa; Pelizzoni, Inghilleri.

Tosca, Duse, Bologna; 24 September; Questa; Turrini, Azzolini.

Aida, Opera, Rome; 2 October; Bellezza; Stignani, Picchi, de Falchi, Neri.

Tosca, Teatro Verdi, Pisa; 7, 8 October; Santarelli; Masini, Polli.

Il Turco in Italia, Eliseo, Rome; 19, 22, 25, 29 October; Gavazzeni; Canali, Valletti, Stabile.

Maria Callas was the surprise of the evening in that she sang a soprano leggiera role with the utmost ease in what one imagines was the style adopted by sopranos at the time this work was composed, making it extremely difficult to believe that she can be the perfect interpreter of both Turandot and Isolde. In Act I she astounded everyone in the theater by emitting a perfectly pitched high and soft E flat at the end of an extremely attractive and vocally difficult aria. . . .

T. de Beneducci, Opera

Parsifal, RAI, Rome; 20, 21 November; Gui; Baldelli, Panerai, Christoff, Pagliughi.

1951

La Traviata, Comunale, Florence; 14, 16, 20 January; Serafin; Albanese, Mascherini.

Il Trovatore, San Carlo, Naples; 27, 30 January, 1 February; Serafin; Elmo, Lauri-Volpi/Vertecchi, Silveri, Tajo.

Norma, Massimo, Palermo; 15, 20 February; Ghione; Nicolai, Gavarini, Neri.

Aida, Comunale, Reggio Calabre; 28 February; del Cupolo; Pirazzini, Soler, Manca-Serra.

Concert, RAI, Turin; 12 March; Wolf-Ferrari. Program: "Ecco l'orrido campo," *Un Ballo in Maschera*; "Io son Titania," *Mignon*; "Leise, leise," *Der Freischütz*; Proch's "Variations."

La Traviata, Massimo, Cagliari; 14, 18 March; Molinari-Pradelli; Campora, Polli.

Concert, Teatro Verdi, Trieste; 21 April; La Rosa Parodi. Program: "Casta diva," *Norma*; "Qui la voce," *I Puritani*; "O patria mia," *Aida*; "Ah, fors'è lui," *La Traviata*.

I Vespri Siciliani, Comunale, Florence; 26, 30, May, 2, 5, June; Kleiber; Kokolios-Bardi, Mascherini, Christoff.

She was I believe not at all well at the time of the first performance but all the same there was an assurance and a tragic bravura about her singing that was frequently thrilling. . . . Her dramatic flair was very much in evidence in the smooth cavatina and exhortatory cabaletta with which she roused the Sicilians against the French in Act I, and the smouldering fury of "Il vostro fato è in vostra man" was extraordinarily vivid. At this performance, her voice showed a tendency to lose quality in the forte passages (apart from a ringing top E at the end of the "Bolero"), but her soft singing in the duets of Act II and IV was exquisite, and the long and crystal-clear chromatic scale with which she ended her Act IV solo made a most brilliant effect.

Giuseppe Pugliese, Opera

Miss Callas is certainly among the best singers on the opera stage in Europe today, and a fine actress as well. Although she was suffering from a cold, she gave a memorable performance. One perhaps could have desired a bit more urgency in the last act; but since the act began after one o'clock in the morning, and came to an end shortly before two, any audible tiredness in her voice could readily be excused.

Newell Jenkins, Musical America

Though Callas had not yet sung and was not even wearing her costume, one was straight away impressed by the natural dignity of her carriage, the air of quiet, innate authority which went with every movement. The French order her to sing for their entertainment, and mezza voce she starts a song, a slow cantabile melody; there is as completely control over the music as there had been over the stage. The song is a ballad, but it ends with the words "Il vostro fato è in vostra man"

(Your fate is in your own hands), delivered with concentrated meaning. The phrase is repeated with even more intensity, and suddenly the music becomes a cabaletta of electrifying force; the singer peals forth arpeggios and top notes and the French only wake up to the fact that they have permitted a patriotic demonstration under their very noses once it is under way. It was a completely convincing operatic moment, and Callas held the listeners in the palm of her hand to produce a tension that was almost unbearable until exhilaratingly released in the cabaletta.

Harold Rosenthal, *Opera*

Orfeo ed Euridice, 9, 10 June; La Pergola, Florence; Kleiber; Tygesen, Christoff.

The Euridice of Maria Meneghini Callas had more to do with the *Sicilian Vespers*, heard several nights earlier, than with the classic style of Haydn. Her voice was rich and beautiful, but was often uneven and sometimes tired. Certainly the role was too heavy for her; but she sang the death aria in the second act with rare insight and fine phrasing.

Newell Jenkins, *Musical America*

Both the strong Maria Meneghini Callas and the extremely agile Juliana Farkas, but especially the latter, pitilessly forced to forms of vocalism that were used at one time and are no longer used . . . had good fun re-creating the stage movement appropriate for the mythological action.

Franco Abbiati, *Corriere della Sera*

Maria Meneghini Callas distinguished herself as Euridice. . . . She has full control of voice in soft singing, and she did coloratura passages with delicacy and accuracy. It was said here that she is an exceptional Norma, and one could well believe it on the evidence of her Euridice.

Howard Taubman, *The New York Times*

Concert, Grand Hotel, Florence; 11 June; Bartoletti (piano). Program: "Casta diva," *Norma*; "Ombra leggera," *Dinorah*; "O patria mia," *Aida*; Proch's "Variations," "Ah, fors'è lui," *La Traviata*.

Well fitted for the "heavy" roles, she seems just as much at home in the role of Titania in *Mignon* or Dinorah in Meyerbeer's opera. . . .

Her high E's and F's are taken full voice, and there seemed no feat which she could not achieve. The audience including many American singers and Rudolf Bing cheered her efforts.

Rock Ferris, *Musical Courier*

Aida, Palacio de Bellas Artes, Mexico City; 3, 7, 10 July; de Fabritiis; Dominguez, del Monaco, Taddei.
Concert, Radio Mexico; 15 July; de Fabritiis. Program: "Pace, pace," *La Forza del Destino*; "Morrò, ma prima in grazia," *Un Ballo in Maschera*.
La Traviata, Palacio de Bellas Artes, Mexico City; 17, 19, 21, 22 July; de Fabritiis; Valetti, Taddei/Morelli.

God wanted to lavish his gifts on Maria: she is a beauty of majestic and distinguished comportment; she has the maximum degree of grace for acting, elegance for dressing, and temperament for attracting and moving, and, above all, a voice for singing. And what a voice! But the voice seems not that of one soprano but of three or four: such is the variety of her notes, from the tiniest thread of emission to the most resonant fortissimo. How well justified is the title "soprano assoluta!"

Junius, *Excelsior*

It would be useless to try to discuss in print each facet of the vocal and stage control; one has to hear her, to see her, to experience her, in order to be able to believe that such a decidedly dramatic voice achieves the perfection of a coloratura in its greatest expression, and in those passages whose difficulty makes almost all the lyric sopranos fail, Maria achieves the incredible in precision, intonation, and beauty; one must hear her in order to be enraptured by the velvet of her middle voice with which she sings the second act, in order to feel the drama of the third, and in order to be driven mad by the profundity of the fourth, in which she achieves an emotional line by means of authentic pianissimos that dignify and crown her incomparable interpretation.

Mariano Paes, *Excelsior*

Norma, Municipal, São Paulo; 7 September; Serafin; Barbieri, Picchi, Rossi-Lemeni.
La Traviata, Municipal, São Paulo; 9 September; Serafin; di Stefano, Gobbi.

Norma, Municipal, Rio de Janeiro; 12, 16 September; Votto; Nicolai, Picchi, Christoff.

Concert, Municipal, Rio de Janeiro. Program: "Ah fors'è lui," *La Traviata*; "O patria mia," *Aida*.

Tosca, Municipal, Rio de Janeiro; 24 September; Votto; Poggi, Silveri.

La Traviata, Municipal, Rio de Janeiro; 28, 30 September; Gaioni; Possi, Salsedo.

La Traviata, Teatro Donizetti, Bergamo; 20, 23 October; Giulini; Prandelli, Fabbri.

Norma, Massimo Bellini, Catania; 3, 6, 17, 20 November; Ghione; Simionato, Penno, Christoff/Wolovski.

I Puritani, Massimo Bellini, Catania; 8, 11, 13, 16 November; Wolf-Ferrari; Wenkow, Tagliabue, Christoff.

Maria Callas has repeated the feat, not unusual in former times, but today almost astonishing, of interpreting two Bellini operas which require two different sopranos. Thanks to the enormous range of her voice and the precious technical devices that allow her to sing with absolute ease of emission, the exceptional soprano demonstrated last evening, in the difficult part of Elvira, the marvelous vocal resources at her disposal.

Franco Pastura, Giornale dell'Isola,
translated by Henry Wisneski

I Vespri Siciliani, La Scala, Milan; 7, 9, 12, 16, 19, 27 December, 3 January; de Sabata/Quadri; Conley, Mascherini, Christoff/Modesti.

The miraculous throat of Maria Meneghini Callas did not have to fear the demands of the opera, with the prodigious extension of her tones and their phosphorescent beauty, especially in the low and middle registers, and with her technical agility, which is more than rare—it is unique.

Franco Abbiati, Il Corriere della Sera,
translated by Henry Wisneski

La Traviata, Regio, Parma; 29 December; de Fabritiis; Pola, Savarese.

1952

I Puritani, Comunale, Florence; 9, 11 January; Serafin; Conley, Tagliabue, Rossi-Lemeni.

This opera must be superlatively sung in order to be bearable, but the performance was a sensation. One can only deal in superlatives in describing Miss Callas's singing—her velvet tone, her exciting phrasing, her hair-raising coloratura, her stage presence, her majesty of bearing, her fine acting. At the end of each act a phenomenon occurred such as I have not witnessed in any Italian opera house or concert hall since the return of Toscanini to La Scala after the war. The audience shouted, stamped, and rushed forward to clamor for Miss Callas in curtain call after curtain call. The orchestra, inured to singers of all types and nationalities, stood in the pit applauding as vociferously as the audience.

Newell Jenkins, *Musical America*

Norma, La Scala, Milan; 16, 19, 23, 27, 29 January, 2, 7, 10 February, 14 April; Ghione; Stignani, Penno, Rossi-Lemeni.

The importance of this performance lay in the consummate artistry of Miss Callas, who is not only Italy's finest dramatic-lyric soprano but also an actress of exceptional gifts and stage presence. She electrified the audience by her very presence even before singing a note. Once she began to sing, each phrase came out effortlessly, and the listeners knew from the first tone of a phrase that she felt instinctively as well as consciously just where and how that phrase would end. She never rushed and she never dragged. Her tones came out round and full, with a legato like that of a stringed instrument. Her agility was breathtaking. Hers is not a light voice, but she negotiated the most difficult coloratura without batting an eye, and her downward glissandi made cold shivers run up and down the hearer's spine. There was occasionally a slight tendency to shrillness and hardness on the high notes, although her pitch was faultless. It is to be hoped that this defect resulted from fatigue, for it would be sad to hear so superb an instrument lose any of its sheen.

Newell Jenkins, *Musical America*

Concert, Circolo della Stampa, Milan; 8 February. Program: "Ah! fors'è lui," *La Traviata*; Bellini aria. Tonini, accompanist.
Concert, RAI, Rome; 18 February; de Fabritiis. Program: "Vieni t'affretta," *Macbeth*; "Ardon gli incensi," *Lucia di Lammermoor*; "Ben io t'invenni," *Nabucco*; "Dov'è l'indiana bruna," *Lakmé*.
La Traviata, Massimo Bellini, Catania; 12, 14, 16 March; Molinari-Pradelli; Campora, Mascherini.

Die Entführung aus dem Serail, La Scala, Milan; 2, 5, 7, 9 April; Perlea;
 Menotti/Duval, Munteanu, Prandelli, Baccaloni.

For the performance, La Scala found in Maria Meneghini Callas
a secure, exceptionally agile, and vibrant interpreter for the difficult
part of Constanza.

Franco Abbiati, Corriere della Sera

She dominated the stage in a memorable interpretation of Constanza: a tremendously difficult role because of the tessitura and perilous
acrobatism of the running passages, which she attacked and conquered
with a vocal virtuosity that earned her unanimous admiration and clam-
orous ovations.

Mario Quaglia, Corriere del Teatro,
translated by Henry Wisneski

Maria Callas scored yet another triumph in the part of Constanza,
which even though it was completely different from the heavier spinto
parts she has been singing at La Scala lately was rendered with delicacy
and feeling, reaching a climax in the difficult aria during the second
act.

Peter Dragadze, Opera

Armida, Comunale, Florence; 26, 29, April, 4 May; Serafin; Albanese,
 Ziliani, Salvarezza, Filippeschi, Raimondi.

Where are such roulades, such trills, runs, leaps, such speed and
fireworks demanded of the singer? One can readily believe that no one
today save Maria Callas, undisputedly the finest woman singer on the
Italian stage, could possibly negotiate the incredibly difficult part and
make it sound like music.

Newell Jenkins, Musical America

It is possible to feel that phrases beneath the florid passages are far
too much overlaid with ornament; but it was impossible to regret it
when Maria Callas was singing them. This American-born Greek soprano . . . deserves fully the considerable reputation she has won, for
she must be one of the most exciting singers on the stage today. Her
presence is imperious, her coloratura not piping and pretty, but powerful
and dramatic. It must be noted that a nasty edge crept into the tone

from time to time; but when she sailed up to a two-octave chromatic scale and cascaded down again (in "D'amore al dolce impero," the aria from the second act) the effect was electrifying. Her brilliance continually startled and delighted, throughout the opera. But whenever tenderness and sensuous charm were required, she was less moving. This seems to be her present limitation; it may well disappear quite soon.

Andrew Porter, Opera

I Puritani, Opera, Rome; 2, 6, 11 May; Santini; Lauri-Volpi/Pirino, Silveri, Neri.

As for Maria Callas, one can only speak of a personal triumph. Without the slightest sign of fatigue from dividing her time between Florence and Rome, there in the enchantments of Armida, and here in the passions of Elvira, she demonstrated not only the agility, extension, and "four voices" which are contained in her throat, but also a rich and vibrant interpretation, the likes of which we have never heard from her.

Giorgio Vigolo, Il Mondo,
translated by Henry Wisneski

Puritani has as its star Maria Callas, who between whiles rushed off to Florence to carry out her formidable assignment in Rossini's *Armida*. This all-purpose soprano, a prototype of the legendary singers of old, makes a buxom Elvira who is vaguely disconcerted when she has no virtuoso flights in view. Her tone is not uniformly beautiful but the general impression is overpowering. Her bel canto style is liable to sudden bursts and protuberances which disappear entirely in passages of agility, so that her descending scales are like rippling water. Add to this her proudly confident sense of the stage and you have one of the singing heroines of the 20th century.

Cynthia Jolly, Opera

I Puritani, Palacio de Bellas Artes, Mexico City; 29, 31 May; Picco; di Stefano, Campolonghi, Silva.
La Traviata, Palacio de Bellas Artes, Mexico City; 3, 7 June; Mugnai; di Stefano, Campolonghi.
Lucia di Lammermoor, Palacio de Bellas Artes, Mexico City; 10, 14, 26 June; Picco; di Stefano, Campolonghi, Silva.

Rigoletto, Palacio de Bellas Artes, Mexico City; 17, 21 June; Mugnai;
  Garcia, di Stefano, Campolonghi, Ruffino.

As an anti-climax came a pedestrian performance of *Rigoletto*, for
Mr. Campolonghi, the jester, was neither vocally nor histrionically up
to Verdi's demands. Mr. di Stefano's Duke, far from outstanding, and
Miss Callas's Gilda, not an ideal role for her, did not improve the
situation.

Solomon Kahan, Musical America

Tosca, Palacio de Bellas Artes, Mexico City; 28 June, 1 July; Picco; di
  Stefano, Campolonghi.

Not in a long time has any one singer stirred so much controversy
as Miss Callas. One faction—the management of the Opera Nacional
and a generous segment of the Mexico City musical press—hails her
as a kind of deity. . . . Another group, whose opinions are more prev-
alent in the lobby of the Bellas Artes than in the press, finds the lady
over-rated. There seems to be no middle ground. . . .

There seems to be no general admiration, even among the strongest
Callas fans, for the basic timbre of the voice. It is her method, her
virtuosity that commands plaudits; and the current debate centers around
the extent of this virtuosity. As to communicative power, her interpretations are intelligently planned, sincerely carried out, but—
perhaps—lacking in spontaneity. Great emotional summits, such as the
"Amami, Alfredo" of *Traviata*, miss the expressive impact. Miss Callas
is at her best in archaic pieces like *Puritani*, which demand her marvelously equalized scales and superb control of the legato line. She is
less successful in standard repertory.

Robert Lawrence, Opera News

La Gioconda, Arena, Verona; 19, 23 July; Votto; Nicolai, Canali, Poggi,
  Inghilleri, Tajo.

[The melodies] relied on two of the most artistically mature and
ample voices of our lyric theater: the voices of Maria Meneghini Callas,
the protagonist, and of the tenor Gianni Poggi. . . .

Franco Abbiati, Corriere della Sera

She is young, pleasant to look at, her black hair is dyed Titian red
to keep from wearing a Gioconda wig in midsummer. She has three

voices, a truly beautiful mezza voce of opulence and warmth, some faked, rather hollow chest tones, and a puzzling top voice.

They tell me she sings high E and F in dazzling coloratura, and it may be that to do this she has sacrificed her dramatic tones. For her Gioconda had trouble with high C, which was wobbly, forced, and shrill. The report is that she will not sing the role again. That would be wise, for she has neither the voice nor the ardent personality to bring it to life.

Claudia Cassidy, Chicago Tribune

La Traviata, Arena, Verona; 2, 5, 10, 14 August; Molinari-Pradelli; Campora, Mascherini.

Hearing Callas sing Violetta was an unforgettable experience. Her acting technique is of the simplest and she appears to make no effort to dramatize the situation physically, as the color of her voice depicts every emotion and sensation she is experiencing. The difficult "E strano" was sung with such amazing ease and lack of effort, that one had the impression that she could go on singing indefinitely without losing the strength and perfect line of her voice.

Peter Dragadze, Opera

Norma, Covent Garden, London; 8, 10, 13, 18, 20 November; Gui/ Pritchard; Stignani, Picchi, Vaghi, Sutherland.

Callas' fioriture were fabulous. The chromatic glissandi held no terrors for her in the cadenza at the end of "Casta diva." Nor did the superhuman leap from middle F to a forte high G. One of the most stunning moments came at the end of the stretta to the Act two trio, when she held for twelve beats a stupendous, free high D. From this point onwards, Callas held her audience in abject slavery. She rewarded them by never letting them down, and by reaching a peak of eloquence in the infinitely moving closing scene of the opera.

Cecil Smith, Opera

To sing "Casta diva" (one of the most trying arias) before one has time to warm up is an unenviable task, and there was a slight sense of disappointment, but this was speedily removed in the succeeding acts. In these, she displayed a voice of sheerest beauty from top to bottom of her register, a cantilena of exquisite line, and compelling dramatic power, especially in the recitatives. She moves on the stage with ease, and has the poise, dignity, and dramatic insight of a fine classic actress.

Arthur Notcutt, Musical Courier

In the title office, Maria Callas revealed her varied gifts to full advantage. She possesses uncommon beauty of tone in well controlled legato and piano, while in bravura passages she supplies both voice and technique necessary to keep the music from becoming choppy. In place of agitated hysteria or theatrical exaggeration, she displayed at all times a firm, majestic mastery both of Norma's music and of her emotional problems. . . . Perhaps the main cause of discussion as to her greatness, and the one which causes people to think her overrated, is a fairly frequent lapse into a masked tone in the middle register, which at times makes her sound as if singing with a mouthful of hot marbles. This feature appears not to be guided by any dramatic or musical purpose, and is consequently hard to explain.

John Freeman, Opera News

Concert, Italian Embassy, London; 17 November. Program: arias.
Macbeth, La Scala, Milan; 7, 9, 11, 14, 17 December; de Sabata; Penno,
    Mascherini, Tajo/Modesti.
    Callas was not in her best voice and at one point was even whistled at.

Peter Hoffer, Music and Musicians

Maria Meneghini Callas bestowed on the satanic character of Lady Macbeth the rare gifts of a crystal-clear voice of astonishing range.

Mario Quaglia, Corriere del Teatro,
translated by Henry Wisneski

We saw Maria Meneghini Callas as a Lady Macbeth whose vocal cords apparently must have been granted some extra strength which gives this voice an almost inhuman quality. Without the slightest attempt to act the part, Callas won success and disapproval in the true Italian manner.

Signe Scanzoni, Opera News

Callas gave her part the depth and feeling that only she now can give to such a dramatic role, with a truly heart-rending climax to the sleepwalking scene.

Peter Dragadze, Opera

Signora Maria Meneghini Callas alternately had satisfactory moments and others less so, as is her wont. She, in particular, did not find that expression of nobility without which one does not have a Lady Macbeth.

Rubens Tedeschi, Unità, translated by Henry Wisneski

Perhaps no other opera can be considered as tailor-made for Callas as *Macbeth*, for which Verdi turned down a soprano with a lovely voice in order to use another, Barbieri-Nini, who was a great actress capable of emitting "diabolical" sounds (according to the adjective in one of Verdi's own letters). This should have been remembered by those two or three who, with prearranged whistles, tried to harass the singer after the great sleepwalking scene, thereby transforming what would have been enthusiastic applause into a triumphant, interminable ovation.

Teodoro Celli, Corriere Lombardo,
translated by Henry Wisneski

La Gioconda, La Scala, Milan; 26, 28, 30 December, 1, 3 January, 19 February; Votto; Stignani, Danieli, di Stefano, Tagliabue, Tajo/Modesti.

And there was, no less dazzling in glories and merits [than di Stefano], but slightly diminished by the too much that she is bestowing upon operatic audiences, a Gioconda equally passionate and delicate, Maria Meneghini Callas.

Franco Abbiati, Corriere della Sera

1953

La Traviata, La Fenice, Venice; 8, 10 January; Questa; Albanese, Savarese/Tagliabue.

La Traviata, Opera, Rome; 15, 18, 21 January; Santini; Albanese, Savarese.

Traviata drew a storm of disapproval from the local press which found in Maria Callas an unsuitable Violetta; the public, undaunted, went to see her in large numbers and quarrelled over her loudly in the foyers. Even the ushers took sides: one would be enchanted by her sheer expertise and the other shocked by her lack of feeling in the part and *la voce troppo forte*. Even the most unprejudiced were startled by the unusual things she put in and the customary things she left out or modified. An exciting, questionable performance, in fact, from a magnificent and highly capricious singer.

The first act succeeded admirably if untraditionally, when one remembers the bird-like coloratura Violetta is used to receiving. This, clear-cut and sturdy, belonged to the Callas of *Armida*: and never have I heard the descending couples of semiquavers (when she hears Alfredo outside) so beautifully handled. She seems to have acquired a new beauty of tone in the high register (although her very top notes are still acid) and the whole voice is becoming better blended. In the second act, however, more than dramatic brilliance and vocal relaxation is required, and here she failed to find true tenderness or to penetrate the pain of the renunciation. . . . "Amami, Alfredo" was disappointing and she disagreed violently with Santini at the difficult rhythmical transition to "Morrò, la mia memoria." The third act was a scene after her own heart, but in the fourth, resplendent in a dressing gown of magenta velvet and ermine, she did not fully exploit the tragedy, using histrionic means instead of the infinite variety of subtle changes which Verdi presents to the singer in this scene.

Cynthia Jolly, Opera

Lucia di Lammermoor, Comunale, Florence; 25, 28 January, 5, 8 February; Ghione; Lauri-Volpi/di Stefano, Bastianini, Arié.
Il Trovatore, La Scala, Milan; 23, 26, 28 February, 24, 29 March; Votto; Stignani, Penno, Tagliabue, Modesti.

This *Trovatore* was worth waiting for, and had the success that it truly merited. The success was not due to the usually dominating figure of Manrico, but to the almost unforgettable singing of Leonora and Azucena taken by Maria Callas and Ebe Stignani. Maria Callas again passed a difficult test and showed once more her remarkable artistic intelligence, her exceptional gifts as a singer, and the fact that she possesses a vocal technique second to none. Her handling of the dramatic content of her part was a masterpiece of artistry.

Peter Dragadze, Opera

Lucia di Lammermoor, Carlo Felice, Genoa; 14, 17 March; Ghione; di Stefano, Mascherini.

Norma, Opera, Rome; 9, 12, 15, 18 April; Santini; Barbieri, Corelli, Neri.

Lucia di Lammermoor, Massimo Bellini, Catania; 21, 23 April; de Fabritiis, Turrini, Taddei, Arié.

Medea, Comunale, Florence; 7, 10, 12 May; Gui; Tucci, Barbieri, Guichandut, Petri.

Her powerful voice and intense dedication to the exacting role gave tragic grandeur to the figure of Medea. In her final scene, while sacrificing her sons to a relentless thirst for revenge, she found accents of true poignancy.

Gisella Seldon-Goth, Musical Courier

Maria Callas has surmounted a challenge that today perhaps no other singer would even be able to attempt. Entrusted with a role ideally suited to her excellent gifts, she displayed a vocal generosity that was scarcely believable for its amplitude and resiliency.

Giuseppe Pugliese, Il Gazzettino,
translated by Henry Wisneski

On stage, Maria Callas was a marvelous interpreter because of her musical security, her understanding of the character, and the sheer intensity of her singing. Her voice, rather rebellious by normal standards, was perfectly suited to Cherubini's remarkable declamation.

Giulio Confalonieri, La Patria,
translated by Henry Wisneski

One can describe Maria Meneghini Callas as the heroine of the evening. With an artist of this magnitude there is no need to enumerate her gifts as a singer and an actress. It is enough to say that her musicality at certain moments was such to make one forget the voice itself, in order to transport the state of mind of the public to a loftier dramatic level of mythical power, such as that of the event being narrated.

Leonardo Pinzanti, translated by Henry Wisneski

The viability of *Medea* depends on the singer who has the tremendous burden of the title role. Yesterday evening Maria Meneghini

Callas was Medea. She was astonishing. A great singer and a tragic actress of remarkable power, she brought to the sorceress a sinister quality of voice that was ferociously intense in the lower register, and terribly penetrating in the high register. But she also had tones that were heartrending for Medea the lover, and touching for Medea the mother. In short, she went beyond the notes, directly to the monumental character of the legend, and she handed it back with devotion and humble fidelity to the composer.

Teodoro Celli, Corriere Lombardo,
translated by Henry Wisneski

Concert, Auditorio di Palazzo Pio, Rome; May. Program: "D'amor sull'ali rosee," *Trovatore*; "Pace, pace," *La Forza del Destino*; "Shadow Song," *Dinorah*. De Fabritiis, conductor.

Lucia di Lammermoor, Opera, Rome; 19, 21, 24 May; Gavazzeni; Poggi, Guelfi, Cassinelli.

Aida, Covent Garden, London; 4, 6, 10 June; Barbirolli; Simionato, Baum, Walters.

After her triumph in *Norma* perhaps Miss Maria Meneghini Callas's Aida was the feature of the performance which was most eagerly anticipated. In the event it had never-to-be-forgotten moments of beauty, power, and subtlety, but also one or two off-setting features due to an excess of emotion which was allowed to disfigure Miss Callas's actual singing. In "Ritorna vincitor," for example, her sense of conflict was so acute that her line (particularly in the beautiful soft ending) was often spoilt by gulps and bulges of tone. Yet "La, tra foreste vergini" in the third act was done with lovely intimate tone and seductive phrasing such as this theater has not heard for many a long day.

The Times

Norma, Covent Garden, London; 15, 17, 20, 23 June; Pritchard; Simionato, Picchi, Neri, Sutherland.

Mme. Callas's singing is remarkable not only for its technical accomplishment but for its great wealth of expressive color. The preposterous plot does at least afford the heroine scope for characterization and Mme. Callas carried the whole opera with authority, having sharpened and amplified the character of the Priestess. In recitative her voice has an edge, in "Casta diva" her line is suave with beautiful mezza voce, in moments of excitement or climax it becomes brilliant.

The Times

Il Trovatore, Covent Garden, London; 26, 29 June, 1 July; Erede; Sinionato, Johnston, Walters, Langdon.

Mme. Maria Callas sang and acted everyone off the stage. That she could dispense roulades and fioriture was a foregone conclusion after *Norma*, but she was also able to make a vivid touching figure of Leonora, whether transported by tempests of the heart, or racked with anguish outside the Aljaferia Palace, or calmly sinking into death. She is not an artist given to gesturing but, like last summer's Azucena, when she moves an arm the audience sits forward, gripped by the stimulus of a dynamic personality in action. The beauty of her vocal line, its plasticity, and its strength, and the easy richness with which she unfolds long phrases, were memorably shown in "Tacea la notte," and especially in the last melody she sings, "Prima che d'altri vivere," when her voice soared up the scale of E flat with a breathtaking blend of tension and effortlessness.

The Times

Her voice—or, rather her use of it—was a source of unending amazement. For once we heard the trills fully executed, the scales and arpeggios tonally full-bodied but rhythmically bouncing and alert, the portamentos and long-breathed phrases fully supported and exquisitely inflected. The spectacular ovation after "D'amor sull'ali rosee" in the last act was still less than the soprano deserved . . . .

Cecil Smith, *Opera*

Aida, Arena, Verona; 23, 25, 28, 30 July, 8 August; Serafin; Pirazzini, del Monaco/Filippeschi/Zambruno, Protti/Malaspina.
Il Trovatore, Arena, Verona; 15 August; Molinari-Pradelli; Danieli, Zambruno, Protti, Malonica.
Norma, Teatro Verdi, Trieste; 19, 22, 23, 29 November; Votto; Nicolai, Corelli, Christoff.
Medea, La Scala, Milan; 10, 12, 29 December, 2, 6 January; Bernstein; Nache, Barbieri, Penno. Modesti.

Bringing this *Medea* to life, imbuing it with a spirit at once pathetic and satanic, cloaking it in agitated singing and pulsating movement, requires, we believe, an interpretation . . . as varied and solemn as that offered last night by Maria Meneghini Callas . . . . Callas's art and technique and intuition had the ideal conditions for expanding in the freedom of bold and excited molding, using deep expressive fervor and striking acting skills to make up for certain limitations in volume, although the singing was nevertheless measured out with incomparable evenness and flexibility of emission . . . .

A huge success. Prolonged and thunderous applause after the three acts, with many curtain calls for the orchestra director, the stage director, and the principal artists.

Franco Abbiati, Corriere della Sera

Il Trovatore, Opera, Rome; 16, 19, 23 December; Santini; Barbieri/
Pirazzini, Lauri-Volpi, Silveri, Neri.

1954

Lucia di Lammermoor, La Scala, Milan; 18, 21, 24, 27, 31 January, 5,
7 February; Karajan; di Stefano/Poggi, Panerai, Modesti.

The fabulous reception accorded her in this aristocratic theater, where so many pundits remembered Toti dal Monte's white-toned clarity as the model for all Lucias, moved Maria Callas to tears, as one photograph witnessed. After the sextet—even before the great scene—she was called to the curtain a dozen times, and flowers rained down on the stage. She picked them up one by one in a graceful allusion to the coming Mad Scene, in which she outdid many a stage Ophelia. She remains more strongly herself with every performance she gives, yet penetrates always more perceptively into the role at hand. It will for instance be difficult to hear "Spargi d'amaro pianto" from another singer (however finished) without finding it pallid. Callas' supremacy among present-day sopranos lies in no mechanical perfection but in a magnificently tempered artistic courage, breath-taking security and agility, phrasing and stage-poise: and in a heart-rending poignancy of timbre which is quite unforgettable.

Cynthia Jolly, Opera News

Callas again had a great personal triumph, holding the public in suspense with the breath-taking clarity and agility of her coloratura, which contrasted with the almost contralto quality of her voice in the recitatives and first act arias. Her mad scene produced an emotional thrill that few other living singers are capable of, and the unusual combination of a dramatic voice, with a soprano leggiero "top," gave a completely new aspect to this role.

Peter Dragadze, Opera

After the risky mad scene, the theater seemed as though it was going to collapse from the deluge of applause. Callas . . . saved her best singing for those celebrated pages, performed not just with a bravura of the highest schooling, but also with a smooth and impassioned flow of musically phrased warbling. This was not the ethereal Lucia one is used to hearing; it was, however, the moving dramatic heroine of which Donizetti perhaps dreamed.

Franco Abbiati, Corriere della Sera

Lucia di Lammermoor, La Fenice, Venice; 13, 16, 21 February; Questa; Infantino, Bastianini, Tozzi.
Medea, La Fenice, Venice; 2, 4, 7 March; Giu; Tucci, Pirazzini, Gavarini, Tozzi.
Tosca, Carlo Felice, Genoa; 10, 15, 17 March; Ghione; Ortica, Guelfi.
Alceste, La Scala, Milan; 4, 6, 15, 20 April; Giulini; Gavarini, Silveri, Panerai.

As Alceste, Maria Meneghini Callas was once again a most fascinating singer. Although the part is less suited to her than others of which she has been a supreme interpreter, she touched most moving heights, sang with exquisite line and with most moving tone and telling expression.

Riccardo Malipiero, Opera

She excelled in personifying the protagonist in a stupendous fashion, artfully interpreting the role with remarkable skill and with exquisite adaptability of voice—deeply moving in the dramatic passages, soft and persuasive in sentimental expressions.

Mario Quaglio, Corriere del Teatro,
translated by Henry Wisneski

Alceste was Maria Meneghini Callas, a singer and actress of rare and perhaps unique dramatic power and intelligence.

O. V., Corriere della Sera

Don Carlos, La Scala, Milan; 12, 17, 23, 25, 27 April; Votto; Stignani, Ortica, Mascherini, Rossi-Lemeni.

Perhaps Callas's voice is not quite suited to Verdi's music; for this wonderful singer, so confident in difficult passages and powerful in dramatic passages, lacks the sweetness and softness necessary in moments of abandon . . . .

Riccardo Malipiero, Opera

. . . the new Elisabetta, Maria Meneghini Callas, whose singing was effective, as always, and more sweet than usual . . . .

Franco Abbiati, Corriere della Sera

It was her last performance of the season at Scala, and this 1953–54 season had seen the greatest triumphs of her career—Donizetti's *Lucia*, Gluck's *Alceste*, Cherubini's *Medea*. In the row behind me a man broke off his applauding to say to his companion, *"La Regina della Scala"*—the Queen of La Scala. And at the end of the last curtain call, a straggler turned to the stage and called, *con amore,* "Arrivederci, Maria!"

Martin Mayer, High Fidelity

La Forza del Destino, Alighieri, Ravenna; 23, 26 May; Ghione; Gardino, del Monaco, Protti, Modesti.
Mefistofele, Arena, Verona; 15, 20, 25 July; Votto; de Cecco/de Cavalieri, di Stefano/Tagliavini, Rossi-Lemeni.
Lucia di Lammermoor, Teatro Donizetti, Bergamo; 6, 9 October; Molinari-Pradelli; Tagliavini, Savarese, Maionica.
Norma, Civic Opera House, Chicago; 1, 5 November; Rescigno; Simionato, Picchi, Rossi-Lemeni.

The voice is excitingly big, vividly colored and meticulously schooled. She molds a line as deftly as she tosses off cruelly difficult ornamentations in the highest register. And she brings to everything a passion, a profile of character and a youthful beauty that are rare in our lyric theater.

It is possible to find flaws in Miss Callas's technique—an occasional spread tone in the high fortissimi; a troublesome tremolo in pianissimo. But the net effect is what counts, and that is grand opera singing in the grandest manner.

It was a great night for Chicago. It may prove an even greater night for opera in America.

Ronald Eyer, *Musical America*

For my money, she was not only up to specifications, she surpassed them. So did Giulietta Simionato, the Adalgisa, who with her made the great duet, "Mira o Norma," something to tell your grandchildren about . . . .

I wouldn't have recognized her [Callas] without the advance pictures. She is wand slim, beautiful as a tragic mask—with a glint of gaiety. She has presence and style, and she sings magnificently. In the shift toward coloratura roles there is a slight unsteadiness in some sustained upper tones. But to me her voice is more beautiful in color, more even through the range, than it used to be. Her range is formidable, and her technique dazzling. She sang the "Casta diva" in a kind of mystic dream, like a goddess of the moon briefly descended. When it comes to pyrotechnics, the glitter of her attack, the feather drift of a falling scale—it adds up to formidable, beautiful song.

Claudia Cassidy, *Chicago Tribune*

Soprano Callas lived up to her reputation. With her lissome figure handsomely clad in white and crimson, she looked almost too young and beautiful to be a pagan high priestess. She made a minimum of stage movement, achieved precise dramatic effects by the tilt of the head or the angle of the body, but also electrified the crowd with slashing moments of violence, as when she confronted her faithless lover in Act II. Her voice ranged from flutey pianissimos that penetrated to the last row of the distant balcony to mezzo-fortes of melting sweetness to fortes of trumpeting and often edgy fierceness. She may not have the most beautiful voice in the world . . . but she is certainly the most exciting singer.

Time

Vocally, the sound Miss Callas produces may best be characterized as peculiar, for it adheres to no conventional concept of tone production. It is substantially an instrumental concept of the human voice she espouses; and like all the great instrumentalists, she uses it for intensely artistic ends. This is no screamer, no calculator of an audience effect. She works on, and with, the voice almost externally. Now shading it to a thin line of filigree in "Casta diva," later exploding its vengeful power in a denunciation of the perfidious Pollione. It is a measure of Miss Callas's increasing command of her remarkable instrument that this "spot" "Casta diva" was more even, better articulated than the recorded one, that she flung off C's with abandon, and a climaxing D at the end of Act II with assurance. One thing seems certain: it will get a lot better before it gets worse. She impresses one as that kind of worker.

Irving Kolodin, *Saturday Review*

La Traviata, Civic Opera House, Chicago; 8, 12 November; Rescigno; Simoneau, Gobbi.

Maria Callas, in a total transformation from the personality of last week's Norma, revealed further the depth with which she has studied her roles. I'd like even to be around when she makes mistakes, for I guess you could rule carelessness out among any possible reasons.

Her acting reinforced last week's impression that she is a brilliant stage personality. The impact of other singers' lines is noticeable in her reactions. She elevates Alfredo and Giorgio Germont so that they "take it from there." It is small wonder that her singing, ranging from "Ah, fors'è lui" and "Sempre libera" to a heart crushing "Addio del passato" is red with the blood of dramatic music, pumped by the pulse of Giuseppe Verdi.

Seymour Raven, *Chicago Tribune*

Lucia di Lammermoor, Civic Opera House, Chicago; 15, 17 November; Rescigno; di Stefano, Guelfi, Stewart.

Maria Meneghini Callas has this town's operagoers bewitched. An innocent bystander wandering into last night's *Lucia* in the Civic Opera House might have thought Donizetti had scored the "Mad Scene" for the audience. Near pandemonium broke out. There was an avalanche of applause, a roar of cheers growing steadily hoarser, a standing ovation, and the aisles were full of men pushing as close to the stage as possible. I am sure they wished for bouquets to throw, and a carriage to pull in the streets. Myself, I wish they had had both . . . .

Remember that Callas, however slender, blonde, and lovely to see, is a dramatic soprano who sings Turandot, Aida, Norma, and not so long ago, La Gioconda. Remember that she just sang a glittering *La Traviata*. Then listen to Lucia's first act, spun like warm silk, sometimes with an edge of steel. It can tell you how she would sound in *Trovatore*. But none of this is fair warning for the "Mad Scene," sung with a beauty and purity of coloratura and fioriture that can set susceptible folk roaring with joy. To use a voice of that size with such superb technical command, and to subordinate that technique to the mood of the music— that is singing in the grand manner.

Claudia Cassidy, *Chicago Tribune*

La Vestale, La Scala, Milan; 7, 9, 12, 16, 18 December; Votto; Stignani, Corelli, Sordello, Rossi-Lemeni.

Maria Callas sang the lead, and it is said that it was only due to her insistence that the work was put on at all. Be that as it may, the role of Giulia is the perfect one for her, covering the entire vocal range and allowing much freedom for acting. She also looked superb. It is a pleasure to watch her, and one begins to believe at last in the action on the stage.

Peter Hoffer, *Music and Musicians*

Among the performers Maria Meneghini Callas sparkled, an artist who without making us forget the Medea of last winter was able to bring the figure of the heroine to life with the powerful breath of her energetic modulations . . . .

An ovation for Arturo Toscanini, present in a box, was . . . provoked at the end of the second act by a lovely gesture of Callas's, who wished to offer the maestro a bouquet thrown to her by the spectators.

Franco Abbiati, *Corriere della Sera*

Concert, RAI, San Remo; 27 December; Simonetto. Program: "Tutte le torture," *Die Entführung aus dem Serail*, "Ombra leggera," *Dinorah*; "Depuis le jour," *Louise*; "D'amore al dolce impero," *Armida*.

1955

Andrea Chénier, La Scala, Milan; 8, 10, 13, 16 January, 3, 6 February; Votto; del Monaco/Ortica, Protti/Taddei.

[Maria Callas was] rather wasted I thought in this part which she nevertheless sustained with dignity.

Riccardo Malipiero, Opera

Maria Meneghini Callas, in the silken gowns of Maddalena di Coigny, imparted amorous rapture and delicate abandon to the role, projecting with admirable talent the rich and plentiful sounds of her extended range.

Mario Quaglia, Corriere del Teatro,
translated by Henry Wisneski

Medea, Opera, Rome; 22, 25, 27, 30 January; Santini; Tucci, Barbieri, Albanese, Christoff.

La Sonnambula, La Scala, Milan; 5, 8, 13, 16, 19, 24, 30 March, 12, 24, 27 April; Bernstein; Ratti, Valletti, Modesti/Zaccaria.

Bernstein lingered dangerously over certain parts of the work, and pushed rather too impetuously in others, risking a disintegration of stage and pit—but nevertheless succeeded in revealing the beauty of a score which normally receives but scant attention. Callas's Amina had something of the same quality; she is, as all know, a great artist and a perfect actress, and despite the strange lapses from her astounding vocal best, it was impossible not to yield to her Amina.

Riccardo Malipiero, Opera

Il Turco in Italia, La Scala, Milan; 15, 18, 21, 23 April, 4 May; Gavazzeni; Gardino, Valletti, Stabile, Rossi-Lemeni, Calabrese.

Maria Callas was brilliant—looking delightful, singing and acting magnificently with the finesse and subtlety and artistic ability that usually one only dreams of.

Peter Hoffer, Music and Musicians

La Traviata, La Scala, Milan; 28, 31 May, 5, 7 June; Giulini; di Stefano/ Prandelli, Bastianini.

Norma, RAI, Rome; 29 June; Serafin; Stignani, del Monaco, Modesti.

Lucia di Lammermoor, Staatsoper, Berlin; 29 September, 2 October; Karajan; di Stefano/Zampieri, Panerai, Zaccaria.

Maria Meneghini Callas is Lucia these days, and one can hardly believe that formerly Maria Malibran and Giulia Grisi could have performed the role more tenderly, animatedly, or passionately . . . . Maria Meneghini Callas's soprano voice has dramatic forte combined with the alluring, sharp timbre of the Italian voice; it has bell-like, tender, sustained pianissimo; it has a modulation for every fluctuation of feeling; and it has the floating lightness of a bird's voice that traces every arabesque in the melody. One does not know what to emphasize most in this performance: the grace of the first aria, the gentle sound of emotion in the departure duet, the rhapsodic declamation of the mad scene, the virtuoso duet with the flute: it was everything together; it was the entire Lucia di Lammermoor with her incomparable romantic magic, and added to that the appearance and acting of the singer, her pale beauty in a white wedding gown—in every way equal to the distraught, deranged figure of Ophelia . . . .

The applause exceeded all normal bounds. The listeners, some of whom had stood for nights to obtain tickets, enthusiastically demonstrated their gratitude. There were flowers, endless cheers, hurricanes of applause.

Werner Oehlmann, *Der Tagesspieler,*
translated by Brittain Smith

Miss Callas, I must say, was tremendous. No more than on other occasions was she a flawless vocalist; but when singing at her best she diffused a kind of rapturous pleasure now virtually inaccessible from any other source; and even when she jolted us with one of those rough changes of register, or emitted one of her cavernous wails, or sang above pitch on a final E flat in alt, she was always the noble, forlorn, infinitely pathetic "Mad Lucia" of nineteenth-century tradition. Nor did her performance end with the Mad Scene; through ten minutes of solo curtain calls she remained with consummate art half within the stage character, with her air of wondering simplicity, her flawless miming of unworthiness, her subtle variation in the tempo of successive appearances and in the depth of successive curtseys, and her elaborate byplay with the roses which fell from the gallery (poetic, chivalrous Berlin!) —one of which, with such a gesture and such capital aim, she flung to the delighted flautist! Oh yes, an artist to her finger tips: the real royal thing. I dare say she will never sing any better than she does now; there is Greek resin in her voice which will never be quite strained away; she will never charm us with the full round ductile tone of Muzio or Raisa or Ponselle. But she has sudden flights, dramatic outbursts of rocketing virtuosity, of which even those more richly endowed singers were hardly capable. Certainly at the present time she is unparalleled.

Desmond Shawe-Taylor, Opera

I Puritani, Civic Opera House, Chicago; 31 October, 2 November; Rescigno; di Stefano, Bastianini, Rossi-Lemeni.

It was most gratifying to watch her madness evolve in Scene three. First came the simple question, "Where is Arturo?", then a realization that something was amiss, followed by the moment of unbearable disappointment leading to her loss of contact with reality, all worked out with the creative detail of a great actress. One remembers still how she took the wreath of white roses from her hair and her anguish when, as if by accident, it dropped to the floor. Unforgettable too was the grand sweep of her mad scene in Act III, the sort of impersonation one rarely experiences even in the spoken theater.

Stewart Manville, Opera

Act I seemed only a prologue to the second and third acts in which Elvira's two mad scenes occur. In both of these Miss Callas projected some affecting and exciting singing though the interpolated high D's were forced and out of focus. But her acting in song, movement, and gesture was memorable; the pathetic droop of her figure during the "mad" intervals is still vivid in the mind's eye. No mistake about it. She is the premier singing actress of today.

Howard Talley, Musical America

Tonight they were waiting for her with palpable excitement. When she stepped on the stage in the second scene of the first act, there was such an ecstatic greeting that the show was stopped dead in its tracks. Thereafter she could do no wrong. Chicago is that way about her.

And you can't blame Chicago. Not that Miss Callas is the perfect singer. She reminded one who had heard her in Italy four years ago that she was capable of uneven work, that she could be strident and off pitch. But she has gained in authority. And when she is in the vein, she is an extraordinary vocalist and technician.

Howard Taubman, *The New York Times*

Il Trovatore, Civic Opera House, Chicago; 5, 8 November; Rescigno; Stignani/Turner, Bjoerling, Bastianini/Weede, Wildermann.

From *Il Trovatore*'s first notes, when she stood in slender profile in her crimson robe and sang of her love for an unknown troubador (tenor Jussi Bjoerling), until she took poison and died in Act IV, her voice contained some of the bite and much of the richness of a clarinet. But its quality was warmed and softened with womanliness. It floated with effortless grace, swelled until it filled the whole block-long auditorium, tapered off sensuously into a decorative vocal arabesque. Whether she was making the most of one of her meaty arias or balancing her tones in ensemble with another singer's, the Callas voice went straight to the listener's solar plexus.

Time

Madama Butterfly, Civic Opera House, Chicago; 11, 14, 17 November; Rescigno; Alberts, di Stefano, Weede.

And here was yet another Callas, unlike any previous characterization—Japanese in movement and mannerism, but deserted Woman epitomized.

Give her further performances and Mme Callas can be the "Butterfly" supreme in our time . . . . Ideally, the Callas Butterfly (or anyone's, faithful both to the libretto and to the score) is scaled for an intimate house—the Piccola Scala, for example. Such a setting would require a measure of less coyness of expression and deportment in the first act, but it would reward all present with the subtle Callas conception of a beloved but fiendishly difficult role—a potentially great conception, and one that may yet find maturity before another week has passed here.

Roger Dettmer, *Chicago American*

For that full throated, soaring ardor was seldom heard from the stage. This was an intimate *Butterfly*, brushed almost from the start by the shadow of the tragedy to come. Not even its love duet was the flood of melody to send pulses pounding. Rather it set the mounting ardor of the man against the muted ecstasy of the woman—and in its own way it told which one kissed and which one turned the cheek. This is not the only way to sing such Puccini—in memory of magnificent love duets I do not say it is even the best way. But with Callas and di Stefano on the stage it is a way of warm Puccini persuasion.

Many an experienced operagoer felt that way about the entire peformance, feeling (with a touch of awe) that Callas had worked out the complicated, taxing role to its geisha fingertips. My own regard for her talents goes higher than that. As a decoration she was exquisite, with the aid of another "Butterfly" beauty of older days, Hizi Koyke, who staged the performance. As a tragic actress, she had the unerring simplicity, the poignant power that thrust to the heart of the score. But in the first scene she missed the diminutive mood, which is that Butterfly's essence. This was charming make believe, but it was not Cio-Cio-San, nor was it the ultimate Callas.

Claudia Cassidy, *Chicago Tribune*

If she were anyone else, I would say the music does not lie in her voice. But Callas has a chameleonic voice, and any minute it could take on Butterfly's color range, just as its owner is capturing Butterfly's wayward, windblown beauty in motion.

So call it, after two performances, a fascinating piece of work in progress, which turns a pretty doll into a woman whose heartbreak holds the fire and pride for such a climax. When the doll of the first act knows the prescience of that coming terror—then I want to see that Butterfly again.

Claudia Cassidy, *Chicago Tribune*

Norma, La Scala, Milan; 7, 11, 14, 17, 21, 29 December, 1, 5, 8 January; Votto; Simionato/Nicolai, del Monaco, Zaccaria.

It had been several years since I had heard her in the part, and though she was a stunning Norma in 1950, she has now become a great one. Her interpretation was strikingly dramatic then, but it has deepened and, at certain points, acquired a new lyric tenderness. Callas was always a passionate singer: but now the passion of love in her Norma is equal to the passion for revenge, which formerly made her such a terrifyingly effective interpreter of the Druid priestess. On opening night (Dec. 7) she was at the top of her form, so splendid that she brought several gasps of admiration and flurries of unexpected applause (for her recitatives!) from the difficult and often apathetic Milanese audience.

William Weaver, Musical Courier

1956

La Traviata, La Scala, Milan; 19, 23, 26, 29 January; 2, 5, 18, 26 February, 9 March, 5, 14, 18, 21, 25, 27, 29 April, 6 May; Giulini/ Tonini; Raimondi, Bastianini/Protti/Tagliabue/Colzani.

Three voices, perhaps too diverse in character and training, three temperaments, perhaps too dissimilar and approachable with difficulty and capable of amalgamation only with even greater difficulty: and where the technique, supreme style and great stagecraft predominate, as they do in the part of the protagonist, performed by Maria Meneghini Callas, the rest seemed out of phase . . . .

A very exhausted audience, endless applause during the performance and at the end of the four acts. And may the reader forgive us if we do not take into consideration either the excesses of vociferous idolatry, or those, even more deplorable, of intolerance, noticed especially during and after the first act . . . .

Franco Abbiati, Corriere della Sera

Il Barbiere di Siviglia, La Scala, Milan; 16, 21 February, 3, 6, 15 March; Giulini; Alva/Monti, Gobbi, Rossi-Lemeni, Luise/Badioli.

Always surprising are the stylistic metamorphoses of Maria Meneghini Callas, who has coined a Rosina nearly worthy of a psychoanalytical study.

Franco Abbiati, Corriere della Sera

Callas's Rosina was far from a conventional conception and most of the critics were up in arms. She played her as a coquette who "knows the ropes" and even flouted tradition to the extent of doing a few steps of dance in which she showed off her ankles. But the voice is in splendid condition and she sings charmingly.

Peter Hoffer, Music and Musicians

Maria Callas made an excitable, nervous, overpowering Rosina, and her familiar unevenness of emission made one regret, rather than forget, the great interpreters of the past.

Claudio Sartori, Opera

Lucia di Lammermoor, San Carlo, Naples; 22, 24, 27 March; Molinari-
   Pradelli; Raimondi, Panerai, Zerbini.
Fedora, La Scala, Milan; 21, 23, 27, 30 May, 1, 3 June; Gavazzeni;
   Zanolli, Corelli, Colzani.

Fedora with Callas in the cast meant full houses and a big success.
Once again she proved that even if she is not the greatest singer she
certainly is one of the world's greatest actresses. However, her voice
seems to have mellowed, and her upper register has lost some of its
strident quality.

Peter Hoffer, Music and Musicians

Maria Meneghini Callas and Franco Corelli led the cast, singing
and acting with dramatic power, perhaps even overstepping the limits
of good style—if indeed good style be desirable in this melodramatic
piece.

Claudio Sartori, Opera

Lucia di Lammermoor, Staatsoper, Vienna; 12, 14, 16 June; Karajan; di
   Stefano, Panerai, Zaccaria.

There is little of the spontaneous brilliance, the seemingly effortless
incandescence, the exquisite shadow play that made her Lyric "Lucia"
an indelible radiance in history's hall of song. But there is superb singing
of enormous skill over what I later discover to be the the kind of
sandpaper throat a visitor can aquire in Vienna's sudden, violent and
unpredictable squalls of chilly, blowing rain. At one point in the pyrotechnics of the "Mad Scene" her voice just simply doesn't respond.
From our high loge we can see Karajan's instant alertness, the almost
pricking ears of the Scala orchestra. But Callas recovers instantly, and
the extraordinarily mournful beauty of that voice makes the scene a
duet of oboe with the Scala's sensitive flute. You might not have noticed
that hazardous moment at all. Just in case you did, a Callas curtain call
touches a hand ever so delicately to her throat. The orchestra men are
a buzz of amused admiration.

Claudia Cassidy, Chicago Tribune

Concert, RAI, Milan; 27 September; Simonetto. Program: "Tu che
   incovo," *La Vestale*; "Bel raggio," *Semiramide*; "Ai vostri giochi,"
   Hamlet; "Vieni al tempio," *I Puritani*.

Norma, Metropolitan, New York; 29 October, 3, 7, 10, 22 November; Cleva; Barbieri, del Monaco/Baum, Siepi/Moscona.

It was a nervous Maria Callas who took to the stage—a tremulous sound in the voice reminded one of Butterfly's entrance last November at Chicago. It was an angry Maria Callas, hissed softly but unmistakably at one point during "Casta diva," who came out for curtain calls to shouts of "Bravo, del Monaco" and "Brava, Barbieri."

Then things, magical things, to Chicagoans familiar, but still and incomparably magical—began happening. It was a smoldering Callas in the cave scene who learned that her Roman lover had been dallying in the Druid forests with Adalgisa. Act III, with the duet "Mira, o Norma," heard the steadiness, intensity and control, of Mme. Callas' best Chicago appearances take the situation in hand. At this turning point on stage, the audience came over.

Act IV with Norma's admission of her own illicit behavior and that great plea for forgiveness to her father . . . heard a Maria Callas singing whom even Chicago did not hear two years ago. Both her musical and stage performance had the overwhelming power that pulls one to the edge of a seat and leaves one afterwards limp.

Roger Dettmer, Chicago American

She spun out the long, extremely taxing phrases of "Casta diva" reticently but with superb control and with admirable refinement where niceties of accent and emphasis were concerned. She went on to tackle the formidable coloratura hurdles of the role with practiced precision, singing nearly everything in tune (a feat noteworthy in itself) and giving each passage an appropriate elegance of style. I can imagine more effortless Normas (Miss Callas seemed desperately anxious the other night to get everything just right), and I was sometimes constrained to admire her zeal, rather than to relax in simple enjoyment, as I should have preferred to do, but this was an astonishingly neat and well-handled one . . . .

Winthrop Sargeant, The New Yorker

Miss Callas' performance of the title role has undergone some interesting changes since this reviewer heard her in it first with the Chicago Lyric Theater two years ago. It is more restrained in action, more deliberate and yet somehow less imposing. She is a fine actress and she obviously has studied every detail of her role with the greatest care. However, she is treating her voice more kindly now and no longer is putting it through the torturous paces in the interest of emotional expression which, in Chicago, made one fear for its safety yet provided such dramatic excitement as to seem well worth the risk. As a result, the voice, which is not a sensuously beautiful one, shows the effects of more cautious manipulation and more care in focusing, both as to pitch and to color, especially in the upper reaches. As a result, too, the so-called "registers" are not so disconcertingly evident, although there is now a certain monotony in the quality. Miss Callas is a highly schooled singer who knows precisely what she is doing at every moment, though what she does may not always enrapture the ear.

Ronald Eyer, Musical America

As for her singing, Miss Callas maintained a standard that one who had heard her in Italy and Chicago rather expected. In a word, the singing was variable. In the "Casta diva" and the third-act scene with the children, when she did not force, her voice had delicacy and point. She phrased with sensitivity; she colored her tones to suit the drama; she was telling in the florid passages.

It is a puzzling voice. Occasionally it gives the impression of having been formed out of sheer will power rather than natural endowments. The quality is different in the upper, middle, and lower registers, as if three different persons were involved. In high fortissimos, Miss Callas is downright shrill. She also has a tendency to sing off pitch when she has no time to brace herself for a high note.

This reviewer can remember only one Norma, Rosa Ponselle, who could sing the entire role without any sense of strain and with unbroken purity. Miss Callas may be forgiven a lack of velvet in parts of her range. She is brave to do Norma at all. She brings sufficient dramatic and musical values to her performance to make it an interesting one.

Howard Taubman, The New York Times

Her voice has flaws, as the critics eagerly pointed out. Notably, on opening night, the notes became shrill in the upper register. But in the low and middle registers she sang with flutelike purity, tender and yet sharply disciplined, and in the upper reaches—shrill or not—she flashed a swordlike power that is already legend. In one of the repertory's most strenuous roles . . . the Callas voice rose from her slender frame with dazzling endurance. No doubt, other great operatic sopranos can coax out of their ample, placid figures tones that esthetes call more beautiful. But just as the greatest beauties among women do not usually have flawlessly symmetrical features, the greatest voices are not characterized by a flawless marble perfection. Callas' voice and stage presence add up to more than beauty—namely, the kind of passionate dedication, the kind of excitement that invariably mark a champ.

Time

For those who have heard Miss Callas elsewhere (as well as on innumerable records) there was a basic curiosity about the marriage of the voice and the house: would they be compatible, or would there be need for a period of trial wedding? A dress rehearsal on the Saturday before left no doubt in this respect: the voice, though not a huge or weighty one, is so well-supported and floated that it is audible at all times, most particularly in the piano and pianissimo effects which Miss Callas delights in giving us. So far as *Norma* is concerned, the singer refuses to force it for volume's sake alone, and it comes clearly to the ear even when she is singing out a top D at the end of the trio with Adalgisa and Pollione.

The kind of voice, basically, requires some consideration. It is what every great artist's means of communication becomes: an extension of her own personality. That personality is dynamic, highly charged, tigerish, and constantly under discipline. So, too, the voice is dynamically dramatic, produced as though it might be torn from the singer's insides, and presided over with an almost visible concern for every word and note she sings. Nothing is thoughtless, left to chance, or without total purpose.

Irving Kolodin, *Saturday Review*

Tosca, Metropolitan, New York; 15, 19 November; Mitropoulos; Campora, London.

There may be sound basis for arguing which singer, of all contemporaries, is the most voluptuous sounding Tosca, the most ample in vocal volume, the most unwilling partner to Scarpia's intentions, but Callas strikes me as the most credible Tosca of our time. She sings her music with the instincts of an actress and phrases her acting with the instincts of a fine musician. Slight in appearance but commanding in manner, she is believable from the first byplay with Cavaradossi, responsively jealous to Scarpia's trickery, and an avenging fury in the moment most foreign to Tosca's true nature, when a knife becomes the key to her dilemma.

Irving Kolodin, Saturday Review

Act II was hair-raising. Callas entered Baron Scarpia's den looking like the Queen of the Night in her black velvet and ermine gown and glittering tiara. Her lip curled shrewishly at Scarpia's overtures, but she staggered when she heard her lover's tortured screams. She wound up her big show-stopping aria, "Vissi d'arte," on her knees just in time to receive the ovation that greeted it . . . . With a start, Callas took the knife from the table, furiously plunged it into Scarpia's chest, then, her head waggling insanely, unable to look directly at the corpse, she placed the candles at his shoulders and made her getaway.

When it was over, and everybody else was killed off too, the audience came back to reality and howled like the West Point cheering section while Maria Callas curtsied, hugged herself and blew kisses through 14 long curtain calls. Tenor Giuseppe Campora, who had given a vocally beautiful performance, doggedly appeared with her every time, although toward the end he began to look rather tired of keeping up with Callas.

Time

As for Miss Callas, she revealed again, only more so, that she is one of the greatest dramatic singers of our time. Her Tosca—coldly beautiful and almost bonily slender—was by turns a rather shrewish minx, a passionate Latin woman of mercurial temperament fully capable of the impulsive murder, and a tender young girl eager for Mario's love. It was a fiery, yet not warm, characterization. It was Miss Callas' own image of the part thoroughly studied down to the last detail and invested with living personality. Everything, including the voice, was thrown into the dramatic requirements of the moment, and as one was swept along by this living, breathing vision of reality, he forgot such purely musical discrepancies as the uneven scale, the hard and sometimes wobbly equality of the full voice in high range and the overconscious manipulation of each tone for both quality and intonation. As a matter of fact, Miss Callas used the voice as an extension, a tool of her dramatic projection, and few will deny that she did it with stunning effectiveness. When she had only to sing, as in the "Vissi d'arte," the voice could be quite beautiful, especially in the middle and low range and in mezza voce.

Ronald Eyer, Musical America

Tosca (excerpts from Act II), Ed Sullivan Show, CBS Television, New
York; 25 November; Mitropoulos; London.

I was not so naive as to expect the whole second act on an hour's variety show. But I had not expected to find it butchered to a jigsaw of 15 minutes, miserably crowded on a clumsy stage, and so horribly photographed that Mr. London resembled a bunch of old bananas and the lovely Callas was turned haggard as a witch.

She sang like a changeling, too. I would not have believed that "Vissi d'arte" if I had not seen it coming out of her mouth, a shrill, shaky ghost of alluring Callas song. Nor would I have thought it possible that she could be so defeated by circumstances, however unfortunate, that she could miss all the drama of the Scarpia death scene, adored of Toscas from Bernhardt on. But there it was, just a dud. Not a spark, not a gleam, just an inexcusable blunder. "Magnificent, wasn't it?" said Mr. Sullivan.

What else could the poor man say? Well, he might have walked out cheerfully, saying, "Frightful, wasn't it?" Or, "If that's opera, you can have it." For what can such a mess possibly prove? People who never go to opera will be contemptuously certain they haven't missed a thing, and people who know opera will be outraged by the travesty.

Claudia Cassidy, Chicago Tribune

Norma, Academy of Music, Philadelphia; 27 November; Cleva; Barbieri, Baum, Moscona.

Taking them in order of their presentation and advance hullabaloo, the Metropolitan Opera production of the Bellini work starred Maria Meneghini You-Know-Who in her local debut. Perhaps such an advance buildup could end up only in a letdown. Callas is a human being, not a goddess. She certainly sang like no goddess—her voice was sometimes tight, sometimes on the verge of cracking on high notes. And, what is no secret, the voice is uneven in color and power throughout its wide range. But there were times when pure beauty of tone poured forth. Maybe next time (next season, perhaps?) Mme. Callas won't be nervous. Perhaps her acting will be more convincing, too.

Samuel Singer, Musical Courier

Lucia di Lammermoor, Metropolitan, New York; 3, 8, 14, 19 December; Cleva; Campora/Tucker, Sordello/Valentino, Moscona.

The power of Miss Callas' personality and performance over her admirers was testified by a tremendous ovation after the Mad Scene that extended almost to 20 curtain calls. But there were others (among them myself) who were less moved by her highly uneven and often unbeautiful singing and her very personalized acting. Most of the time, one had the impression that Lucia di Lammermoor was appearing as Maria Callas, rather than that Maria Callas was appearing as Lucia . . . .

Miss Callas' singing was at its best in passages which were fluid in tempo, not too heavy in texture and not too high. If she hurried phrases and skimmed over the tones a bit, she nonetheless sang several such passages in the Mad Scene with virtuosic flexibility and smoothness. But no more than "Regnava nel silenzio" in Act I was needed to reveal a disturbing tremolo in her sustained tones, and the notes above the staff in climaxes frequently approximated screams. It is only fair to add that they were rewarded with thunders of applause from her worshipers. What it all boils down to is that either one falls under the spell of this artist's fascination and willingly accepts her limitations in exchange for it—or one does not.

Robert Sabin, Musical America

Each of the successive showpieces—"Regnava nel silenzio" in the first act, the duet with Raimondo in the second, and Lucia's part of the sextet—were treated within a dramatic framework that made the Mad Scene an illogical climax to an illogical part. Here, instead of indulging in useless wanderings about the stage with the surface suggestions of dementia, Miss Callas concentrated on interpreting the words with a simplicity and power that absorbed the attention of the capacity audience. When she finished "Ardon gl'incensi," sung with steady accuracy, a full measure of musical meaning, and strongly executed embellishments, the roar of applause was house-wide. The succeeding "Spardi d'amaro pianto" showed some signs of vocal weariness, and the final top E flat (not in the score) was barely struck before she dropped to the floor, ending "life" and all incidental difficulties. Her previous top D's (also unsolicited by the composer, but expected by the audiences) were exclamation points rather than periods.

Irving Kolodin, Saturday Review

From the technical point of view, Miss Callas' Lucia, on Monday evening last week, was less impressive than her Norma. It was so because of one specific and rather damaging flaw—an athletic rather than an artistic one, in that she failed to negotiate her high notes with any ease whatever. Those in the first act emerged like desperate screams, while one in the first part of the Mad Scene was passed up in favor of the optional lower octave, and the final one in the scene ended in complete disaster. Except for these faulty notes, however, I found her interpretation of the role interesting, and occasionally even thrilling. Her coloratura was extraordinarily agile and accurate, the quality of her voice in *mezza voce* was warm and expressive, and her handling of accent and phrasing was always scrupulous, elegant, and authoritative. Miss Callas, in sum, again showed herself to be a remarkable singer, but she also showed that her striking physical resources have their limits.

Winthrop Sargeant, The New Yorker

The "Regnava nel silenzio" opening air and the following duet with the tenor were delectably and realistically sung; the customarily dull scene with Ashton in Act II held impact and a new appeal. . . . When Callas reached the "Mad Scene" one settled back and said, "This is it. This is what we have read about in the stories of divas of the Golden Age. This is at last the true soprano voice as it should be." Dishevelled in appearance (she cares nothing for being constantly a beauty), ravishing in vocal timbre, rivalling the flute in flexible speed, with limpid warmth and cumulative emotional intensity (up until the final note, which went agley), she was superb.

M. C., Musical Courier

In fairness to Callas and those who know her at her dazzling best, neither the Metropolitan nor the Vienna performances matched the unforgetable *Lucia* that set Chicago blazing two years ago. Vienna's was technically more glittering than the Metropolitan's, but the Metropolitan's at its best was warmer, richer, more appealing and to me more beautiful . . . .

She sang the "Sextette" as well as I have ever heard her do it, with that muted oboe luster at its warmest and most beautiful. And up to that unfortunate curtain her "Mad Scene" was magnificent. I don't know where else you can hope to hear such exquisite coloratura, such spun silk fioriture, such gossamer chromatic scales.

Claudia Cassidy, *Chicago Tribune*

Almost the whole first act of *Lucia* is a concert without the slightest dramatic force or even implication. Here Miss Callas was at a disadvantage because her excellent acting was of no avail. On the other hand, since her voice lacks in sheer sensuous beauty, she could not keep the concertizing on a high enough vocal plane.

Then, in the second act, this operatic profligate suddenly gives us real music drama and everything comes to life. There are few ensembles in the entire literature that can match the celebrated sextet.

Here, and in the famous mad scene in the third act, Miss Callas was a different person. In fact, the mad scene was ravishing—as long as it was sung quietly and without forcing the voice. She made an appealing figure, forlorn and tormented. But the minute she reached out for the high and soaring ones, the voice became edgy and some of the scene-ending high notes were really embarrassing, totally devoid of musical definition.

Paul Henry Lang, *New York Herald Tribune*

Concert, Italian Embassy, Washington; 17 December; Schaefer (piano). Program: "D'amor sull'ali rosee," *Il Trovatore*; "Casta diva," *Norma*; "Ah, fors'è lui," *La Traviata*; "Vissi d'arte," *Tosca*; "Regnava nel silenzio," *Lucia di Lammermoor*.

1957

Concert, Civic Opera House, Chicago; 15 January; Cleva. Program: "Ah, non credea," *La Sonnambula*; "Ombra leggera," *Dinorah*; "In questa reggia," *Turandot*; "Casta diva," *Norma*; "D'amor sull'ali rosee," *Il Trovatore*; "Il dolce suono," *Lucia di Lammermoor*.

It seemed as if the enthusiasm of this Chicago audience, never undecided in its likes and dislikes, drew forth unplumbed reserves of tonal color and feeling. The concert ended with the first part of the Mad Scene from Donizetti's *Lucia*, sung with superb control and a full measure of communication.

Howard Talley, *Musical America*

She began so quietly even the noisiest latecomer had to listen. From her wide choice of heroines afflicted with coloratura dementia she chose the sleepwalker of *Sonnambula*, the brooding aria with the lovely lyrical Bellini line, and she sang it superbly in its haunted world of troubled dreams. This was the Callas voice at its most magical, with the sound of the oboe in it, a dark lustered, poignant voice, to make you believe anything it chose.

Then she turned to the shadow song from Meyerbeer's *Dinorah*, whose heroine plays so gaily with shadows happier than reality. It was in its fey way gayer than a lark, for what lark was ever paid $10,000 for a single concert. But it didn't rise to heaven's gate for the climax. It got there, but the sound was harsh and shrill.

It was right then that Callas showed her mettle. She put down her bouquet, rested a foot on the podium, folded her arms, and sang "In questa reggia" from Puccini's *Turandot*. *Turandot*, as all operagoers know, is plain dynamite. The soprano tessitura is mercilessly high. Callas said of it three years ago when she dropped it from her repertory, "I am not so stupid." But she is about to record it for Angel . . . . It got them cheering, but at what cost?

It meant that a superb singer, who is also an artist, and so doubly valuable, sang that cold, cruelly beautiful aria with every ounce of strength she could summon, driving it like nails into the consciousness of the audience. It was not beautiful, for it was forced to a degree altogether perilous to the human voice so mistreated. But it was, for sheer courage and determination, for winning at all costs, magnificent . . . . It was a triumph for Callas, unless you value her so highly you want her restored to her incomparable best.

Claudia Cassidy, *Chicago Tribune*

Norma, Covent Garden, London; 2, 6 February; Pritchard; Stignani, Vertecchi, Zaccaria, Collier.

Mme. Callas's Norma is a feat of rare personality. It cannot be said that the voice itself has become more beautiful: the upper tones sometimes sounded pinched, sometimes hard and inexpressive, and the singer's sense of pitch was apt to stray in either direction—"Casta diva" ended very sharp: was this perhaps because Mme. Callas now sings it a tone lower than she used to? In the middle of the voice the timbres often do not so much mix as curdle. Her singing is still glorious, at once epic and pathetic in effect. Her breath control is still astonishing, enabling her to draw out a legato as suave as that of the finest instrumentalist, subtly shaded but always even in quantity. Fioritura never sounds vacuous when she sings it, for she understands and can convey the shades of emotion and temperament that Bellini intended in any given roulade; most expressive of all are the descending chromatic scales which are so characteristic of Norma's music, and which she weighs with a curious, highly individual melancholy that stabs to the heart. Her histrionic presentation of the role is of the art that conceals art: it is her colleagues who appear to be acting, while Norma herself is real, a guardian of her people and their rites, a mother, and a woman scorned in love yet unshaken in tenderness and magnanimity even when she is seen to bare her teeth or flash an eye like a stiletto. The varied facets of the part do not conflict: they are all in Norma's character.

The Times

Her voice proved less rich than before, with occasional shrillness and a new hard edge. But she has grown in artistic stature; her style is now well-nigh impeccable, her singing uniform throughout its range, whereas before one could hear her move from one register into another. She identifies herself with the character she is playing almost as completely as Ulanova. Her lower notes are more caressingly beautiful than ever, and her breath control is now so perfect that she can produce a legato as effortlessly and suavely as an expert cellist.

Frank Granville Barker, *Opera News*

Miss Callas' voice was in excellent fettle, and apart from the now-accustomed sour note and occasional off-pitch singing, we found her better than ever. The voice is more beautiful and more closely knit than formerly, and her interpretative powers greater than ever.

At the end of each of the two *Norma* performances she received a standing ovation from the capacity audience. And at the second performance, after the "Mira, o Norma" duet . . . such pandemonium reigned that the conductor . . . had no alternative but to grant an encore of the cabaletta.

Musical America

La Sonnambula, La Scala, Milan; 2, 7, 10, 12, 17, 20 March; Votto; Ratti, Monti/Spina, Zaccaria, Cossotto.
Bellini would have liked Callas's Amina.

L'Europeo

Popular delirium for Callas's return. We share it fully, because in the revival of *Sonnambula* at La Scala we had the best Callas one could wish. That is, a very great artist, a sublime performer such as Malibran must have seemed to Bellini.

Callas made of Amina a pathetic and at times sad character, perfect in every phrase, in every expression. Callas sang Amina with Bellini's music in her heart, and works of ineffable longing on her lips, such as Bellini certainly conceived. We did not have the good fortune to live during the golden age of Bellini opera, and we have tried to relive Pasta's and Malibran's successes through descriptions of them. But at La Scala we have truly relived those times, listening greedily to every one of dear Amina's phrases. Callas has become a mistress of interpretation and of bel canto.

Bruno Slawitz, *Musica e dischi*

To have tried to find a revelatory expression not just in the flowing melodies but in even the slightest bits of recitative; to have found, even, two ways of expression, one for Amina awake and aware of herself and the other for Amina rapt in her painful drowsiness: that is what Maria Callas has done, restoring to Bellini's girl not attitudes, movements, voice, but soul. And it seems to us, therefore, that we can repeat about this artist what a New York critic wrote of Enrico Caruso, December 4, 1920, after a memorable performance of *Samson and Delilah:* she "sang gloriously."

Teodoro Celli, *Oggi*

Here are some jottings by a Callas fan—I really think the term should be fanissimo—who prefers to remain anonymous:

Of *Sonnambula*—"Needless to say, Mme. Callas's performance was unique and superb. Her voice is much better than when I heard her last—if that is possible. She improves all the time, and I'm sure will be a great singer for 20 years or longer. Not to go on too long about it, the great aria of the whole opera, 'Ah! non giunge,' comes at the end. Callas approaches the front of the stage and begins the superb and most difficult aria; then very gradually the lights in all the tiers of boxes come on, and afterwards, the lights in the house itself—toward the end of the final, great aria the whole of La Scala is brilliantly lit and the opera ends a few minutes later in full light. Most extraordinary and exciting effect. As you can imagine, the entire audience rose to its feet to applaud and one could hear neither orchestra nor singers at the end of the opera."

Claudia Cassidy, Chicago Tribune

Anna Bolena, La Scala, Milan; 14, 17, 20, 24, 27, 30 April, 5 May; Gavazzeni; Simionato, Carturan, Raimondi, Rossi-Lemeni.

An unparalleled success. Even Callas' London triumph, which now makes London her favorite audience, did not equal this one . . . .

The opera had not been done anywhere since 1850 or so, and one can see why. The first act is pretty slow, but all leads up to the last act and especially the last scene in the Tower when, of course, Anne Boleyn loses her reason. And truthfully, the mad scene of *Lucia* just isn't in it for excitement and fantastic difficulty and beauty.

Claudia Cassidy, Chicago Tribune

As Anna, Signora Meneghini Callas called to mind her greatest performances of Medea and her first of Norma. Her vibrant voice, stage deportment, the artistry of her singing, and stupendous stylization, everything makes of her an Anna who can have no rivals today.

E. M., Corriere della Sera

Iphigénie en Tauride, La Scala, Milan; 1, 3, 5, 10 June; Sanzogno; Albanese, Colzani, Dondi.

With her noble dignity of bearing and authoritative command of the stage, Callas as the humane priestess of the barbaric Scythians who would see no end to their human sacrifices was a constant and exciting joy. She is in fine vocal state at present; and, since the tessitura of the role lies comfortably within her range, her singing caused none of the momentary discomfort that has sometimes seemed to go with her slimmer figure. Following the storm and narration of Iphigenia's dream, she begins in tones of melting softness, "O toi, qui prolongeas mes jours," Iphigenia's agonized prayer to Artemis. . . . Her "O malheureuse Iphigénie" was another moving experience. Only Callas can invest with so many overtones of meaning a single exclamation, as for example, in Iphigenia's recognition of Orestes, where joy at meeting, sad regret for past separation, sorrow at his impending sacrifice, and an overwhelming love, were all intermingled in the single word "fratello."

Lionel Dunlop, Opera

Last night, for Gluck's *Iphigénie en Tauride*, a vacuum was created—an admiring, exclamatory vacuum, a vacuum of concentric reflectors—around the art of Maria Meneghini Callas. We do not know whether it resulted spontaneously from the difference in class between the distinguished prima donna and the rest of the vocal ensemble or whether it was artificially induced by the producer and orchestra director through a calculated dosage of stage effects, by surbordinating themselves in any event to the singing and the person of the protagonist. But the vacuum was created, and with it, a lack of equilibrium.

Franco Abbiati, Corriere della Sera

Concert, Tonhalle, Zurich; 19 June; Moralt. Program: "Ah, fors'è lui," *La Traviata*; "Ardon gli incensi," *Lucia di Lammermoor*.
Lucia di Lammermoor, RAI, Rome; 26 June; Serafin; Fernandi, Panerai, Modesti.
La Sonnambula, Opernhaus, Cologne; 4, 6 July ; Votto; Monti, Zaccaria, Cossotto.

The fact that the visitors also brought with them their most famous vocal star, the soprano Maria Meneghini Callas, who sang the title role in Bellini's *La Sonnambula*, transformed this evening into an operatic event almost without comparison. When she stood on stage and traced the gentle arc of the cantilenas one could forget everything else around, not only the forces of the masterful ensemble, but also the naïve, old-fashioned arrangement of this old-fashioned opera, which would hardly be capable of survival without the vocal and dramatic miracle of this towering artist.

One has heard or read often enough that as a singer, Callas is something extraordinary—now we have experienced her with our own eyes and ears and found this artist's legendary fame confirmed in the most complete fashion. One tries in vain to describe the luminous beauty of the voice: melting sweetness in floating pianos, metallic brilliance in fortes, and in its coloratura, a perfect plasticity that one would only approximate very imprecisely with the usual comparisons from the instrumental realm.

But most important is that as an actress, the owner of this precious soprano voice must be reckoned among the greats. She played the role of a Swiss village beauty who, as a sleepwalking apparition, falls into discredit and loses her lover . . . with tender, charming gestures and sensitive tone, exactly as one sees this unfortunate Amina on the title page of the old piano score. In fact, the entire nineteenth-century operatic tradition is preserved here in a form that has become foreign to us, but that is, however, truly delightful.

Kölnische Rundschau, translated by Brittain Smith

Concert, Herodes Atticus, Athens; 5 August; Votto. Program: "D'amor sull'ali rosee," *Il Trovatore*; "Pace, pace," *La Forza del Destino*; "Ai vostri giochi," *Hamlet*; "Liebestod," *Tristan und Isolde*; "Regnava nel silenzio," *Lucia di Lammermoor*.

Mme. Maria Meneghini Callas last night gave a memorable operatic recital in the 1,800-year-old outdoor theater of Herod Atticus. Last Thursday Mme. Callas refused to sing because the dry climate of Athens had affected her voice. Some people than claimed that the reason was "cold feet" rather than "dry throat." There had been much criticism of her and the Greek Government for the high fee paid her. Last night a large number of policemen were on the look-out for vociferous critics, but they were not needed.

The Times

La Sonnambula, King's Theater, Edinburgh; 19, 21, 26, 29 August; Votto; Monti, Zaccaria, Cossotto.

Proceedings began with *La Sonnambula*, starring "La Divina," Maria Meneghini Callas, not in her most divine voice. The premiere had uneasy moments, and by the third performance almost every sustained note around F threatened to crack and collapse: "Ah, non credea" was a painful experience for everyone in the theater. Despite which, there was engrossing art in her impersonation . . . .

After four performances, the diva ("tired") flew back to Milan, and Renata Scotto took over.

Andrew Porter, High Fidelity

The soprano was in varying voice throughout her appearances, and after four Aminas she had to cancel her fifth, as she was not well. According to reports, opening night found her in far from good voice. The second and third performances, which were broadcast, displayed the singer at her very best and very worst; in the fourth, which I heard, the soprano was in excellent voice, and her performance ranked with her Normas in London of last winter.

This is not to say the voice was always perfectly produced, or that all the sounds she made fell pleasantly on the ear; but the musicianship, intelligence and intensity with which she invests her roles were in evidence throughout the evening, and her singing of "Come per me sereno" in the first scene and "Ah! non credea" in the last were intensely moving. Dramatically her interpretation was a tour de force; by very nature Miss Callas is an imperious figure more suited to the great tragic roles of the lyric stage, and yet although Amina is a Giselle-like figure, the soprano was able by her personality to make us believe in the figure she created.

Harold Rosenthal, Musical America

Concert, Civic Opera, Dallas; 21 November; Rescigno. Program: "Tutte le torture," *Die Entführung aus dem Serail*; "Qui la voce," *I Puritani*; "Vieni t'affretta," *Macbeth*; "Ah, fors'è lui," *La Traviata*; "Al dolce guidami," *Anna Bolena*.

She opened with a Mozart aria from *The Abduction from the Seraglio*, which she did in harsh, mediocre style. With two arias from Bellini's *I Puritani*, Callas hit her stride, rippling down her famed arpeggios, her tone pure and vibrant.

At the end, Callas appeared in a black lace sheath and a blazing diamond necklace. She sang the final aria from Donizetti's *Anna Bolena*, in which the wronged queen, about to be beheaded, forgives her enemies. At the last exultant phrase ("Only my blood is lacking to finish the crime, and this will be shed!"), Callas took a single step forward —so dramatic that people all but jumped. She raised a commanding hand over her head, then threw arms wide and sent that last full note straight up through the roof.

Time

Un Ballo in Maschera, La Scala, Milan; 7, 10, 16, 19, 22 December; Gavazzeni; Ratti, Simionato, di Stefano, Bastianini/Roma.

As soon as the turbulent Maria Meneghini Callas appeared, extravagantly costumed as ever, we realized that she had set her stamp on Amelia. She was in voice and sang superbly. Callas is never dull. When not held in check she is prone to exaggeration; when guided by an intelligent and trusted *régisseur*, her acting is convincing and exciting. Her personality is without doubt the most imposing on the operatic stage today. Others may have more beautiful voices, but at the moment there is only one Callas, just as there was only one Mary Garden.

Ernest de Weerth, *Opera News*

Concert, RAI Television, Rome; 31 December. Program: "Casta diva," *Norma*.

1958

Norma (Act I), Opera, Rome; 2 January; Santini. Pirazzini, Corelli, Neri.

How did Callas really sing the first act? Over the radio an adequate judgment is difficult. What was clear was that she was singing under effort, especially as the act wore one. She began with an admirably clear-cut recitative taken monumentally slowly, slightly muffed the effect of the "sacro vischio" but recovered a lovely quality in the opening of "Casta diva." The rest—particularly in the cabaletta—was a question of covered and hardened tone: nothing that does not happen constantly in performance, but which is unacceptable to a perfectionist of Callas's ferocious sensibility. Couple this dissatisfaction with all the other factors (the Corelli-Pirazzini success which ended the act, the over-expectant public, her battle with her own physical state) and the story is told. But as an eminent conductor pointed out, who knows but that with less entreaty and a little more diplomatic firmness she could have been persuaded to go back to reap the inevitable success of the succeeding acts?

Opera

Concert, Civic Opera House, Chicago; 22 January; Rescigno. Program: "Non mi dir," *Don Giovanni*; "Vieni t'affretta," *Macbeth*; "Una voce poco fa," *Il Barbiere di Siviglia*; "L'altra notte," *Mefistofele*; "Ai vostri giochi," *Hamlet*; "Ben io t'invenni," *Nabucco*.

And it [Chicago] also heard some singing. Some magnificent singing that in our time only Callas can achieve. There are beautiful voices in the world, never too many or even enough, but some. Callas takes a beautiful voice and goes on from there. She has a marvelous technique, a deeply probing, vividly projected sense of drama, and the widest range of any singer I have known.

Here in one evening she sang the noble aria of Mozart's Donna Anna, the "Non mi dir" from *Don Giovanni*, with its full complement of coloratura. She sang the tiger's brew, that of Lady Macbeth's Letter Scene from the Verdi opera. She picked up a bewitching bouquet and became the Spanish coquette of Rossini's "Una voce poco fa."

Even then she had barely started. For "L'altra notte," Margherita's haunting aria from the prison scene of *Mefistofele*, caught the mourning dove note that to me is the loveliest of all the Callas gifts, lovelier even than the fey carillons of Ophelia's mad scene from Thomas' *Hamlet*, and deeply akin to the eerie beauty of the chromatic cascades of her coloratura, the wonderful Verdi line of the great aria from his first triumph, *Nabucco*.

Was everything perfection? Of course not. Great things are seldom perfect. But this was Callas at her crest except for some notes more bold than beautiful, and even those had the beauty of courage, of the indomitable will to win.

Claudia Cassidy, *Chicago Tribune*

Maria Callas sounds to be in big vocal trouble—how serious only she is equipped to measure. But last night, heard for the first time in 12 months, her voice was recurrently strident, unsteady and out-of-tune. It seems to have aged 10 years in one.

There always have been blemishes in the production: a heavy pulse nearing C in alt and above, and a tone not in itself quite sensuous higher than the middle register. But there always has been the Callas control, the sheer will power, that disciplined and integrated defects —made them strengths, urgent and electrifying, by means of a musicianship no singer today can equal or imitate.

Last night sheer musicality saved her more than once. In Verdi's Letter Scene from *Macbeth* and later in Abigaille's big Babylonian aria from *Nabucco* there were sounds fearfully uncontrolled, forced beyond the too-slim singer's present capacity to support or sustain.

Roger Dettmer, *Chicago American*

La Traviata, Metropolitan, New York; 6, 10 February; Cleva; Barioni/ Campora, Zanassi.

Taken as a whole, her interpretation of the part was far and away the finest that I have encountered at the Metropolitan or anywhere else in all the years I have been listening to opera. The high notes again wobbled very slightly now and then, but I am beginning to accept the reedy tone quality as a characteristic of Miss Callas' vocal personality; when one has become used to it, it seems to add intensity to her singing. Hers is not a pure, innocent voice (pure, innocent voices are a dime a dozen) but a fiery conveyance for female passion, and it is used with amazing skill to underline each shifting mood of this extremely subtle role. What emerges is a highly personal interpretation of Violetta, in which is it impossible to disentangle the dramatic elements from the vocal ones. . . The entire interpretation, from the aria, "Sempre libera," in the first act, to Violetta's death, just before the final curtain, was one of those electrifying fusions of music, theater, and personality that operagoers are only occasionally privileged to witness, and are seldom able to forget.

Winthrop Sargeant, *The New Yorker*

She made Violetta an appealing figure, spirited in the first act and touching later on. Her costumes were attractive, and she immersed herself in the psychology of the role. In the first act she was rather busily preoccupied as Alfredo declared his love, but thereafter she did not forget that she was Violetta. She was particularly moving in the scene with the elder Germont.

Miss Callas sang better than at any time last season. She has a fine grasp of the Verdi style and especially this role. She phrased with sensitivity. In the second act she spun out a memorably colored pianissimo in "Dite alla giovine" and her farewell to Alfredo had an anguished intensity. Through the second act her tones were firm, well-focused and admirably molded, and in the third she continued to sing in a way that would justify her reputation.

There were places where Miss Callas' singing was not worthy of her station in the operatic world. If it is sustained beauty of tone you want in your Violetta, the soprano does not fill the bill. Her singing had its variable moments, as it did last year. Top tones grew edgy and shrill, and sometimes they wavered like the chart of a persistent, low fever.

Howard Taubman, The New York Times

Miss Callas doesn't command the beauty of sound to be ideal in any part, but hers is the best rounded Violetta offered here in years.

For all the throaty "covered" quality she purveys, Miss Callas makes her voice an instrument of dramatic purpose from first to last. For all its weightiness in the middle register, she sang the first act in the written key, with precision, and an emphatic top D flat. And although she could broaden her line eloquently for "Amami, Alfredo," she could also pronounce the beautiful phrase "Alfredo, Alfredo, di questo core" (Act III in the Metropolitan version) with the sounding equivalent of the *con voce debolissima e con passione* which Verdi directed. Those who reported on the occasion without hearing the fourth act left the public uninformed of a memorable "Addo del passato," in which the lovely half-voice effects, the swells from piano to pianissimo, and the obedient delivery of the final A with *un fil di voce*, as the score requests, were sermons on the text of what operatic art is all about.

Binding these isolated details together was a sense of total characterization, a unity of sound and movement that made her work consistently absorbing . . . . For all the disparagement of her "ugly" sound—and I regard this observation to be on a par with the discovery that the Venus de Milo has no arms—Miss Callas makes an effect of pleasure or poignance with any tone she utters. As a vitalizing force, Miss Callas obviously contributes much the Metropolitan—or any other repertory theater—must cherish. In her current vocal form, she commands the attention of all who regard opera as something more than a concert in costume.

Irving Kolodin, *Saturday Review*

As Violetta, she was equally compelling as the heartless courtesan and the pitiful dying consumptive. Her voice, always more sharply exciting than buttery beautiful, fluctuated under full steam but accomplished the loveliest of pianissimos.

When the curtain fell, Maria Callas had achieved what had never been hers before: a twenty-minute full-throated ovation in her own home town, complete with eighteen curtain calls, twelve for her alone. Utterly exhausted, the only words she spoke were: "I'm numb, I'm numb. I still can't believe it's finally happened."

Newsweek

When Maria Meneghini Callas, in a gleamingly white hoop-skirt gown, stepped demurely before the Metropolitan Opera's golden curtain after the first act of Verdi's *La Traviata* last week, plainclothesmen planted themselves at the head of the aisles near the stage. Nobody was sure who was supposed to be protected from what, but the cops' presence was clearly unnecessary. On her first Met appearance this season, soprano Callas carried the house from the moment she lifted her first note across the orchestra pit.

Time

Lucia di Lammermoor, Metropolitan Opera, New York; 13, 20, 25 February; Cleva; Bergonzi/Fernandi, Sereni, Moscona/Scott/Tozzi.

The soprano, singing the role for the first time this season, was in beautiful voice, and she achieved a vocal consistency that this listener has never heard from her.

As is well known, the upper extremes are not Miss Callas' most comfortable habitat. This tends to obscure the fact that in quiet singing over most of the vocal register up to a B or so, her voice is one of the most liquidly beautiful before the public today. It is produced easily, penetrates over the orchestra, and has a pure melting sound.

What is more, Miss Callas is no mere soprano mouthing notes and roulades. She brings a high quality of imagination and musicianship to her singing. Her first-act "Quando rapita" brought down the house, and it should have. . . .

Her Mad Scene was carefully adjusted, with much . . . metrical freedom. She sounded just a shade tired here, but she nevertheless literally made most present-day Lucias sound like amateurs. She was rewarded with eight solo curtain calls.

Harold Schonberg, *The New York Times*

In *Lucia* . . . Callas had a more supple, responsive vocal organ at her disposal than . . . last year. Thus, she was able to execute, in depth, the concepts which sometimes were only on the surface previously. In the requirements of Donizetti, the voice was free, limpid, and beautifully true to its own evocative timbre throughout . . . .

Irving Kolodin, *Saturday Review*

Tosca, Metropolitan Opera, New York; 28 February, 5 March; Mitropoulos; Tucker, Cassel/London.

To this reviewer, who heard her in one of last season's *Toscas*, her performance last night had more concentration and fire. It was comparatively underplayed and pallid a year ago. But this time it grew out of an inner flame. Not that Miss Callas exaggerated. But she performed as if every faculty was alert and engaged.

The part lies well for her voice. It has no coloratura in the high regions, and even the occasional reediness of Miss Callas' soprano becomes an asset as it seems to give fiber to her struggle with Scarpia. She is fully in command of phrase and style, and her musicianship is impeccable. Her "Vissi d'arte" was a fine job of communicative singing, even if the climactic top tones wavered and took on an edge.

The audience, which had been waiting for the end of a full-fledged aria by the prima donna, applauded and shouted its approval. Miss Callas stood there, in the position she had taken in the final measure of "Vissi d'arte," without stepping out of character. It was a sustained ovation, but the chances are that it did not strain the soprano's patience.

Howard Taubman, *The New York Times*

Miss Callas, we thought, was in fine, glossy voice and acted with great spirit . . . . But when she came out for her first solo bow after that act [the second], which includes the heroine's big aria as well as the extravasation, somebody booed. . . . The real contest came after the finale. The boos—enunciated, it seemed to us, with professional malignity—punctured the applause, which began as simply well bred. The applause lost its breeding as the pro-Callas majority got mad. The sound produced by human hands is inferior in volume to that produced by the larynx, so somebody shouted "Bravo!" Timidly, then with increasing resolution, others followed. An old gentleman in the first row of the grand tier hammered with his hearing aid on the railing. He thus achieved a double purpose—making a noise and shutting out the noise the opposition made . . . . The soprano, smiling, took curtain call after curtain call. The intervals between curtain calls became longer and longer, but half the audience wouldn't go home, and the types who work the curtain must have collected overtime. The lower tiers made most of the noise, pro-Callasites massing in the front half of the orchestra to shout even after the management had dimmed the house lights. The gallery, which usually produces the best-orchestrated demonstrations, was this time relatively apathetic, except for the booers, who could not have been more than a dozen. When they shut up, everybody went home, after a final, unconfused "Bravo!"

We came away happy and bruised, our musical education complete.

"The Talk of the Town," The New Yorker

Concert, Cinema Monumental, Madrid; 24 March; Morelli. Program: "Casta diva," *Norma*; "D'amor sull'ali rosee," *Il Trovatore*; "L'altra notte," *Mefistofele*; "Ai vostri giochi," *Hamlet*.

The first sensation that one has when listening to her . . . is of adverse signs. The timbre of the voice does not seduce . . . . The color of the voice is unequal—the colors are various: it seems to be beginning to be nasal at certain moments, and it is evident in others, in the upper register, that it is out of tune.

And how then can one speak of an exceptional figure? Because of other things. Because of the temperament, the intelligence, the personality, the stage mastery of unmistakable originality. Because of the technique. An improbable technique that astonishes us with the full, very extensive voice, when it displays fabled agility, gorgeous trills, descending chromatic scales with the perfection of an instrument. As in "L'altra notte" from *Mefistofele*, and above all, in "Ophelia's Scene and Aria" from *Hamlet*, the most greatly applauded, and rightly so . . . .

Antonio Fernández-Cid, ABC

La Traviata, São Carlos, Lisbon; 27, 30 March; Ghione; Kraus, Sereni.
Anna Bolena, La Scala, Milan; 9, 13, 16, 19, 23 April; Gavazzeni;
    Simionato, Carturan, Raimondi, Siepi.

The final scene in the Tower of London is the greatest thing in the opera, and it also showed Mme Callas at the summit of her powers both as singer and as tragic actress. . . . We have here no conventional mad scene with flute obbligato, but a long chain of arioso, arias and recitatives . . . . Interpreted by such an artist as Maria Callas, and directed with perfect taste by Visconti, this was a scene of high tragedy.

Could *Anna Bolena* enter the international repertory? With Callas, yes; without her, or some comparable soprano of whom as yet there is no sign, no. Many people think it a flaw in these old operas that they depend on the availability of great singers; but what would be the fate of the standard violin and piano concertos if there were scarcely a player who could even get his fingers round the notes, let alone fill them with a lulling charm or a passionate intensity?

Desmond Shawe-Taylor, *Opera*

Five minutes of cheering and five curtain calls were the soprano's reward as the star of Donizetti's *Anna Bolena*. It was her first performance in Italy since she walked out on a Rome Opera gala audience on January 3. . . .

Associated Press

Over 200 policemen were in and around the theater on this occasion, as violent demonstrations for and against the soprano were expected. However, the evening passed fairly normally, and ended in a triumph for Miss Callas.

Her performance was excellent, and although she did not have the physical strength and power behind her voice as in the past, her supreme mastery of the art of singing made it a joy to listen to her.

Peter Dragadze, *Musical America*

Il Pirata, La Scala, Milan; 19, 22, 25, 28, 31 May; Votto; Corelli, Bastianini.

Maria Callas's interpretation was flawless. Never perhaps has a singer been better adapted by her own means of expression to play the part of Imogene; and never avoided so well those strongly dramatic accents so as to limit herself almost entirely to the meaningful recitatives (which Mme Callas knows how to utter in the only convincing way) and to those lyrical mezza voce sections, meditative and with slackened tempo, which have become a predominating characteristic of her interpretations . . . .

Claudio Sartori, Opera

The work is exceptionally difficult to sing, accounting in part for its infrequent performances. In the role of Imogene, Maria Meneghini Callas had a triumph second only to her unforgettable Medea. She brought the cold Milan audience to its feet, cheering and applauding almost hysterically for over 25 minutes after the final Mad Scene. In the first two acts, the soprano's voice was sometimes harsh and forced, but her remarkable musicality, style, vocal agility and personality, combined with a warmed-up voice in the last act to give us as much pleasure and excitement as of old.

Peter Dragadze, Musical America

After the tragic madness of Lucia and Medea, the stupefaction of the sleepwalking Amina, after Anna Bolena's bewilderment, Imogene's anguish: these are the summits of Maria Meneghini Callas's latest interpretations, those of a singer who seems to draw the best of her transformations of art in scenes divorced from life's reality and situated at the borders of a mystery inaccessible to humans . . . . She is a very great interpreter of others' torments, an interpreter without equal.

Franco Abbiati, Corriere della Sera

Concert, Covent Garden, London; 10 June; Pritchard. Program: "Qui la voce," *I Puritani*.

American-born Maria Meneghini Callas brought down the Royal Opera house tonight during a gala 100th anniversary performance in the Covent Garden landmark.

The soprano took eight curtain calls amid great applause after she had sung the Mad Scene from Act 2 of Bellini's *I Puritani*.

Reuters

Bellini himself was represented by the scene from *I Puritani* in which the aria "Qui la voce" occurs. Here the long tradition of great singers coming from far and near to sing at Covent Garden was observed by the appearance of Mme. Maria Meneghini Callas, who gave a present demonstration of that vocal art which had come down from the eighteenth century and was the artistic justification of the otherwise anemic operas of Bellini and Donizetti, that were made for this sort of virtuosity.

The Times

Concert, BBC Television, London; 17 June; Pritchard. Program: "Vissi d'arte," *Tosca*; "Una voce poco fa," *Il Barbiere di Siviglia*.
La Traviata, Covent Garden, London; 20, 23, 26, 28, 30 June; Rescigno; Valletti, Zanasi.

In the first act Callas showed us a brittle, highly strung Violetta, unable to be at rest; the charming hostess who talks to as many of her guests as she can, who does not want to spoil the party when she feels ill, and who can only joke at first over Alfredo's declaration of love. For this Violetta, love does not come in the duet, but in the middle of the "Sempre libera" when she hears Alfredo's "Amor, amor e palpito." As Callas uttered the simple word "Oh?" and then "Oh, amore!" we knew the truth, just as earlier in the scene, when she looked at herself in the mirror and sighed, "Oh, qual pallor!" we knew that this Violetta realized she was a dying woman. And what other Violetta has been able to use the coloratura in "Un di felice" so naturally to suggest, as Callas does, the nonchalant carefree life of the courtesan?

The second act Violetta had become softened, and was wholly and utterly devoted to her Alfredo. The long central scene with Germont was outstanding, and here Callas was supreme. From the moment she drew herself proudly to her full height at the words "Donna son'io, signore, ed in mia casa," through the changing emotions of the conversation with Germont . . . to the resigned "È vero! è vero!" as Germont pointed out that she would one day grow old and Alfredo would tire of her, and on to the great moment of renunciation—"Ah, dite alla giovine": this was operatic singing and acting at its greatest. The beginning of "Dite alla giovine" was a moment of sheer magic, with the voice curiously suspended in mid-air; and the final request to Germont to embrace her as a daughter was profoundly moving.

In the writing of the letter and the short scene with Alfredo, Callas achieved a great intensity. At the first two performances under review the "Amami, Alfredo" passage was rather subdued; at the final performance she rode the orchestra, opened up her voice and achieved the maximum degree of intensity, which aroused the audience to a spontaneous outburst of applause.

In act 3 . . . Callas successfully depicted the conflicting emotions of Violetta in the party scene. Again it was the odd word and phrase that assumed a new significance, as for example, the heartfelt "Ah! Taci" to Alfredo before the denunciation—and at the same time the nervous hands touched her face and patted her hair. Then in the great ensemble, "Alfredo, Alfredo, di questo cor" was sung as if Violetta's heart was truly breaking.

Callas's last act was superb. Dramatically one felt how Violetta suffered, one saw the effort with which the dying woman dragged herself from bed to dressing table, from dressing table to chair. "Oh, come son mutata" brought a lump to the throat as she eagerly scanned the telltale glass for some glimmer of hope. The reading of the letter was quiet and intimate, and then came a moving "Addio del passato." When Alfredo was announced, Violetta hurriedly tried to tidy her hair and look her best, and then came the reunion, with Violetta's hands (and how Callas had made the most of her beautiful long fingers throughout the evening) clasping at the longed-for happiness, and hardly believing that Alfredo really was a flesh and blood figure. "Ah! Gran Dio! Morir sì giovine" was sung with terrific intensity—and at the final performance Callas took the whole phrase in one breath without a break.

The drama moved to its close, and gently Violetta gave Alfredo the locket. The death scene was almost horrific, the last "È strano!" was uttered in an unearthly voice, and as Violetta rose to greet what she thought was a new life, a glaze came over her eyes, and she literally became a standing corpse. This was at the first night, but the death scene varied from performance to performance.

Harold Rosenthal, *Opera*

And then Callas does after all sing. She may not on Friday have done so with beauty of tone, but in almost every other respect it was a performance of outstanding distinction and musicality, full of detail that again and again illuminated the part as though for the first time. Her rebuke to Germont père, "Donna son'io, signore, e in mia casa," was turned with unassertive authority that in voice and gesture bespoke a great singing actress. But perhaps the most marvellous moment of the evening was the long sustained B flat before Violetta descends to the opening phrase of "Dite alla giovine." This is the moment of decision on which the whole opera turns. By some miracle Callas makes that note hang unsuspended in mid air; unadorned and unsupported she fills it with all the conflicting emotions that besiege her. As she descends to the aria, which she opened with a sweet, distant mezza voce of extraordinary poignancy, the die is cast.

There is no other singer in the field of Italian opera today who can work this sort of poetic magic. And even if one strikes Maria Callas on an evening on which this magic is only intermittent and fleeting, it remains for me a haunting shadow of the perfection that opera so constantly strives for and so rarely achieves, in which drama and music effect a mutual reconciliation and illumination.

Peter Heyworth, *The Observer*

No less an event was the Callas *Traviata*, which culminated in a blaze of controversy. There were the inevitable hard high notes, and there was an uncomfortable ragged moment at the close of an otherwise magical "Addio del passato." But there must have been many Verdi-lovers who felt that at last they had come face to face with Violetta herself, so completely integrated was this unforgettable performance, and her singing was of rare musicianship, with floating mezza voce passages that no other artist today can match for sheer expressive beauty.

Opera News

Concert, BBC Television, London; 23 September; Pritchard. Program: "Un bel dì," *Madama Butterfuly*; "Casta diva," *Norma*.
Concerts, Municipal Auditorium, Birmingham, 11 October; Municipal Auditorium, Atlanta, 14 October; Forum, Montreal, 17 October; Maple Leaf Garden, Toronto, 21 October; Public Music House, Cleveland, 15 November; Masonic Auditorium, Detroit, 18 No-

vember; Constitution Hall, Washington, 22 November; War Memorial, San Francisco, 26 November; Shrine Auditorium, Los Angeles, 29 November; Kiel Auditorium, St. Louis, 11 January; Rescigno. Program: "Tu che invoco," *La Vestale*; "Vieni t'affretta," *Macbeth*; "Una voce poco fa," *Il Barbiere di Siviglia*; "L'altra notte," *Mefistofele*; "Quando me'n vo," *La Bohème*; "A vos jeux, mes amis," *Hamlet*.

The vocal artistry and blistering emotional intensity of soprano Maria Callas bore her first Atlanta audience to musical and spiritual heights seldom attained in a concert hall here . . . . To judge from the stillness that prevailed while she sang and the loud, sustained applause when she stopped, the audience was well satisfied. . . . She gives her all to the music. She can look like a pixie or like a devil; she can croon like an angel; she can wail like a banshee . . . .

Richard Gray, Atlanta Constitution

She could one moment move her audience to shouts and vigorous applause with her finely-drawn coloratura performance of a Rossini aria. And then, almost child-like, she could not resist a giggly peek over her shoulder at all the hullabaloo as she disappeared into the wings.

Her widely noted (but really quite rare) hard or awkward tones would be followed immediately by the most beautiful sounds one could imagine.

Her innate dramatic gifts and obvious stage deportment were in evidence throughout every phrase she uttered, yet, quite distractingly, she was unable to cope with her chiffon stole. It appeared, as the program went on, in every conceivable drape and position, but it would never stay put.

Miss Callas' scales, trills, and roulades were impeccably placed and always contributed to the total artistic and dramatic effect.

Frank Hruby, Cleveland Press

The lights in the auditorium were darkened, leaving the orchestra in high relief with its music stands bathed in reading lights. A spotlight was thrown on the wings and the lady entered escorted by Signor Rescigno.

The progress along the white strip of carpet which led to a spot beside the podium was triumphant. Mme. Callas held her head, with its cap of bronze hair, high, and fiddled with several yards of gauze which draped her shoulders.

Her gown was of cloth of gold in the highest of style.

It became evident that after such an entrance, the lady could not dare do less than sing better than any other singer in the history of opera.

And sing she did, capably and with the tremendous dramatic force that has made her a star of nearly every important opera house of the world.

The voice did not come up to all expectations, largely because the expectations had been so immensely enlarged. There is a marked vibrato which detracts from the firmness of a held tone, and there are parts of the vocal register which are rather unpleasantly reedy. . . .

Nevertheless, the production of the tremendous invocation from Spontini's *La Vestale* was a chilling performance filled with the super-natural terror of the opera.

The program continued the high dramatic vein, with the great oral recitative and florid aria of Lady Macbeth from the Verdi opera . . . .

On the concert stage, Mme. Callas turns out to be surprisingly tall. She is endowed with a rather deliberate grace in movement. Her manual gestures are extraordinarily effective.

J. Dorsey Callaghan, *Detroit Free Press*

And the concert setting, in a single static spotlight, led Callas to enact a role in which she didn't look anywhere near as genuine as she can in *Lucia*.

The role was that of Maria Callas herself—a hammy throwback to old prima donna artificiality—ogling broadly, smirking coyly, her features flickering unaccountably between demure anguish and gaiety, while she hugged a long satin stole of shocking pink around her white-gowned tall figure, as if to keep out some imaginary frost. In fact, it was a warm evening.

Now, how does Callas really sing?

She has magnificent vocal qualities, along with one bad weakness. The weakness is that her full top tones—from B natural upwards—are unpleasantly shrill. The shrillness hurt when she sang out for forceful climax.

What's strong about her is that her voice is an intensely sensual, personal instrument. It hits its tones on the bull's eye of pitch (and if you think it didn't where you sat on Wednesday, I'd blame it on the auditorium's silly acoustics). It's a tone that purrs or pours out always with fascination and meaning. . . .

At the end, Callas—slouching and lilting and spurting on and off stage—sweetly refused encores. One man in the audience (silly fellow) leaped onto the platform and kissed her on both cheeks.

And the hypnotic way in which the crowd massed up to the stage—just to look at Callas silently, or to yell eagerly, "More! Maria, Sing!"—is a subject I recommend to psychologists, sociologists, and students of the occult. It was astounding.

Alexander Fried, San Francisco Examiner

The "Mad Scene" from *Hamlet* by Thomas, for example, was managed with the finest delicacy and, even as a vocal production alone, was truly elegant. What gave the scene its poignancy, however, was the emotional intensity with which she revealed the plight of a young girl who feels reason and her life slipping away from her and remembers only her love . . . .

In contrast to her reputation as a fireball, Mme. Callas was notably relaxed and modest in her stage demeanor. She wore a smart but subdued sheath gown, acknowledged her several ovations with an inclination of the head and a friendly wave of the hand rather than an elaborate bow, and in general reserved her temperament for the music.

There was little doubt at any stage of the performance that she had the power to stir an audience; and it was evident, as well, that her means of doing so were those of a first rank artist.

Thomas B. Sherman, St. Louis Post-Dispatch

La Traviata, Civic Opera, Dallas; 31 October, 2 November; Rescigno; Filacuridi, Taddei.

Mme. Callas can't be touched for presence and a magic brewed with one of the shrewdest, most reliable techniques in the business. She is that rarest of creatures, a genuine artist, by which we mean a musical intelligence first and foremost. Roles are not just sung for vocal opulence and applause of the moment. They are created to such a fine degree that their impact as vocal communications will be remembered as long as great artistry is catalogued.

Such was her Violetta, a triumph of a complete art and not just of the sounds that can be made. And just who is it that is supposed to have a monopoly on pianissimos? Her use of same Friday evening stilled the house unforgettably. In moments of passion or emotional disturbance she was unerringly the mistress of mood. Even the famous Act 1 scene that embraces the coloratura powers of the "Sempre libera" were skillfully negotiated for great theater, even if the ear was ready with a tense concern that never quite materialized.

Raul Askew, Dallas Morning News

Medea, Civic Opera, Dallas; 6, 8 November; Rescigno; Carron, Berganza, Vickers, Zaccaria.

Madame Callas, who has been described as "the most sincere opera artist in the world," sang her Colchian Sorceress better than even you have heard her before in opera or concert or, for that matter, in the recorded *Medea* album of recent issue.

One is conditioned to accept the questionable, even exacerbating vocalism of this intense soprano-actress. Thursday evening, however, she intoned like the demi-goddess she portrayed, almost never assaulting the ears. Much of it, too, was fortissimo in a tortuous high tessitura. Evaporated for the nonce were the ludicrous tremolos, rasping "spread" notes and other vocal outrages.

In their places were some mezza voce velvet, a vivid palette of well-produced vocal color, and then ringing and clarion-clear dramatic metal. It was as if she were trying to prove something especially to a four-letter name indicating an unkind New York impresario. . . .

Medea is a great and universal theme if you can do it. Madame Callas was one who could. And by the splendor of her singing she elevated some interesting, significant but hardly violent music to the Olympian plane of the tragedy.

John Rosenfield, Dallas Morning News

Concert, Opera, Paris; 19 December; Sebastian. Program: "Casta diva," *Norma*; "D'amor sull'ali rosee" and "Miserere," *Il Trovatore*; "Una voce poco fa," *Il Barbiere di Siviglia*; *Tosca*, Act II, with Lance, Gobbi, Mars.

Let it not be said that the spectators, near or far, did not get their money's worth; it was a very good show indeed. Callas may be difficult, unreasonable, temperamental, impossible, or what you will. But when she is on stage, she is very much *there*. . . . The curtain rose and a graceful figure sang the aria "Casta diva" from Bellini's *Norma*—sang it well, but not sensationally. In Leonora's aria from the fourth act of *Trovatore*, Mme. Callas began to hit her stride. The "Miserere" . . . brought down the house, and after "Una voce poco fa" . . . pandemonium broke loose . . . .

After the intermission Mme. Callas was joined by Tito Gobbi and others in the second act of *Tosca*—this time with costumes and scenery. The ovation she received for this performance was entirely warranted. "La Callas" had demonstrated that the prima donna of the "good old days" is still alive in her person, and *tout Paris* seemed to find delight in this fact and in paying homage to the singer who could elicit such rapture. They hadn't had so much fun since the time of "La Malibran" . . . a mere 110 years ago.

Everett Helm, Saturday Review

1959

Concert, Academy of Music, Philadelphia; 24 January; Ormandy. Program: "L'altra notte," *Mefistofele*; "Una voce poco fa," *Il Barbiere de Siviglia*; "A vos jeux, mes amis," *Hamlet*.

Il Pirata, Carnegie Hall, New York, 27 January; Constitution Hall, Washington, 29 January; Rescigno; Miranda-Ferraro, Ego.

For the concluding number, one of those mad scenes in which Italian composers of the early nineteenth century liked to have their prima donnas expire, the lights were doused. Only the lamps on the instrumentalists' desks remained on and a spotlight played on Miss Callas. This wasn't the Met, but it was the atmosphere of the opera house.

Miss Callas rose to the occasion here. . . . She sang the introductory recitative and then the aria, "Col sorriso d'innocenza," with commanding artistic resource. She had been in good voice all evening, though her attack at the outset, probably because of tenseness, had had the impact of a buzz saw.

She had sung with a grasp of the Bellini style and with enormous conviction. At times the voice had been ingratiating: at others it had

had an edge. Top notes had been a gamble: either shrill or brilliantly in focus. But now at the end she did not fail. This was Maria Callas living up to her reputation.

Then came the tumult and the shouting. Hundreds debouched down the aisles to the footlights. They applauded and yelled and screamed, "Brava Maria!" Miss Callas returned again and again for curtain calls. Finally a man came out and turned off the lights, and the worshippers departed.

Howard Taubman, The New York Times

And, of course, that brings us to the heart of the matter, for without a singer of Miss Callas's special endowments and acquired resources, *Il Pirata* would founder on Imogene's first entrance. Made from her place on stage . . . it put her to the test of an unaccompanied recitative in cadenza form, followed by an aria rising to a top D. Her voice was hardly loose, at this point, but it was all fervor and solidity. Much could be made of the extremes of range with which she coped impressively well, but there was much more art and expression in her finely controlled delivery of the legato line and its embellishments, in her sense of the tragic accent appropriate to the words and their meaning, and the kind of spell she casts with a covered sound as against an open one.

Throughout Act II and coming to a proper climax in the final "Mad Scene" (which she sang alone on a darkened stage in a spotlight) Miss Callas disposed vocal powers not previously at her command in New York. The pleading "Tu m'apriasti in cor ferita" . . . was an example of warmly colored cantabile singing . . . which attested to her ability to make an emotional appeal without bravura or other exhibitionistic devices. To labor the superb delivery of the "Mad Scene" is hardly necessary.

Irving Kolodin, Saturday Review

As the other soloists filed out, all the lights but those over the exits and the musicians' desks suddenly went out. Slowly Miss Callas rose, drew close her red stole, and an eerie glow fell on her face. At that ghostly juncture Miss Callas made the most of her strange and haunting timbres. It was something to be left in the dark with the voice of Maria Meneghini Callas.

Louis Biancolli, New York World-Telegram and Sun

The voice, which Miss Callas uses more as an extension of her dramatic personality than as a musical instrument, was not always beautiful, at least not in the popular sense in which beauty is equated with the quality of sweetness. Sometimes it was strident . . . . But it performed its function, in collaboration with the singer's impeccable musicianship and her unerring sense of authentic drama, in lifting the performance leagues above the kind of surface theatricality that commonly prevails in opera.

Ronald Eyer, Musical America

At the evening's conclusion, after Miss Callas had gone theatrically "mad" in the final scene, crowds massed at her feet and throughout the house, as if they had caught her fever. More or less hysterical, and including a few less noisy if articulate dissenters, they, for the most part, kept yelling "bravo" and "Callas." Only after an attendant came out to dismantle the prompter's box and the lights went low, did they disperse.

Harriet Johnson, New York Post

Concert, Teatro de la Zarzuela, Madrid; 2 May; Rescigno. Program: "Non mi dir," *Don Giovanni*; "Vieni t'affretta," *Macbeth*; "Bel raggio," *Semiramide*; "Suicidio," *La Gioconda*; "Col sorriso," *Il Pirata*.

In *Semiramide* . . . Callas gave, without doubt, the best and the worst of her art: an uneven, very unpleasant, and hard upper register, followed by a chromatic descending scale right out of the textbook, prodigious in quality, timbre, instrumental purity, and human emotion. The counterpart is encountered in the imperfection of several high notes, the vocal muddying of a sufficient number of phrases, the wavering in timbre in long notes, the unevenness of color of the voice, quite noticeable. If it is a matter of measuring the pros and cons, the triumph of the former would be obvious . . . .

Antonio Fernández-Cid, ABC

Concert, Liceo, Barcelona; 5 May; Rescigno. Program: "Tu che le vanità," *Don Carlo*; "L'altra notte," *Mefistofele*; "Una voce poco fa," *Il Barbiere di Siviglia*; "Vissi d'arte," *Tosca*; "Quando m'en vo," *La Bohème*; "Col sorriso," *Il Pirata*.

Madame Callas is undoubtedly an artist of personality, temperament, and clear diction in the diversity of her accents. Her voice, pliant
and ductile in general emission, shows a light tremolo in the high notes
and an imbalance of timbres. The artistry of the singer, whom one
should hear in a complete opera for a more thorough judgment, is pure
and allows her to obtain effects that lead directly to success . . . .

The reception accorded the artist could not have been more cordial
or more enthusiastic.

U.F. Zanni, *La Vanguardia Española*

Concerts, Musikhalle, Hamburg, 15 May; Liederhalle, Stuttgart, 19
May, Deutsche Museum, Munich, 21 May; Kursaal, Wiesbaden,
24 May; Rescigno. Program: "Tu che invoco," *La Vestale*; "Vieni
t'affretta," *Macbeth*; "Una voce poco fa," *Il Barbiere di Siviglia*; Tu
che le vanità," *Don Carlo*; "Col sorriso," *Il Pirata*.

Maria Meneghini Callas's first appearance in Munich was celebrated tumultuously last night. The audience, for the most part in
evening dress, gave the Italian [sic] diva tumultuous ovations . . . .
The concert went off without incident.

Friedrich Müller, *Süddeutsche Zeitung*, translated by Brittain Smith

Medea, Covent Garden, London; 17, 22, 24, 27, 30 June; Rescigno;
Carlyle, Cossotto, Vickers, Zaccaria.

Fury hot, and fury cold, are the gamut of Medea as Callas plays
her, with a striking pattern of gesture, but some facial expressions that
tend to become over familiar. Act III fortunately provides her with the
new emotion of concern for her children, but it is in the triumphant
note of horror she achieves at the end, after she has struck them down,
that Maria is most Medea. Vocally, Callas appears to have profited
from a period of relative idleness . . . for the sound was fresh, responsive, endlessly expressive in her veiled, *chalumeau* manner. But the
range continues to contract, with a lunge for a C in Act II that came
out merely as a shriek.

Irving Kolodin, *Saturday Review*

Callas made a heroine of burning passion and intensity and sang
at her exhilirating best; her voice was full and round, now tender and
coaxing, now dark and commanding.

Frank Granville Barker, *Opera News*

From her first appearance, standing between two huge pillars, and wrapped in a huge cape which exposes nothing but her eyes, heavily rimmed with black and filled with well-composed hatred to her last, when the temple in which she has murdered her children tumbles to the ground showing her in a snake-entwined chariot with their corpses at her feet, Callas builds her performance into one powerful line of ever-increasing tension. It is the kind of performance which spoils one for anything less from the opera stage . . . .

And just as it is with her broad movements and the character she creates as a whole, so is it with the details. Her eyes seemingly can match the thought of the moment and reveal the next move simultaneously. She can tower as a pillar of outraged fury one moment and lie in a heap the next. Part of her plea to Creon is sung from the floor and addressed to his big toe. In addition, the range of her hand movements, already so celebrated in all her roles, is given full play in *Medea*. She can even make and wave a fist, an action few divas could afford to make.

George Louis Mayer, American Record Guide

Concerts, Concertgebouw, Amsterdam, 11 July; Théâtre de la Monnaie, Brussels, 14 July; Rescigno. Program: "Tu che invoco," *La Vestale*; "Ernani involami," *Ernani*; "Tu che le vanità," *Don Carlo*; "Col sorriso," *Il Pirata*.

Preceded by the now inevitable spate of advance publicity, Maria Meneghini Callas came, sang, and conquered Amsterdam in her Dutch debut on Saturday night. The Amsterdam burghers, rather like our staid Victorian forefathers, have the reputation of being cool and reserved. Whether that be true or not, all reserve vanished on this occasion, and Mme. Callas was welcomed like some visiting royalty. The audience rose to greet her at her first entrance; and during the course of the evening excitement mounted, so that the ovation that she received after the final item, the Mad Scene from Bellini's *Il Pirata*, was something not easily to be forgotten . . . . Ridiculous? Hysterical? No more so than the kind of receptions that were accorded Jenny Lind or Patti.

The Times

One must thank Callas for having revived a personage of whom there existed nothing more than the memory, that of the diva, the imperious and fantastic grand performer whose tradition extends from the Congress of Vienna to the last Russian Grand Dukes . . . . The program presented by Maria Callas Thursday evening . . . was austere. But it is that very austerity that permits the artist to exercise over her public the genuine magnetism that characterizes her and that allows her literally to bewitch her listeners, to the point that they remained contemplative and silent during the intervals between pieces.

L. V., Le Soir (Brussels)

Callas entered. A royal step, a muse reincarnated whose voice nourishes the grooves of hundreds of thousands of long-playing records. There was the shock, immediate, stunning. Brussels had already capitulated.

Callas smiled. A goddess sure of her power, her lovely hands . . . crossed over her chest, she made a sign to the orchestra director, maestro Nicola Rescigno.

The miracle worked.

The miracle.

Henry Lemaire, Le Soir (Brussels)

Concert, Coliseo Albia, Bilbao, Spain; 17 September; Rescigno. Program: "Tu che le vanità," *Don Carlo*; "A vos jeux, mes amis," *Hamlet*; "Ernani involami," *Ernani*; "Col sorriso," *Il Pirata*.

Concert, Royal Festival Hall, London; 23 September; Rescigno. Program: "Tu che le vanità," *Don Carlo*; "Col sorriso," *Il Pirata*; "À vos jeux, mes amis," *Hamlet*; "Una macchia," *Macbeth*.

Concert, BBC Television, London; 3 October; Sargent. Program: "Sì, mi chiamano Mimì," *La Bohème*; "L'altra notte," *Mefistofele*.

Concert, Titiana Palast, Berlin; 23 October; Rescigno. Program: "Non mi dir," *Don Giovanni*; "Ernani involami," *Ernani*; "Tu che le vanità," *Don Carlo*; "A vos jeux, mes amis," *Hamlet*.

Concert, Loew's Midland Theater, Kansas City, Mo.; 28 October; Rescigno. Program: "Non mi dir," *Don Giovanni*; "Regnava nel silenzio," *Lucia di Lammermoor*; "Ernani involami," *Ernani*; "Col sorriso," *Il Pirata*.

A bomb hoax interrupted a Maria Callas concert for 40 minutes last night but the tempestuous soprano brushed it off as "ridiculous."

The orchestra was playing an overture when a man called the box office and police headquarters. He told the police dispatcher: "There's a bomb planted in the orchestra pit at the Midland Theater that's set to go off at 9:30."

Larry Kelly of Dallas, concert producer, hurried backstage and told Mme. Callas a few minutes before 9 o'clock.

"What time is it supposed to go off?" she asked. Told that it was 9:30, she replied, "Then I will go out and sing and let the people know I am here. If I don't they will say, 'Well, that Maria Callas.' I'll take the risk . . ."

Kansas City Banner

Lucia di Lammermoor, Civic Opera, Dallas; 6, 8 November; Rescigno; Raimondi, Bastianini, Zaccaria.

Madame Callas made the fourteen-minute episode [the "Mad Scene"] theatrical, telling, rather pitiable and certainly full of meaning. When singing in mezza voce and in the middle of her voice she produced superlative sound. The screeched high notes had to go with it and also some badly aimed attacks which she barely covered by roulades downward into the more comfortable register.

Withal, it was a finer Mad Scene than New York ever heard in her Metropolitan Opera days . . . . No doubt there will be many to say: "I have heard Callas as Lucia and must get her out of both my eyes and my ears before I can accept another."

John Rosenfield, Dallas Morning News

[Callas's Lucia] revealed once more that, all sensational and controversial publicity aside, she is at her best an artist of high rank. Granted that there are possessors of more beautiful voices in the world today; granted, too, that this or that famous soprano may surmount intricate, technically difficult passages with more ease and flawlessness. But no one is able to infuse even seemingly less important phrases with precisely the same dramatic power as Callas does. It must be said, in all justice, that in the higher range a disturbing tremolo occurs at times. Her artful phrasing is, however, expert; so is the floating and subdued coloring even of certain passages often unduly neglected by others; and in the Mad Scene, the phrase "Alfin son tua, alfin sei mio" emerged with a wondrous intensity and a ravishing vocal timbre which were incomparable. The huge audience was entranced, and responded with a long, standing ovation.

George Saxe, Musical Courier

Medea, Civic Opera, Dallas; 19, 21 November; Rescigno; Williams, Merriman, Vickers, Zaccaria.

1960

Norma, Epidaurus; 24, 28 August; Serafin; Morfoniou, Picchi, Mazzoli.
Poliuto, La Scala, Milan; 7, 10, 14, 18, 21 December; Votto/Tonini; Corelli, Bastianini, Zaccaria.

But although [Callas' voice] is not quite the same as it was some time ago, before the soprano reportedly started her exaggerated "slimming cure," which was not very successful, her voice sounded warm and beautiful, her acting was dignified and restrained. Thus the vociferous applause that greeted her entrance and the equally boisterous acclaim that broke out at the end of each of her scenes, was well motivated.

Gisella Selden-Goth, Musical Courier

And what of the great prima donna? Your correspondent looked forward to the event with a certain amount of trepidation, and discovered that in part—let us face things squarely—Callas is not what she once was. A magnificent stage presence, yes: when she appears, her personality simply singes the edges off everyone else, dramatically. She is a magnificent actress . . . . But when she reached B or high C, her voice became tight, metallic, unpleasant. As the evening wore on, she showed the strain, too—something which she never did before. In the last act, the critics in the press box winced, and there was an audible hiss of sympathy from the audience when she flattened—and flattened like a ton of bricks—in several high notes. It was a memorable comeback, but not a flawless one.

H. C. Robbins Landon, High Fidelity

Two decades of singing an extraordinarily wide repertory have left some scars on the Callas voice, particularly in her high notes, which are not always so firm or secure as before . . . . Her qualities as an interpreter, however, once more reigned supreme. The force of her phrasing remains miraculous; all the coloratura was articulated expressively, every melody shaped from its inner source to an appropriate, secure profile . . . .

Fedele d'Amico, Opera News

On the first night, she was clearly not in good voice. She is, of course, a highly wrought singer, and the feverish excitement that surrounded the evening probably took its toll, for her voice sounded strained.

Her movements, gestures, and general stagecraft were, of course, as consummate as ever. What actress uses her hands as Mme. Callas does? And there were moments when she achieved a poignancy that no other singer can rival.

Peter Heyworth, The New York Times

It is precisely those demands [of Poliuto] which exposed the old flaws in the soprano's vivid artistry: the heavy vibrato and occasional sourness on sustained high notes, the lack of richness in long-drawn phrases and of sheer volume of tone in ensembles. The voice has not greatly altered since I last heard it. She still has the capacity to color a phrase with unrivaled dramatic expression, from anger to grief and all points between, but Poliuto afforded her scant chance to show it.

Her movements and gestures, "calculated in the dark and shaped by instinct," as she once said, are still surpassingly grand, in the play of her supplicating or accusing hands, the carriage of her head and body and the scorching flash of her great, black, anxious eyes. She commands the stage with consummate technical mastery to underpin a voice which, if it were more comfortable, would likely make her a lesser artist.

Noel Goodwin, The Observer

Mme. Callas was far from being in good voice at the third performance, and although at the fifth the voice was under firmer control, on both occasions her first act was vocally poor. There seemed to be more voice at the singer's disposal than when she was last heard at Covent Garden, but a lot of the time the tone sounded empty and hollow, and she seemed to produce more of those strident top notes than usual. Then suddenly would come a few minutes of sure and exquisite singing, of phrases so full of significance that little thrills would run down the spine . . . . Dramatically, too, she produced many of her familiar thrills, yet on both evenings in the first act one had the curious impression that one was witnessing an artificial performance by Callas imitating Callas being Paolina. A strange experience, and one I have never before had at a Callas performance . . . .

Harold Rosenthal, Opera

1961

Concert, St. James's Palace, London; 30 May; Sargent (piano). Program: "Casta diva," *Norma*; "Pleurez mes yeux," *Le Cid*; Tu che le vanità," *Don Carlo*; "L'altra notte," *Mefistofele*.

Medea, Epidaurus; 6, 13 August; Rescigno; Glantzi, Morfoniou, Vickers, Modesti.

Though no city, not even a village, is to be found near Epidaurus, its fourteenth-century-B.C. amphitheater drew a capacity crowd of 17,000 who streamed in all afternoon, seemingly from nowhere. Their goal: to hear Maria Callas impersonate Cherubini's Medea, whose original prototype lived in nearby Corinth. Nor were they disappointed, for seldom in recent years has Callas been in such excellent form. Few singers with steadier top notes could approach her for dramatic impact, musicianship (style and phrasing), the unfailingly right coloration of voice and body movement that she brings to the role, having made it so much her own since the 1952 Florence revival.

Trudy Goth, Opera News

Medea, La Scala, Milan; 11, 14, 20 December; Schippers; Tosini/Rizzoli, Simionato, Vickers, Ghiaurov.

Speaking of Callas is like walking over burning coals. There are those who adore her with a sort of inclination to fetishism. There are those who detest her on the basis of the gossip, often tendentious, of a certain part of the press enamored of rumors. We are with neither the former nor the latter. The fact remains for us that this Medea of hers is unique for the psychological penetration of character, for the intimate warmth of the molding, manifested in a stupendous way, for the moving vocal thrill . . . not minimized, certainly, by the slight and sporadic oscillations of the upper register with which the miracles of a vocal technique of a clearly superior class cope.

Franco Abbiati, Corriere della Sera

It was not the same Callas in 1961 as the one who had sung this same opera in 1953 as her Scala debut. She was then a stout figure, typical of an old-style soprano who opened up the entire range of classical opera by demonstrating that she could sing anything written for a female performer. Now "the tigress," as she is called by the "scaligerans," is a svelte, long, and fine-boned figure, incredibly transformed by her own indomitable energy and ambition. And if her voice at times is a bit frayed and wobbly—and takes painfully wrong notes occasionally—it still retains all the lyric intensity, the emotional inflections and nuances, and the dramatic projection that no singer of her time can equal. She is the example of her own belief that beautiful sound can at times be sacrificed for powerful drama.

Trudy Goth, Opera News

Anyone who heard the performances of *Medea* some years back and now hears this new production cannot but notice that the youthful impetuosity, the almost savage passion that Callas brought to the character of Medea and to her gestures, words and cries have become somewhat dimmed with the passing of the years. Stylistically, there has perhaps been an improvement: the interpretation is more severe, more homogeneous, the utterance more studied, the characterization better built up, but all to the detriment of the sincerity and brilliant improvisatory quality that made a miracle of the earlier performances. Formerly one listened only to Callas. Now, thanks to her more modest interpretation, to her new respect for the opera and the character, and to her purer singing, there is even time and opportunity to realize that the score of *Medea* is a continuous fabric of gems and a masterpiece.

Claudio Sartori, Opera

1962

Concert, Royal Festival Hall, London; 27 February; Prêtre. Program: "O don fatale," *Don Carlo*; "Pleurez mes yeux," *Le Cid*; "Nacqui all'affanno," *Cenerentola*; "Al dolce guidami," *Anna Bolena*; "La luce langue," *Macbeth*; "Ocean, thou mighty monster," *Oberon*.

These recitals, indeed, are perhaps Mme. Callas's new visiting cards: they no longer read, "Prima soprano assoluta: all roles studied, rivals routed, managements flouted at short notice," but indicate a gentler artist whose voice is matching the change in temperament by finding its true range on a slightly lower specific gravity. Her *Cenerentola* finale reflected not breathless, bubbling joy but hesitant acceptance of happiness: the scales and runs were not a burst of exuberance but a kind of elaborate vocal caress, with the notes lightly touched in a near-glissando as the voice passed easily across them. At the end, a sudden shriek of all the old sourness indicated how much care she had been exercising; just as the beautifully cradled tone of "O mia regina" in Eboli's aria was immediately preceded by a violent low register snarl. Even Lady Macbeth raged and flashed only through sharp-edged phrasing and superbness of rhythm. Though happier at this dynamic and emotional level, the voice is still an untamed organ.

Of the strictly soprano arias, it was Massenet's "Pleurez, mes yeux" which most successfully caught the imagination—and here, too, the effect was achieved less by pliant stroke than by the yielding cadence of the phrase and by such strokes as the subtly soft consonants (the gently touched, barely rolled "r" in the repeated "pleurez"), the quickly stifled tone at "Hélas!" In the *Anna Bolena* Mad Scene, late in a long evening, tiredness was added to other difficulties: the piece . . . exposed more weaknesses than strengths. Nor was "Ocean, thou mightly monster" (in the original English) a success, for it demands glorious security of intonation and breath control, exulting coloratura and—where Callas was severely tested—absolute steadiness of tone and line through a slowly rising scale.

John Warrack, Opera

Concerts, Deutsches Museum, Munich, 12 March; Musikhalle, Hamburg, 16 March; Städtischer Saalbau, Essen, 19 March; Beethoven Halle, Bonn, 23 March; Prêtre. Program: "O don fatale," *Don Carlo*; "Pleurez mes yeux, *Le Cid*; "Nacqui all'affanno," *Cenerentola*; "Habanera" and Séguedille," *Carmen*; "Ernani involami," *Ernani*.
Concert, Madison Square Garden, New York; 19 May; Wilson (piano). Program: "Habanera" and "Séguedille," *Carmen*.
Medea, La Scala, Milan; 23 May, 3 June; Schippers; Rizzoli, Vickers, Simionato, Ghiaurov.

Her voice, now smaller in scope and distinctly nasal in quality, sounded even and steady after a few warm-up measures; dramatically she left no doubt who remains the outstanding figure on the operatic stage.

G. F., Opera News

Concert, BBC Television, London; 4 November; Prêtre. Program: "Tu che le vanità, *Don Carlo*; "Habanera" and Séguedille," *Carmen*.

1963

Concerts; Deutsche Oper, Berlin, 17 May; Rheinhalle, Düsseldorf, 20 May; Liederhalle, Stuttgart, 23 May; Royal Festival Hall, London, 31 May; Falkoner Center, Copenhagen, 9 June; Prêtre. Program: "Bel raggio," *Semiramide*; "Casta diva," *Norma*; "Ben io t'invenni," *Nabucco*; "Quando m'en vo," *La Bohème*; "Tu, tu piccolo iddio," *Madama Butterfly*; "O mio babbino caro," *Gianni Schicchi*.

What is Maria Callas, the artist, today? What is achievement, what is myth? The evening could not provide an answer to the questions. What is the magic that she exerts based on? Suffice it to say that it is still there; she is the mistress of the evening . . . she is simultaneously personality and idol, and it is difficult to separate the two forms of her existence.

She begins with Rossini, with Semiramide's aria. From the first note the enticement of the wonderful, dark-toned voice, capable of every powerful expansion and of every light, sweet tenderness, has its effect; with the first phrase she displays the unparalleled stylistic taste that is certainly the most admirable aspect of her performance. . . . When the performer begins to sing Norma's cavatina . . . everything is fervor, everything soaring, breathing melody, flowing *melos* that twice soars to radiant climaxes and descends again assuaged. And if the coloratura of the allegro was hurled out violently and imperfectly, the will and capacity for attaining dramatic effect captivate completely here, too.

The second half of the evening brings yet another moment of vocal intensification with Abigaille's aria from *Nabucco*; once more the voice's power of expression masters the astringent alto tone of the lower register and the plangent or radiantly soaring metallic timbre of the high notes. Then Maria Callas allows herself the less demanding effects of Puccini's Musetta and Butterfly . . . .

Werner Oehlmann, *Der Tagesspieler*, translated by Brittain Smith

The flirtation with the mezzo repertory seems to have been abandoned, and we are now back with the soprano roles. Mme. Callas has obviously been putting in some very hard work on the voice, and it certainly sounded far better than at any time I can recall since she last sang at Covent Garden . . . . The famous wobble on which her detractors so eagerly fasten was still there—but it was far less in evidence and the voice was under far better control. The breath control is less perfect than it was, one feels that this slim little figure just cannot meet all the demands the singer puts on the voice; the dramatic instinct is all it ever was, and the phrasing and musicianship are still unsurpassed.

The *Semiramide* aria which began the evening was interesting but not overwhelming; "Casta diva" was sung mostly with an exquisite tone, but the cabaletta was only an echo of what it used to be. Do you remember how every note in the descending scale used to be crystal clear? The *Nabucco* extract was outstanding on any count . . . . Musetta's Waltz Song came up new and unhackneyed, and with *all* the character of that wayward lady well and truly captured. The short final scene of *Butterfly* was over before it had begun—but in the few minutes that it lasted, Mme. Callas managed to tug at the heart-strings. "O mio babbino caro," the encore, was likewise sung for all it was worth, plus what the soprano thought it was worth!

Harold Rosenthal, Opera

Concert, Champs-Elysées, Paris; 5 June; Prêtre. Program: "Bel raggio," *Semiramide*; "Nacqui all'affanno," *Cenerentola*; "Air des lettres," *Werther*; "Adieu notre petite table," *Manon*; "Ben io t'invenni," *Nabucco*; "Quando m'en vo," *La Bohème*; "Tu, tu piccolo iddio," *Madama Butterfly*; "O mio babbino caro," *Gianni Schicchi*.

Maria Callas has been one of the enchantments of our age, she has renewed the meaning of a tired bel canto and created a style of dramatic and lyric interpretation that will mark a milestone . . . but I did not find the Callas of the great days. Of course she sings with a miraculous legato. Of course she retains that phrasing, so intelligent, so beautiful, and which gives the most mediocre or facile music an essential significance that the majority of singers weighed down by concerns for the throat have lost sight of. Of course she still has, in some notes, that so rare quality of timbre owing to the generous emission that has always characterized her vocal part. But what unsteadiness in the voice! In the first place, an unsteadiness which in the upper register gives birth to sounds indefinable in pitch, and which often becomes trills, at times trills with an interval of a third. Some aficionados discreetly call it a vibrato. Perhaps. But all the same is it a lot of vibrato. Moreover, the upper register becomes rather white and flat under pressure. People have often reproached Maria Callas for having a weak middle register. One should admit that it seems to be somewhat stronger. But the passages that lead there are quite labored. In the lower register—of which this role [concert singer] did not allow her to make a great display—there are some very beautiful notes sung with the chest voice just as needed. Would this not be the proper region to cultivate today? But even so, I fear that Callas the great mezzo will never make me forget the other Callas, so imprudent and so sublime.

Claude Rostand, *Le Figaro Littéraire*

Has Maria Callas retained all her trumps? No. But she plays the ones she still has in her hand with a consummate skill. I do not find her reputation overblown: she offers us a festival of intelligence, charm, and beauty.

Marcel Schneider, *Combat*

1964

Tosca, Covent Garden, London; 21, 24, 27, 30 January, 1, 5 February (9 February: Act II for BBC Television); Cillario; Cioni, Gobbi.

And how did she sing? I will be asked. Well, the voice was far better at all the three performances I heard than at any time since the 1957 *Traviatas*. At the performance on February 1 it was at its best, but the voice is so much part of the whole of a Callas performance that one cannot really separate it from the acting. She colors her voice much as a painter does his canvas, and if it is still not as large and sumptuous as it once was, it still is an amazing instrument, and its timbre highly individual.

Harold Rosenthal, *Opera*

It is the hallmark of a great artist to capitalize on his defects, and there is honor rather than disgrace in admitting that Maria Callas and Tito Gobbi played Tosca and Scarpia coolly and intelligently because neither has the same purely vocal gifts as formerly.

Miss Callas dispenses with all the traditional props and mannerisms of the 19th-century diva. Dressed and made up to resemble Mlle. Mars, the great French tragedienne, she combines the natural accents, intonations and gestures of a woman simply in love with the hands and arms of a great ballet dancer. Everything about her is expressive, even her silences, and the only moment of severe disappointment was her "Vissi d'arte." True, she had arrived with a heavy cold and was said to be singing on the first night with bronchitis and a middling high fever. Whatever the reason, her sustained legato singing was only patchily beautiful, and the whole excitement of her performance lay in her parlando or arioso singing but supremely in her acting.

Martin Cooper, *Musical America*

Both the press and the segment of the public lucky enough to get into the house were almost unanimous in praise; but some of those who heard the broadcast second performance (when Miss Callas was indeed in somewhat rougher voice than at the premiere) wrote angry letters to critics, asking what had become of their standards that they could rave about such squalling and wobbling on all sustained notes above the staff. Later still, a TV showing of Act II largely restored the status quo, in that Callas' amazing intensity and subtlety as a singing actress became manifest to millions and explained why theater audiences can willingly accept vocalizing so faulty and at moments painful.

The fact is that the compensations are immense, and such as no other artist now offers . . . .

Desmond Shawe-Taylor, *Opera News*

True, there were times when the lamp of her art burned low, but it was always bright. You want *more* power and support behind those shrieks of anguish in Act II. But how superb the whole delivery in the first act: what detail, what caressing and isolating of key words. All the detail was lovely; some of it unforgettably striking. I have not known Callas so magnificently in control of the situation (if not of the top of the voice) for a long time. . . .

The audience roared at her for twelve minutes at the end of the murder scene in which she had for nearly forty minutes gripped them.

Philip Hope-Wallace, *The Guardian*

Norma, Opera, Paris; 22, 25, 31 May, 6, 10, 14, 19, 24 June; Prêtre; Cossotto, Craig/Corelli, Vinco.

No one among the melomaniacal Friday-night gallery gods who booed her peak peacock cries could have been ignorant that the once fabulous Callas voice no longer reliably functions above an F or a G in her esthetically thinned body, so their booing sounded particularly uncouth. . . . For a majority of Paris listeners even on Friday, and certainly on Monday, the compensations in the Callas extended vocal artistry could properly be called magical—in the purling sounds of her impeccable bel canto, with notes rising fountainlike at the opening (not at the end) of the famous "Casta diva" aria; in the throttle depths of her chest tones; in the emotional colors shading her voice so that she seemed to be singing with a painted voice in the final scene of Act IV, when, freed from the earlier fears of the evening and backed by the chorus, she poured into her voice all the dramatic audible color that was consonant with complete and great lyric vocal acting . . . .

This writer first heard of and heard Callas in the spring of 1948 in Naples, singing Puccini's *Turandot* at the Teatro San Carlo. We had been warned in advance that she was fat, young, unknown, and temperamental, with a great and gorgeous, still inexperienced voice—which all turned out to be true. Today even without its upper reaches, she has been truly sensational as a belated operatic newcomer in Paris . . . .

Genet, The New Yorker

By the fifth evening the tempest in the auditorium (which had included hectic boos, cheers, and cheek-slappings on earlier occasions) had simmered down to a series of rhythmical hand-clappings after each act; the tempest on the stage, however, reached and maintained an intensity for which only the diva's Hellenic ancestors can account. Except for a few shrieks above the staff, Callas sang with all the eloquence and variety of her art.

Mary Ellis Peltz, Opera News

Only a little applause greeted her aria "Casta diva," sung in a very uneven manner and with skirted high notes. There even some "boos!" coming from the balconies . . . . But it was even worse a bit later, when the entire audience gave an ovation to Norma's rival, Adalgisa, performed by the young Italian mezzo-soprano Fiorenza Cossotto, with a powerful and colorful voice. A feeling of uneasiness ran through the house. Would Callas accept this setback or would the diva, long famous for her caprices, refuse to appear in the second act? When the curtain fell, the applause rang out for Cossotto while the "boos" kept coming to greet Callas from the same spectators in the balcony. Fortunately, Callas, in a very elegant fashion, certified her rival's success by advancing toward the audience and pointing out Fiorenza Cossotto to the entire house. People breathed. Callas was displaying the best personality in the world!

In the second act, passions erupted. Maria Callas, sublime in pink voile, demonstrated a fabulous elegance in her gestures and an equally fabulous musical sense, unfortunately hampered by some quite unorthodox sounds, while at her side Fiorenza Cossotto deployed all the seduction of a timbre of surprising richness. Scarcely had the curtain fallen when the show continued in the balcony: the parties were showering each other with abuse, and two spectators were taken to task in a lively way. It almost came to a fist fight. . . .

The third act achieved adhesion: Maria Callas had finally recovered the sureness of her voice, her fullness and sweetness without equal in mezza voce. The 2,200 spectators shouted with enthusiasm, as a single person, at the end of the famous duet "Mira o Norma," interrupted in the middle by applause from people who did not know the work. The audience . . . beamed with joy, and after four curtain calls, the two triumphant victors of the evening came back three more times to greet the delirious house.

Finally, in the last act, there was no longer anyone on stage except Maria Callas. Effacing all her partners, the diva surpassed herself, her voice became more fabulous and more moving than ever, and she flung out in full voice an ascent of two octaves that made the audience shiver with pleasure: the high notes, like the low ones, became sensational, and Maria Callas again truly became the superstar of legend in her duet with the tenor and the great final ensemble, which attained incomparable heights. The audience shook the rafters with applause: Maria Callas had definitely won the battle and conquered all of Paris, but the struggle had been close-fought.

René Sirvin, *L'Aurore*

I went to the second performance to discover that hearing Callas shape Bellini's melody is still one of those revelatory experiences comparable, perhaps, to hearing Casals play Bach. Eloquent line can never have been more beautifully moulded.

Callas has a superlative technique to draw a subtle, flexible line, exquisitely controlled, and ravishing in timbres raging between soft compassion ("Oh, di qual sei tu vittima") and fierceness ("In mia man"). Only at climaxes above the stave is the line drawn with a slate pencil. The voice will not take pressure today; it could not ring out as it once did to dominate the great twin climaxes of the finale, and an attempt to throw out a bold, ferocious high C ("e di sangue roman scorgeran torrenti") brought momentary disaster. Yet I feel sorry for anyone who, after 99 perfect notes forming one sublime paragraph, then finds all spoiled by a single horrid, or fairly horrid, sound.

True, the ugly notes were uglier than ever before. But there was also a new sort of vocal ease and happiness in the performance: as if Callas had accepted the fact that some parts would never come right, and that we and she should make the most of what *was* memorably sung—by far the greater part of the role. She gave a noble, dedicated interpretation, a performance so rapt and serious that it created its own atmosphere and made one oblivious of the extra-musical tensions which inevitably build up around everything she does. She is the greatest musician on the stage today.

Andrew Porter, *Musical Times*

Even now with her flawed vocal technique, Callas can get more out of this Bellini role than anyone else, and the weight and vocal color she gives to individual words and phrases is still an object lesson to all . . . . I found it difficult to relax during most of the first two acts . . . though by the time she had reached the Norma-Adalgisa-Pollione trio she had struck form, and as she rounded on Pollione with the words "Tremi tu? e per chi?" flashing her scornful eyes at him and pointing at him accusingly, the drama flared to life, and we were almost back in 1952. . . . Then in the last scene the miracle happened—in the dramatic recitative before the "Guerra, guerra" chorus, there was a slight vocal mishap which seemed to act as a spur, and from that moment until the end of the evening (some twenty-five or so minutes) she produced a stream of tone, firmly-based, such as I had not heard from her since those first Covent Garden *Normas*. She raged, she pleaded, she was in complete command of the stage, and had an electrifying effect on her companions. The audience went mad, and rightly so, for once again the Callas magic had worked.

Harold Rosenthal, Opera

Tosca, Opera, Paris; 19, 22, 26 February, 1, 3, 5, 8, 10, 13 March; Prêtre/Rescigno; Cioni, Gobbi.

Tosca, Metropolitan Opera, New York; 19, 25 March; Cleva; Corelli/ Tucker, Gobbi.

When the act was well under way, several things were apparent. This was going to be one of the best-acted *Toscas* in Metropolitan Opera history. It was also apparent that Miss Callas was singing with great care, trying to make the best of her vocal resources, avoiding as cannily as possible the vocal traps of the role.

And that, in sum, is the report of Miss Callas' evening. Her conception of the role was electrical. Everything at her command was put into striking use . . . . Her face mirrored every fleeting expression implicit in the music during her colloquy with Scarpia. This was supreme acting, unforgettable acting.

But now we come to matters vocal, and the story is less pleasant. Miss Callas is operating these days with only the remnants of a voice. Her top, always insecure, is merely a desperate lunge at high notes. She sings almost without support, and her tones are shrill, squeezed, and off center. It can be said that she avoided the sheer vocal desperation of her Covent Garden Tosca, singing with much more care. And in her biggest aria, the "Vissi d'arte," she sang in a subdued, almost reflective manner that made the most of the emotional content of the music, even if the purely technical vocal aspects sometimes went by the board.

Harold Schonberg, The New York Times

At the first offstage sound of her voice calling for her paramour, "Mario! Mario!", a wave of expectant murmuring swept the galleries. Then she swirled onstage and the audience erupted in a three-minute ovation. The prodigal daughter had returned . . . .

But *Tosca* is not a play; the singing's the thing. And even Callas could not make it otherwise. Never an instrument of luscious quality, her soprano last week was a thin and often wobbly echo of the voice that fled the Met in 1958. Her high notes were shrill and achingly insecure, and seemed all the more so by contrast with the rich, ringing tenor of Franco Corelli as Mario. In the poignant "Vissi d'arte" aria, Callas relied almost wholly on dramatic rather than vocal brilliance to carry her through—which, in her case, is admittedly a compelling compromise. The audience certainly thought so. At the curtain, a shower of roses and confetti rained down from the galleries, and the house bravoed on for half an hour of curtain calls.

Time

The voice I heard last night was not the voice of a woman that, in some respects, was in any sort of vocal trouble whatever. It had a creamy lightness to it which summoned up memories of her earliest recordings. She has somehow achieved this without losing her astounding ability to make the voice the servant of the drama . . . . It was— simply as singing—one of the most remarkable achievements in my memory . . . . What she did with her voice in the first act was an extension of the totally delightful, girlish conception she had devised. What she did with it in the second act was even more remarkable, because it stripped this piece of old-fashioned melodrama down to human proportions. Her "Vissi d'arte," soft and floating, became what it is supposed to be: a prayer from a frightened, confused, trapped human being. The whole act, in fact, was a stunning study in humanity.

Alan Rich, *New York Herald Tribune*

Concert, Paris Television; May; Prêtre. Program: "Adieu notre petite table," *Manon*; "Ah, non credea," *La Sonnambula*; "O mio babbino caro," *Gianni Schicchi*; Duparc, "Invitation au voyage" (not broadcast).

Norma, Opera, Paris; 14, 17, 21, 24, 29 (minus Act IV) May; Prêtre; Simionato/Cossotto, Cecchele, Vinco.

The fact that the famous singer, suffering from a fall in blood pressure such as would have caused a normal being difficulties in standing, had the courage to sing, in that state, the most arduous role in the international repertory, demonstrates a rare professional conscience. That she managed, with obviously diminished means, to transform this performance into a personal triumph such as she herself has rarely known, seems a veritable miracle. . . . It must be said that if the singer's voice seemed weaker, her singing did not show that in the least. The aria "Casta diva," performed that way in a floating pianissimo, testified to obvious precautions, but also provided for a sheer miracle of technique, and the legato of the great despairing cantilena that opens the third scene, this time again, was unsurpassed by any other contemporary singer. In the last act all that one could miss were certain outbursts of fury directed at Pollione that a diminished bravery does not permit Callas to make ring out as usual. "The essential thing," she said after the performance, "for me was to have sung the duets with Adalgisa acceptably. I would not have wanted to spoil Simionato's debut in Paris!"

Jacques Bourgeois, Arts

The singer, even with a voice at times inaudible still managed to fill the house with her more impalpable pianissimi, while the forced and awkwardly supported sounds got lost or were deformed in the immense space. For those who saw her final evenings . . . there will no doubt remain certain unforgettable phrases, words, inflections: without doubt, in the last act, Norma's famous invective that Callas has made her own "In mia man alfin tu sei," or better still the opening of the duet with Adalgisa "Ah, perchè, perchè," murmured in a painful dream, but over and above everything, those several phrases in the second act where, after having pronounced her "Oh rimembranza" in such a personal way, Maria Callas, with the voice of Norma evoking her first moments of happiness with Pollione, with the help of the phrase "Così trovava del mio cor la via," managed to hold an ethereal and smooth high A, as clean and transparent as those of her best years.

Roland Mancini, Opera International

Tosca, Covent Garden, London; 5 July; Prêtre; Cioni, Gobbi.

1973 and 1974

Concerts, Hamburg, 25 October; Berlin, 29 October; Düsseldorf, 2 November; Munich, 6 November; Frankfurt, 9 November; Mannheim, 12 November; London, 26 November and 2 December; Paris, 8 December; Amsterdam, 11 December 1973; Milan, 20 January (private); Stuttgart, 23 January; Philadelphia, 11 February; Toronto, 21 February; Washington, 24 February; Boston, 27 February; Chicago, 2 March; New York, 5 March; Detroit, 9 March;

Dallas, 12 March; Miami, 21 March; Columbus, 4 April; Brookville, N.Y., 9 April; New York, 15 April; Cincinnati, 18 April; Seattle, 24 April; Portland, Ore., 27 April; Vancouver, 1 May; Los Angeles, 5 May; San Francisco, 9 May; Montreal, 13 May; Seoul, 5 and 8 October; Tokyo, 12 and 19 October; Fukuoka, 24 October; Tokyo, 27 October; Osaka, 2 November; Hiroshima, 7 November; Sapporo, 11 November, 1974; with di Stefano. Accompanists: Ivor Newton, Robert Sutherland, Vasso Devetzi. Program (with variations from city to city): "Una parola Adina," *L'Elisir d'Amore*; "Garden Scene," *Faust*; "Final Scene," *Carmen*; "Qual prode el tuo coraggio," *I Vespri Siciliani*; "Tu qui Santuzza," *Cavalleria Rusticana*; "Ah per sempre o mio bell'angelo," *La Forza del Destino*; "Io vengo a domandar grazia," *Don Carlo*; "Habanera," *Carmen*; "Voi lo sapete," *Cavalleria Rusticana*; "O mio babbino caro," *Gianni Schicchi*; "Sola, perduta," *Manon Lescaut*; "Adieu notre petite table," *Manon*; "Air des lettres," *Werther*; "Suicidio," *La Gioconda*; "Sì, mi chiamano Mimì," *La Bohème*; "Vissi d'arte," *Tosca*; "Tu che le vanità," *Don Carlo*.

Callas the actress knows precisely how much movement on stage is desirable in such circumstances (almost none). Her words were as clear and impressive as ever, in every item except perhaps the first duet (from *Don Carlos*) in its first few minutes. Her intonation is still flawless, her phrasing skilled the more because her breath control has been inactive for so long.

This means not only that she has difficulty in sustaining long phrases and therefore breaks them up discreetly but that the quality of tone has become more breathy or less ringing, the gear change between the lower and upper registers very evident, as it was not when she was singing all the time. The low chest notes were strong and cogent in "Suicidio" and "Voi lo sapete" and the final *Carmen* duet, the middle of the voice rather colorless . . . , the top often characteristic, bringing recognition of the voice we had come to hear, but husbanded in volume and intensity.

Cavalleria (solo and duet) induced her to try singing out: she did not force, and there was little of the acid wobble which used to thrill some and repel others, but she did not attempt a true fortissimo, and wisely. The real Callas is to be experienced in the theater, with orchestral backing; she is clearly not yet returned to training pitch for vocal feats on such a scale. Meanwhile, in "O mio babbino caro," her encore, she reminded us of the phrasing and coloring and expressiveness that we remember, fined down and miniature. The Bizet duet, and the last cries of "Signor" in that from *Don Carlos*, gave me to hope optimistically that she may yet give us her Carmen in the opera house.

William Mann, *The Times*

Vocally "O mio babbino caro" was impossible—the piece doesn't work as a cornet solo—but the girlish skip with which Callas rounded the bend of the piano, the pleading of the eyes, the teasing of the mouth were irresistible. Best of all was the *Cavalleria* aria, which is a narrative piece: vocally secure, Callas told Santuzza's story with variety and agony and eloquence, the hands another register of the voice, another enactment of the soul.

It was moments like these that turned the frantic, fabricated enthusiasm of the crowd [in Boston] into an authentic ovation at the end . . . . Though the evening brought those musical illuminations we had demanded but dared not expect, it moved me mostly because it was such a human triumph, the triumph of an artistic personality, the triumph of a will, still daring and risking much when it sets out to dominate ever more refractory means. I do not think we can expect to see Maria Callas on stage in an operatic role again, but her human and artistic adventure is not yet done.

Callas has long commanded our attention, our respect, our gratitude, our awe. Now in her struggle and in her exhaustion she asks and earns, at cost to herself and to us, what she had never before seemed to need, our love.

Richard Dyer, *The Nation*

If they had not been Callas and di Stefano, the evening would have been truly painful. As it was, collective throats tightened in sympathy. Once, Callas was the Tosca of the century: now she could not get through "Vissi d'arte" without an off-pitch slur and a painful pause while the music caught up with her shortness of breath. She commands the stage effortlessly, changing emotional registers with the skill of a great actress . . . .

But what a pity for [her career] to resume like this. At one point, while announcing her next number, Callas told the audience—or at least those who could hear her—"If I don't sing they say I am temperamental and am doing it on purpose. I am tired and Giuseppe has a cold."

Later, when she announced, "Vissi d'arte," a man in the audience shouted back, "Thank you." To him and the audience she replied, "You are welcome, though I can't promise how I'm going to sing it." How sad that she felt the need to apologize, and how strange it seems to feel sorry for her.

Thomas Willis, Chicago Tribune

It would be silly to pretend that Miss Callas has much voice left. But, unlike the tenor, she remains an artist. She gave her best, and every now and then the old Callas sound came out. Vocal considerations aside—in public statements the past few months Miss Callas has been preparing us for the deficiencies in her voice—she knew exactly how to project a line, what tempo to choose, what the emotional meaning of the music was.

To the audience, nothing could go wrong. It was understandable that the concert was a representation to them of the singer that was, not the singer who is. And Miss Callas was able, even with her limited resources, to give an idea of the kind of temperament and musical understanding that never has deserted her. She looked not a day older than in her last appearance here almost ten years ago, and everybody washed her with oceans of love. She, at least, deserved the tribute.

Harold Schonberg, The New York Times

Callas Speaks

∷≡∷≡∷≡∷≡∷≡ ∷≡∷≡∷≡

Callas's Memoirs, 1957

EDITOR'S NOTE: *Callas's memoirs, as transcribed by Anita Pensotti,
originally appeared in the Italian magazine* Oggi *in 1957. It is obvious that
Pensotti substantially reshaped the materials that Callas dictated to her, because the style and composition of the memoirs are far removed from the
patterns of speech and thought that Callas revealed in direct interviews.
Nevertheless, and in spite of certain inaccuracies in matters of dates and
performances, the resulting document certainly bore Callas's stamp of approval
and represents the image of herself that Callas wished to project to the
world—at least in 1957. As with so many of Callas's pronouncements, the
memoirs reveal a personality fraught with contradictions and raise almost more
questions than they answer.*

PART 1

I have lately been asked many times by Italian and foreign journals,
among them the American magazines *Time* and *Life,* to publish my
memoirs. I have always refused. First of all because memoirs are usually
written when one is advanced in years or when, presumably, one will
have nothing more to say. In the second place—excuse me for saying
this—I have not accepted because of my reticence. I hate talking about
myself, so much so that I have always declined every proposal for

reminiscences about my trips in order to avoid, which would have been impossible, any allusions to my successes, always allowing others to speak at my expense, convinced that I was dealing with intelligent, kind, and generous people. Unfortunately, however, by dint of allowing others to speak, I find myself at the center of innumerable rumors that are circling the globe. And it is frankly in order to correct so many inaccuracies that I have made up my mind now, although reluctantly, to clear up the most important points of my private life and of my career as an artist. This story, therefore, has no polemical pretext, much less—God help me—any polemical intent. This story begs to be followed in the same spirit in which I have dictated it.

Let's begin then with my birth, as is obligatory in any biography. I came into the world in New York, under the sign of Sagittarius, the morning of the second or fourth of December. I cannot be precise with regard to this circumstance, as I am in all things concerning me, since my passport shows the date of birth as the second, while my mother maintains that she brought me into the world on the fourth. You choose the date you prefer. I prefer the fourth of December, first, because I have to believe what my mother says. Second, it's Saint Barbara's Day, the patroness of the artillery, a proud and combative saint whom I like in a special way. The year: 1923. The place: a clinic on Fifth Avenue, that is, right in the heart of New York and not in Brooklyn, where, I don't know why, certain journalists want at any cost to have me born. Not that there's anything ugly or shameful in the fact of being born in Brooklyn (I believe that that section was the birthplace of many famous people), but purely out of love of accuracy.

I was registered at the Hall of Records as Maria Anna Cecilia Sophia Kalogeropoulos. My parents are both Greek: my mother, Evangelia Dimitriadu, who comes from a family of soldiers, is from Stilida, in the north of Greece, while my father is the son of farmers and is a native of Meligala, in the Peloponnesus. After their marriage they took up residence in Meligala, where my father had a prospering pharmacy. They probably would not even have moved from there if they had not had the great sorrow of losing their only son, Vasily, at just three years of age. From that moment my father began to become intolerant, to want to distance himself as much as possible from the place where his son had died, and gradually the decision to move to America matured in him. They left in August 1923, four months before my birth, taking with them Jackie, my older sister, who was then six years old.

In New York, too, my father opened a very lovely pharmacy, and at the beginning everything went well. The business prospered, and we lived in an elegant apartment in the center of town. Then came the terrible crisis of 1929, which shook our family too; the pharmacy was sold, and from that time on my father was little aided by good fortune. I should add that perhaps he is too honest and too much a gentleman to succeed in elbowing his way into the business jungle. Moreover, he has always been troubled by poor health. He now works as a pharmacist in a hospital in New York and has a good position. He wouldn't leave America for anything, because he's lived there for 34 years and has become perfectly accustomed to it; but during my Mexico City and Chicago tours I always took him with me (my mother came with us once, too), and I had the joy of seeing him every evening in the theater, seated beside my husband, while I sang.

Turning to my childhood, I have no particular recollection, except the vague intuition that my parents were not suited to each other. In fact, they now live apart, a thing that grieves me very much.

As for my vocation, there were never any doubts. My father tells of how I sang while still in the cradle, hurling vocalises and high notes so unusual for an infant that even the neighbors were stupefied. My mother's family, by the way, always boasted an aptitude for singing. My grandfather had a magnificent dramatic tenor, but he was a career officer and understandably never thought of cultivating it. We're not speaking, though, of women. It would have been a scandal, an unbearable dishonor, to have "a woman of the stage" in the family. My mother, however, was of a different mind, and as soon as she became aware of my vocal gifts decided to make of me a child prodigy as quickly as possible. And child prodigies never have genuine childhoods. It's not a special toy that I remember—a doll or a favorite game—but, rather, the songs that I had to rehearse again and again, to the point of exhaustion, for the final test at the end of a school year; and above all the painful sensation of panic that overcame me when, in the middle of a difficult passage, it seemed to me that I was about to choke, and I thought, in terror, that no sound would emerge from my throat, which had become parched and dry. No one was aware of my sudden distress because, in appearance, I was extremely calm and continued to sing.

After grade school all my companions enrolled in high school or other secondary schools, and I would very much have liked to follow their example, to become a high school student. But I couldn't: my mother had decided that I should not steal even a moment from a day spent in studying singing and piano. So, at eleven years of age, I put my books aside and began to get to know the enervating anxiety and the waiting involved in contests for child prodigies: I was regularly entered in them, for radio contests or for scholarship competitions. I always studied thanks to scholarships, because after '29 we were far from rich, and also because I was always full of pessimism about my possibilities. Even now, though I am charged with being conceited, I never feel secure about myself and torment myself with doubts and fears. Even as a child I didn't like the middle way: my mother wanted me to become a singer and I was quite happy to second her, but only on the condition that I be able one day to become a *great* singer. All or nothing: I certainly haven't changed in that regard with the passing of the years. The fact, therefore, of winning scholarships represented for me a firm guarantee that my parents were not deluded in believing in my voice. Comforted by that, I continued studying voice and piano with a kind of fury.

Toward the end of 1936 my mother wanted to return to Greece to see her family and to take Jackie and me with her. My sister set out on her own somewhat before us; we were reunited in January or February 1937. In America, for ease of pronunciation, my father had shortened our last name, keeping only the first part and changing "Kalous" to "Callas," two more harmonious syllables. I don't know whether he did that for any special reasons, but I remember that at school, too, I was regularly called Mary Callas. In Greece, on the other hand, I again became Maria Kalogeropoulos. When I arrived in Athens I had barely turned thirteen, but I looked older because I was as tall as I am now, stout, and altogether too serious, in my face and clothing, for my young age. My mother tried first to enroll me in the Athens Conservatory, the most important one in all of Greece; but they laughed in her face. What were they to make—they said—out of a thirteen-year-old girl? So, claiming to be sixteen, I entered another conservatory, the National, where I began studying with a teacher, probably of Italian origin, Maria Trivella. Barely a year later, however, I succeeded in achieving my aim and moved on, after a test that I passed brilliantly, to the Athens Conservatory, where I was entrusted to the wonderful teacher who had an essential role in my artistic formation: Elvira de Hidalgo.

It is to this illustrious Spanish artist, whom the public and the old subscribers at La Scala will certainly recall as an unforgettable and superlative Rosina and as a splendid interpreter of other very important roles, it is to this illustrious artist, I repeat, with a moved, devoted, and grateful heart, that I owe all my preparation and my artistic formation as an actress and musician. This elect woman, who, besides giving me her precious teaching, gave me her whole heart as well, was a witness to my whole life in Athens, including both my art and my family. She could say more about me than any other person, because with her, more than with anyone else, I had contact and familiarity. She tells the story of how I turned up for my lesson every morning at ten and stayed to hear all the other lessons, until six in the evening. If I know such a vast operatic repertory, I perhaps owe that precisely to that fact, to that thirst for advice and instruction of which I wasn't even aware then. At that time, in October or November 1938, or eighteen years ago, my stage debut took place. For the first time, at less than fifteen years of age, I faced the footlights in the authoritative garb of the prima donna. My role was that of Santuzza in *Cavalleria Rusticana*, and everything went very well. But I was in despair because my face was swollen and contorted by a tremendous toothache. It has always been like that, at every important turn in my career. As you will see from the rest of the story of my life, I have always had to pay for all my triumphs immediately without fail, personally, with a sorrow or a physical ailment. That first success, however, opened the way for me to other auditions, and a few months later I was chosen to sing the part of Beatrice in the operetta *Boccaccio* at the Royal Opera House of Athens.

I remember that at that period my only preoccupation was my hands. I never knew where to put them: they seemed useless and cumbersome. My teacher, however, bemoaned my incredible clothes—and now I understand that she had a thousand reasons for doing so. Once, after have entreated me insistently to put on my most chic outfit, because she was going to introduce me to an important person, she saw me turn up in a dark red skirt, a blouse another shade of red—gaudy and strident—and on my head, atop rolled-up braids, I had a ghastly hat of the "Musetta" type. I thought myself quite elegant and was very crestfallen when Madame Elvira tore off that absurd headgear, yelling that she would not give me any more lessons if I didn't make up my mind to improve my appearance. To tell the truth, even as it was I didn't know my looks. My mother was the one who thought about selecting my clothes, and she didn't allow me to stay in front of the mirror for more than five minutes. I had to study, I couldn't "waste time with nonsense," and certainly I owe it to her strictness that now, at just thirty-three, I have vast and extensive artistic experience. But on the other hand, I was deprived entirely of the joys of adolescence and of its innocent pleasures, those that are fresh, naïve, and irreplaceable. I forgot to say that, by way of compensation, I got fat. Using the excuse that in order to sing well one needs to be hefty and blooming, I stuffed myself, morning and night, with pasta, chocolate, bread and butter, and zabaglione. I was rotund and rosy, with a quantity of pimples that drove me mad.

But let's continue in order. After *Boccaccio* the director of the Royal Opera House chose me again, for *Tosca*. The rehearsals lasted more than three months, without interruption, and I got so tired that even today that opera occupies the last place on my scale of preferences. And so we arrive at the most painful period of my life, the very, very sad war years, of which I don't like to speak even with the people closest to me, so as not to irritate wounds that have not yet healed. I remember the winter of 1941. Greece was invaded by the Germans; the population had already been reduced to starvation for several months. It had never been so cold in Athens: for the first time in twenty years the Athenians saw snow. We were rehearsing d'Albert's *Tiefland*, the opera that is considered the German *Cavalleria*, and because of the fear of bombing we had to perform in semidarkness that was diffused by acetylene lamps. For the whole summer I had eaten only tomatoes and boiled cabbage leaves, which I managed to obtain by covering kilometer after kilometer on foot and begging the farmers in the neighboring countryside to spare me a few of their vegetables. For those poor people a basket of tomatoes or some leaves of cabbage could mean execution, because the Germans were implacable; nevertheless, I never returned empty-handed. But in the winter of '41 a friend of the family, then engaged to my sister, brought us a little cask of oil, corn flour, and potatoes; and I can't forget the incredulous stupefaction with which my mother, Jackie, and I looked at those precious goods, almost fearing that through witchcraft they could disappear at any moment.

No one who has not experienced the miseries of occupation and starvation can know what liberty and a tranquil and comfortable existence mean. For all the rest of my life I will never be able to spend money needlessly and will suffer—it's stronger than I am—at the waste of food, even if it's a bit of bread, a piece of fruit, or a little bit of chocolate. Later on, when the Italians came, we began to live a little better. His pity stirred by my progressive emaciation, a man who admired my voice, the owner of a butcher shop requisitioned by the invaders, introduced me to the Italian official in charge of distributing provisions to the troops. Once a month, for a paltry sum, he sold me ten kilos of meat, and I strapped the package to my shoulders and walked for an hour under the sun, even in the hottest months, as lightly and happily as if I were carrying flowers. That meat, in fact, was our greatest resource. We didn't have a refrigerator and so we couldn't keep it. But it was resold to our neighbors and with the proceeds we could get along by acquiring indispensable things.

Later the Italians "requisitioned" a group of opera singers, of which I was a part, for some concerts, and in accordance with our request they gave us provisions instead of money. Finally, after about a year, I was able to eat rice and pasta again and to drink good milk. In essence, the Italians were always good to me. At that time Madame de Hidalgo insisted that I learn Italian. "It will be useful for you," she would repeat, "because sooner or later you will go to Italy. Only there will you be able to begin your real career. And in order to interpret and express well, you must know the exact meaning of every word." I listened to her and tried not to allow myself to be charmed. Italy and La Scala represented an impossible dream for me, as though I might find myself on Mars or the moon, and I rejected them even at the back of my mind so as to avoid delusions. Nevertheless, I bet my teacher that in three months I would manage to converse in Italian with her. But I didn't know how to do it. I certainly couldn't go to the head office of the fascists, as some people suggested I do, because my compatriots naturally would have considered me a traitor. I couldn't manage the money for private lessons. At that time I had struck up a friendship with four young doctors who had studied in Italy, and I don't know how, perhaps because I immediately liked the language of Dante enormously, within three months I had won my bet.

In the summer of 1944 I had my first scrapes with colleagues. They were going to put on *Fidelio* and another prima donna had put herself out a great deal to get the part and had succeeded in getting it, but she was entirely too busy to learn it. Since the rehearsals had to begin immediately, I was asked whether I could replace her, and I naturally accepted, because I knew the score to perfection. I'm telling you this episode in order to show that my only weapon—a very powerful and fair one—is always to be prepared, because nothing holds up against bravery. On the stage, before the curtain rises, you can do everything to support an artist, but when the curtain rises, the only thing that speaks is courage. They say that I always win. These are my means: work and preparation. If you consider those means "harsh," then I really don't know what to say.

Immediately after the performances of *Fidelio*, which were given in the marvelous amphitheater of Herodes Atticus, came the "liberation," and then began the attacks against me on the part of my colleagues. But we will speak of them again later. In the meantime, finally, the administration of the Royal Opera House granted me three months of vacation, and my mother, without losing any time, immediately found a job for me at the British headquarters, where I was assigned to the office of distribution of secret mail. We started work at eight, but I had to get up at six thirty because in order to save money I made the whole trip on foot, and our house, at 61 Patissiou, was very far from the office. The British offered us an abundant noon meal, and rather than taking it at headquarters, I had it put in a pot and carried it home to share with my mother. (At that time my sister Jackie wasn't living with us.) I had a break of an hour and a half in all, so I had a quarter hour, more or less, at home. I went on like that until the winter: but even now, when I'm well, I feel the effects of the exhaustion that was left to me, like a sad inheritance, by liver complaint and a blood pressure reading of 90 at the most.

Excuse the digression and let us continue. We are at 1945: the time had come to renew my contract with the Royal Opera House, but I found out from a maternal uncle, a doctor at the Royal House (Professor Constantine Louros), that Ralis, then the head of the Greek government, had received my colleagues en masse. They had gone to protest to him, threatening a full-dress strike in the event that I were again engaged as a prima donna at the Royal Opera House. It was a disgrace, they railed, that a girl of twenty-one be compared to artists of their talent and their age. My uncle didn't know what to advise me; but since there's always a beneficent God to help those who travel the straight and narrow and never do any harm to anyone, when I least expected it, the American Consulate offered me a ticket to America. I would repay the money, I was told, when I could.

The director of the Royal Opera House was very embarrassed when he had me summoned to explain to me that I would no longer be engaged as a prima donna. I allowed him to stammer out a bunch of excuses, then announced to him that I was leaving for America, adding, "Let's hope that you won't have to regret this one day." But before departing I wanted to give a last sample of my skills and I sang Millöcker's *The Beggar Student*, an operetta as difficult as anything for a soprano: they were obliged to entrust it to me because no one else could sing it.

I left on the *Stockholm* (the ship that collided with the *Andrea Doria* last July). I hadn't written my father that I would be arriving; my mother had advised against it; I don't know why. Or perhaps I do, but there's no need for me to state it. I took three or four dresses with me and didn't have a cent in my pocket. My mother and my sister refused to accompany me to Piraeus: they said they wouldn't have been able to stand the commotion. On the other hand, some friends came, among them the tuberculosis specialist Papatesta, who lived in the apartment below ours.

They gave me a farewell dinner. I remember very well: it was two in the afternoon. A few minutes before embarkation I was fervently advised: "Be careful and don't lose your money. Where have you put it?" "There's no danger," I replied, "I don't have any." They couldn't believe me. They took my pocketbook, turned it inside out, and didn't find anything. The *Stockholm* was to leave Piraeus at three, and at that hour the banks were closed. None of them could help me, but I waved at them happily. I was going to meet the unknown; nevertheless, at that moment I felt with extraordinary clarity that I need not be afraid.

PART 2

At twenty-one, alone and without a cent, I boarded a ship at Athens —as I've told you—headed for New York. Now, at a distance of twelve years, I realize exactly what grave consequences I could have encountered and what incredible risks I was facing in returning to America at the end of a world war, with the prospect of not being able to track down either my father or my old friends. But, as I said, I was not afraid; and it was not just a question of courage, or rather, the unawareness appropriate to my very young age. It was something deeper: an instinct, unlimited faith in the divine protection that—I was sure of that—would not fail me.

You will see for yourselves, as my story continues, how the hand of God has always been above my head—permit me this expression—at all the most dramatic moments of my life. I first experienced that when I was six years old. I was walking with my parents, and suddenly I saw Jackie, who was playing ball on the other side of the street, with our housekeeper and a cousin. It often happens with me—it's a characteristic side of my personality—that I'm seized by sudden tender impulses and feel ashamed of them immediately afterward, I don't know why, perhaps because of excessive modesty about my feelings. At that time, too, catching sight of my sister, I ran to her to give her a kiss and then ran away, red and embarrassed, precipitously crossing the street just at the moment when a car was coming along at great speed. I was knocked over and dragged to the end of the street. The American newspapers (that was the first time they took an interest in me) called me "lucky Maria" on that occasion, because I managed to recover in almost miraculous fashion, after being unconscious for twelve days and when everyone, from the chief physician to the janitor at the hospital, considered me a hopeless case.

I have good reason to say that I also merited the appellation "lucky Maria" in another very grave hour of my life, which goes back to the Greek period. On December 4, 1944—I remember it very well because it was my birthday—civil war erupted in Athens. As I have said, I was then working for the British Command and my superiors recommended that I not leave headquarters, because, having occupied such a delicate post as that of distributing secret mail, I would undoubtedly be a victim of communist reprisals and subjected to inevitable torture. But our house was located in the zone occupied by the Reds, and I did not want to leave my mother on her own. For that reason I had myself taken, in a jeep, to Patissiou Street, and for several days I stayed locked in my room. I was racked with fear; moreover, I was sick thanks to a box of very old beans that, for the lack of anything else, I had decided to eat (and by the way, I have a real and genuine allergy to every kind of dry legume). In that condition I couldn't even think of procuring provisions for my mother and myself, and I might have died of starvation (many people died of it at the time) if I hadn't had the help of my friend Doctor Papatesta, who brought me some of the little food that he had at his disposal.

At a certain moment I received a visit from a pale and poorly dressed boy—he looked like a coal vender—who asserted that he had been charged with a mission concerning me by an official of the British Command. Terrified, suspecting a trap, I tried to chase him away in a rude manner; then, since his insistence had become unbearable and nearly rabid, I resigned myself to listening to him. He was in reality a secret agent whom the British had sent to beg me to return to headquarters, because they feared for my life and were amazed that the communists had not yet arrested me. The fellow found it very hard to convince me; but at last he persuaded me that it was absolutely essential for me to go back to the British zone, and without wasting time I called Doctor Papatesta to entrust my mother to him.

Our house (my mother and sister still live there) is on a beautiful avenue, very spacious and tranquil, that comes out on Concord Square. But when I think of that avenue I always see it in my imagination as I saw it that morning, literally covered with broken glass and all sorts of wreckage that had fallen out of windows as a result of the constant machine gun fire: gray and silent. A tremendous, unnerving silence that would last sixty seconds, to be broken, once a minute, by the communists' terrible "blind volley," shots at regular intervals that could hit anyone and had the specific aim of wearing down the populace's nerves. Even now I can't explain to myself how I could have run desperately through the midst of that devastation, under fire, and arrive safe and sound at British headquarters.

I've told this episode only to show—and you will hear me repeat this often—that the good Lord has always helped me. Do you know, in fact—to pick up the thread of the conversation—whom I found waiting for me when I disembarked in New York? Precisely the person whom I would have least expected: my father, who had learned of my arrival from one of the Greek-language newspapers that are published in America. I really don't know how to describe the limitless relief with which I drew myself to him, hugging him as though he had been raised from the dead, and crying on his shoulder from joy.

I've already had occasion to tell you that my father is hardly rich; but in that year and a half that I lived with him he treated me like a queen, making it up to me for everything that I had suffered. He got a new, very pretty bedroom set for me, clothes, and elegant shoes. I was happy and was beginning little by little to regain faith in myself, because every time that a Greek ship dropped anchor in port, sailors or officers turned up at our house, wanting to greet "the famous singer Maria Kalogeropoulos." And they told my father that many of them, at the time of *Fidelio*, made their way on foot from Piraeus to the Acropolis (a preposterous thing, if you know Athens), braving the German roundups, simply in order to hear me sing. Their words did me good: in those years, as you have seen, I thought only of studying and of earning a living, taking advantage of the natural gift of my voice, without even realizing that in the meantime fame and the public's favor had risen around my name.

Comforted by that evidence, I decided, with courage, to win a place for myself in New York. In the final analysis, I told myself, I was a singer who had seven years of an intense career behind her. I hoped, ingenuously, to find some engagements. But who in America knows poor little Greece? And who can lend an ear to a twenty-one-year-old girl? I realized very quickly, with bitterness, that I would have to start all over again from the beginning.

At that time, not having much to do, I often went to the pharmacy where my father worked; and there one morning the owner of the store introduced me to an ex-singer who invited me to her home to hear her pupils and give my opinion of them. I spent three or four hours with her, every Saturday, and sometimes I helped, giving advice to her students. I remember that one of those Saturdays—it was getting close to Christmas—a Mr. Edward Bagarozy came to say hello to this ex-singer, his friend, to give her his greetings. I was invited to sing. After having listened to me attentively, Mr. Bagarozy proposed that I participate in the opera season that he intended to call the United States Opera Company. He promised that I would be the prima donna in *Turandot* and perhaps also in *Aida*.

Meanwhile, I had obtained an audition at the Metropolitan, but I could not agree with the administration because I was offered parts that I believed unsuited to my possibilities at that time, namely, *Fidelio* (which I didn't want to sing in English) and *Butterfly*, which I refused without hesitation. I was in fact convinced that I was a "fatty." In reality I weighed 176 pounds and 176 pounds is a lot, but not excessive for a tall woman like me, five feet eight inches. I had received other offers that I refused, and I was given a letter of introduction, by Elvira de Hidalgo, to Romano Romani, the maestro for the famous Rosa Ponselle. In response to my request for lessons, Maestro Romani said, "I don't see the necessity. You need above all and only to work." I was also heard by poor Maestro Merola, from San Francisco, who, after paying me a number of compliments, gave way to the usual tired refrain: "You're so young . . . what guarantee can I have . . . who will assure me! First," he concluded, "make a career in Italy and then I'll sign you up." "Thank you," I replied, dejected and furious, "thank you very much, but when I've made my career in Italy, I'm certain that I will no longer have any need of you."

I remember very well that at that time I went from one movie house to another, not to see the films, but so as not to go out of my mind from torturous thoughts about my uncertain future. Then, finally, came the time when I was to sing *Turandot* with the United States Opera Company. But the season fell through for lack of funds. Among famous colleagues who suffered because of that were Galliano Masini (who was at the height of his popularity), Mafalda Favero, Cloe Elmo, the tenors Infantino and Scattolini, the baritone Danilo Checchi, Nicola Rossi-Lemeni, Max Lorenz, the Konetzki sisters, various artists of the Paris Opera, poor Maestro Failoni, and others whose names I don't recall.

In great haste they had to organize a concert to collect the money necessary for tickets home, and immediately afterward the Italian singers all returned to Italy. Rossi-Lemini remained in New York, attracted by vague promises of work. While waiting for better times, Nicola and I studied together at Bagarozy's apartment, because I didn't have a piano at my house, and it was Rossi-Lemini who told me one afternoon: "I've been signed up for this year's season at the Verona Arena, and I've heard that Giovanni Zenatello, the famous tenor, the director of the Arena, is having trouble finding a Gioconda to his taste. Do you want me to ask for an audition for you? He's staying here in New York, and the thing can be managed immediately." I said yes, of course.

At that time the name Verona had no meaning for me at all. I would never have been able to imagine that precisely in that city, which is now so dear to me, the most important events of my life would come to fruition. As I will relate later, in fact, I met my husband in Verona; I had my first Italian success in Verona; and I met Renata Tebaldi in Verona.

So I went to Zenatello and got a contract for *La Gioconda* with a fee of 40,000 lire per performance. Meanwhile, I knew that my mother and father were not swimming in money—in fact, they had to work hard just to get along. My mother had wanted to return to New York at all costs, and in order to be able to pay for the trip I had had to borrow the money from my godfather, Professor Leonidas Lantzonis, the assistant director of the Orthopedic Hospital of New York. When the time came for my departure for Italy, I was forced to turn to him again.

So there I was, having to take the sea route again, still poor as a church mouse (I had fifty dollars, all that my father could give me), but—it's appropriate to say—with an enormous baggage car of hopes and with the incredible joy of one who sees, almost with fear, an impossible dream coming true. I landed at Naples on June 29, 1947, where the heat was hellish. With me were Rossi-Lemeni and Mrs. Louise Bagarozy, Edward's wife, who intended to attempt a singing career in Italy. We left our trunks in Naples. They reached us later, after having become noticeably lighter during storage. We took the train to Verona. We found only one empty seat and took turns sitting there all night without managing to close our eyes, because the two who were standing didn't stop looking impatiently at their watches, waiting for their turn. On the very morning of my arrival in Verona I was met at the Hotel Academia (where a room had been taken for me) by my poor and very dear Gaetano Pomari, the assistant director of the Arena, and Giuseppe Gambato, the municipal secretary and a lover of the arts. They came to invite me to a dinner in my honor that was to take place the following day. I went, of course, and there, twenty-four hours after setting foot on Italian soil, I shook the hand of my future husband, Giovanni Battista Meneghini.

Allow me to recount in all the details the meeting with my life's companion—a chapter that all women, after all, recall with extraordinary pleasure. At that time my husband shared a place with poor

Pomari, because his apartment had been requisitioned during the war; and since he loved opera, he took willing part in all the great discussions that precede every opening of the Verona season. The evening before my arrival he had asked jokingly: "And what task do you entrust to me for the production of *La Gioconda*? Let me take care of the ballerinas this time." "No," they replied, "you will take care of the prima donnas. The American one is arriving tomorrow, and we've been thinking of entrusting her to your care." Battista was very tired those days; the large brick factories of which he was director and co-owner took up his days entirely. When he left his office and the time came for him to participate in the dinner, he decided that, all in all, it would be better to go rest: he had to leave very early the next morning, as usual. As he was going up the stairs (the apartment was directly over the Pedavena, the restaurant where we were eating) he was overtaken by a waiter—a certain Gigiotti, I still remember his name—who told him, in Veronese dialect, "Come downstairs, sir, or Mr. Pomari will be furious." Titta (that's what I call him) pretended not to have heard; but since the waiter insisted, after a few moments of hesitation—decisive ones for my life —he turned around and hurried down the stairs.

I remember that when we were introduced—he was dressed in white—I thought to myself: "This is an honest, sincere person. I like him." Then I forgot him, because he wasn't seated next to me at the table, and without my glasses (as is well known, I'm very nearsighted) I could make him out only obscurely. At a certain moment, however, Louise Bagarozy, who was beside me, passed on to me an invitation from Meneghini. Battista wanted to take her, Rossi-Lemeni, and me to Venice the next morning. I agreed at once, but changed my mind the next day: my trunk had not yet arrived and the only dress I had was the one I was wearing. Rossi-Lemeni, however, did so much and talked so much that he managed to persuade me. To conclude, I went to Venice with Battista, and during that trip our love was born at a single stroke.

I should say, at this point, that up to that time Titta had not yet heard me sing. That happened some twenty days later, when Maestro Serafin arrived from Rome. He—I was immensely proud of that—was to conduct *Gioconda*. The audition took place in the Adelaide Ristori Theater and went off in the best possible way. I was very happy, Serafin was enthusiastic, and Battista was even more enthusiastic than he.

But as usual, during the dress rehearsal at the Arena, I had to pay the price of my success in hard cash. In the second act, in order not to run into the artificial sea surrounding the ship, I wound up in one of those entrances through which wild animals at one time exited. Fortunately, there was a wooden chute; otherwise I would have cracked my head on those rocks. I sprained my ankle, and instead of having it bandaged immediately, I chose to continue the rehearsal. (I often have these attacks of conscientiousness, which always end in harm for myself.) At the end of the third act the ankle was so swollen that I couldn't even allow my foot to touch the ground. A doctor was called, but by then it was already too late, and because of the tremendous pain I didn't manage to close my eyes the whole night. I remember the gratitude and tenderness I felt that evening for Titta, who stayed by my bed until dawn, seated on a chair, to help me and comfort me.

That is just a little episode that shows the nature of my husband, for whom I would be willing to give my life, immediately and with joy: it was then I realized that I would never meet a man more generous than he and that God had been very good to me in placing him on my path. If Battista had wished, I would have abandoned my career without any regrets, because in a woman's life (I mean a real woman) love is more important, beyond compare, than any artistic triumph. And I sincerely wish anyone who lacks it a fourth or even a tenth of my conjugal happiness.

Let's return to *Gioconda*. I made my debut at the Arena, then, with a bandaged leg, scarcely able to drag myself around that enormous stage. But I had completely recovered when, at Castelvecchio, I attended a reception given in honor of all the singers of the Verona season. On that occasion I saw for the first time my dear colleague Renata Tebaldi, whom I have always admired and whom I still admire very much. Renata—that's what I called her at the time of our friendship, and I don't see any reason why I should alter that—had sung in *Faust*, and perhaps because of an involuntary oversight on the part of our hosts, she wasn't introduced to me during the party. But I haven't forgotten the agreeable impression made on me by that beautiful girl, by that wholesome, happy, and cordial face.

I'll have to return to the topic of Renata many times in the installments that follow.

PART 3

After the performances of *Gioconda* at the Verona Arena, I deluded myself by thinking that I would obtain many engagements. On the contrary, I received a single offer, from the theatrical agent Liduino Bonardi, who offered me *Gioconda* at Vigevano. I refused, but I was to regret that bitterly a short while later when finally, for lack of anything better, I decided to accept the offer and it was already too late: he found someone else. Meanwhile, La Scala asked me to audition, and Maestro Labroca, then the artistic director of the theater, had me sing excerpts from *Norma* and *Ballo in Maschera*. Trembling, I waited for his evaluation and heard him say that my voice had too many defects. "Try to correct them," Labroca added, "and in a month I'll call for you. But return home calm. I assure you that you'll have the part of Amelia in *Ballo in Maschera*."

I waited a month, two months in vain (how many tears on Titta's shoulders); then the good Lord decided to help me again. One day Maestro Serafin decided to mount *Tristan* at the Fenice in Venice, and for the part of Isolde he thought of the young American singer whom he had conducted in *Gioconda* at Verona. He asked the director of the Fenice, Maestro Nino Cattozzo, to locate me, and Cattozzo telephoned a friend of my husband in Verona (I prefer to keep his name a secret) to have him furnish my address that very evening and to tell him whether I knew the part and was disposed to accept it. I, of course, knew nothing about any of this. But in the evening, guided by a sure presentiment, Battista advised me to go back to Liduino Bonardi the next day to find out whether there was any possibility of contracts for me. And whom did I find there as soon as I entered the agency? Maestro Cattozzo, who, not having received the desired response, had gone to Milan to look for another Isolde. "I'm happy to see you," he said, "Have you changed your mind?" "About what?" "But weren't you asked about *Tristan* at the Fenice?" I came down to earth and understood everything, with great sadness.

Cattozzo also told me that Serafin would come to Milan the next day for the audition and asked me whether I knew *Tristan*. Out of fear of losing the likely engagement I answered yes without hesitating, and when Serafin arrived in Milan I went to see him at the beautiful home of Carmen Scalvini, whom I was seeing for the first time and who was very nice to me. The rehearsal went well and the maestro wanted to congratulate me, but I couldn't keep from confessing the truth to him, and that is that I had learned only a little of the first act of *Tristan*, and that had been a long time ago. Serafin wasn't frightened; he suggested that I go to Rome for a month to study the opera with him. That's what I did, and I signed a contract with the Fenice, a contract that included not only *Tristan* but *Turandot* as well. The fee, not without a certain effort, was raised: imagine, from the 40,000 at Verona to 50,000 per performance! No one protested at that time!

One evening, during the run of *Tristan*, while I was removing my makeup in my dressing room, I heard the door open, and in the doorway, all of a sudden, was framed the tall figure of Tebaldi, who was in Venice to sing—I don't know if it was for the first time—*Traviata*, with Serafin. As I've already said, we knew each other only by sight, but this time we shook each other's hands warmly, and Renata gave me such spontaneous compliments that I was enchanted. "Good heavens!" she said, "if I had had to perform such an exhausting part, they would have had to pick me up with a spoon!" I think that very rarely, between two women of the same age and same profession, could there arise an attraction as fresh and immediate as that which was born between us. My attraction to her became authentic affection sometime later, at Rovigo, where Tebaldi was singing in *Andrea Chénier* and I in *Aida*. At the end of the aria "O patria mia" I heard a voice from a box seat cry out, "Brava, brava Maria!" It was Renata's voice. From that time we became—I can well say so—dearest friends. We were often together, and we exchanged advice about clothes, hairdos, and even about repertory. Later, unfortunately, our schedules did not allow us to enjoy fully that friendship any longer. We met only in passing, between one trip or another, but always, I think, I'm even quite sure of it, with mutual pleasure. She admired my dramatic force and physical endurance; I, her very sweet singing. At this point I want to make it clear that if I so often followed her performances with attention, I did it exclusively in order to try to understand the quite special way in which Renata sings; and I'm infinitely sorry to hear such a ridiculous accusation leveled against me as that I want to "intimidate" her. The public, Renata, and much more so the people with whom she surrounds herself, can't understand that I—and I'm by no means ashamed of this—always discover something to learn from the voices of my colleagues, not just the famous ones like Tebaldi, but even from the humble and mediocre ones. Even the voice of the most modest student can offer instruction to us. And I, who torture myself, hour after hour in the exhausting search for continual improvement, will never be able to give up listening to colleagues sing.

Before entering into this long digression about Tebaldi, I was telling about my performances of *Tristan* and *Turandot* at the Fenice. Even though it's not for me to say so, I had a great success in both operas. Then I sang *Forza del Destino* in Trieste (where the critics, who have always been rather hard on me, accused me of not knowing how to move on stage), *Turandot* at Verona, in Rome, at the Baths of Caracalla, and lastly, *Tristan* again, at Genoa, in May 1948. Often, when recalling that *Tristan* at Genoa, I laugh to the point of crying. Since the Carlo Felice Theater, seriously damaged by bombings, had not been restored, the opera was performed in the Grattacielo Theater, that is to say, in a movie house with a very tiny stage. Imagine the company that I was part of, with my plentiful 165 pounds (thirty-three more than now), Elena Nicolai, very tall and robust, Nicola Rossi-Lemeni, also tall and robust, Max Lorenz, the same size, and the baritone Raimondo Torres, of no smaller size.

Imagine all these colosusses moving around in a tiny, tiny little theater, struggling with an opera that requires ample, solemn, and absolutely dramatic gestures. I remember that when as Isolde I ordered Nicolai (Brangäne) to run to the prow of the ship to tell Tristan that I wished to speak with him, I couldn't at all manage to keep a straight face. In fact, not having any room, Elena could only move away slightly, at most two or three meters, and in order to allow the time expected for the stage action to pass, she kept pirouetting around, stirring up our hilarity. It was a stupendous performance, however, and the Genoese haven't forgotten it.

A few months later, while I was in Rome preparing *Norma* with Serafin, with which I was to inaugurate the season at the Communale in Florence, the first symptoms of appendicitis appeared. I decided not to pay any attention to those annoyances, but in December, during the opening performance of *Norma*, I realized that the cramps in my right leg were becoming more and more insistent, so much so that kneeling cost me tremendous effort. I had to have an operation, giving up *Aida* in Florence, and for three or four days after the operation I had a fever of 41 degrees centigrade [105 degrees Fahrenheit].

Battista feared for my life. I recovered rather quickly, but I was still convalescing when I threw myself, with my usual fury, into preparing *Walküre* for the Fenice in Venice. I want to clarify a specific notion of mine: one shouldn't confuse duty and ambition. Coming from a long theatrical career, I have learned this inexorable law to perfection: the show must go on, even if the protagonists die. That's why I'm so tenacious in my work, only because it's a question of duty, not of ambition.

During that period of intense activity my greatest regret was being forced to be away from Titta too often. I often loathed my career because its requirements forced me to be apart from him, and I dreamed of abandoning it.

So, we have arrived at January 1949. I was engaged in performances of *Walküre* in Venice, and I learned that Margherita Carosio had fallen ill with the flu and would not be able to sing *Puritani* (again, at the Fenice). I was in the lobby of the Hotel Regina, with Serafin's wife and daughter, and almost mechanically, on learning that news, I moved to the piano and began leafing through the score, reading at sight and ad-libbing a few arias. Mrs. Serafin sat up in her chair. "As soon as Tullio arrives," she said, "you'll sing that for him." Thinking that she was joking, I calmly said yes. But on the next day, at ten—I was sound asleep—I was awakened by the phone, again by Maestro Serafin, who ordered me to come downstairs immediately, without even washing my face, so as not to lose any time. I put on my dressing robe and went down half asleep, without realizing what was wanted of me. In the music room I found, besides Serafin, Maestro Cattozzo and a substitute maestro, who ordered me, almost in chorus, to sing the aria from *Puritani* that I had ad-libbed the night before. I looked at them with bewilderment: I swear that at that moment I suspected that they were mad. But then I surrendered, sang, and stayed to hear them propose to me right away, without batting an eyelash, that I prepare *Puritani* in order to replace Margherita Carosio. They were giving me six days and I didn't know the opera at all; in addition, I had performances of *Walküre*. It still seems incredible to me, but we managed it. That very day, Wednesday, I studied *Puritani* for several hours and sang *Walküre* in the evening; Thursday, several more hours of study; and again on Friday, with a performance of *Walküre* in the evening. Saturday afternoon, with a nervousness that I hope is understandable, I went through the first dress rehearsal of *Puritani*; the next day, the last matinee of *Walküre* and the dress rehearsal of *Puritani*.

I Puritani went on stage punctually on Tuesday, with a happy outcome. Then I sang *Walküre* in Palermo, *Turandot* in Naples, *Parsifal* in Rome (I learned it in five days), and between one performance and another I took part in my first radio concert, at Turin, with the following program: the "Liebestod," "O patria mia," "Casta diva," and the aria from *Puritani*. I'm telling you this in perhaps excessive detail because I've often been accused by people, or rather by my adversaries, of wanting to sing everything. As you have been able to observe, I have never wanted anything: it was only chance and my friends' insistence, not my exaggerated ambition, that opened the way to such an unusual and rich repertory.

I have said that in spite of my growing success, I wasn't content. I wanted, in fact, the warmth of my own home and the tranquillity that every woman derives from a happy marriage. I would have married Titta the day I met him, but there is a distinct difference in age between my husband and me, and Titta, being the honest person that he is, didn't want to push me into a step that I might regret. He wanted me to be sure, to take time to think calmly, but at the beginning of 1949 I had thought enough. I was to leave in the spring for a round of performances in Buenos Aires, and I preferred to have Maria Meneghini on my passport instead of Maria Callas.

So we decided to get married and began taking steps to obtain the necessary marriage documents. Since I'm an adherent of the Orthodox faith, I had to have the Vatican's approval; but a priest from Verona, Professor Mortari, assured Battista that once we had all the papers, we would be able to resolve that problem without any trouble. The Vatican posed no difficulties. In April my documents had arrived from New York and Athens in good order, and Titta's were also ready. My departure date was fixed for April 21st, and there was no longer time to organize a wedding ceremony with lots of flowers, "Ave Maria," and a reception, as I would have liked. Therefore we decided to defer the wedding until August 15, my name day, when I would be back from

Argentina. My husband, however, with the prudence characteristic of businessmen, wanted to have in his hands all the documents, which in the meantime had been taken to the Archbishopric for the certification of the marriage license, already obtained.

The morning of April 21, a few hours before I left Verona, Battista sent his secretary to retrieve the documents. But at noon the woman, who was usually capable and businesslike, had not yet returned. When she finally appeared, her clouded face told us that unforeseen obstacles had turned up. She said, in fact, that at the Archbishopric she had been assured that the documents weren't ready; she then added that—it seemed to her—what must be in our way was some great difficulty interjected by the family. In reality it became known later that two individuals had taken the trouble to present themselves at the Archbishopric to whisper that it would be very appropriate, on the part of the religious authorities, to create insurmountable obstacles for the marriage. Neither my husband nor I wish to name the two because these are matters that concern only our families and their economic interests. In any event, Battista wasted no time. He told me (I received the news with enormous surprise and great joy) to be ready, because at three in the afternoon we would be married at Zevio, near Verona, at the town hall. Then he hurried to the Archbishopric, where, in sorrowful and firm tones, he asked Monsignor Zancanella to return all the papers to him because since we could not be wed in a church, we would be united in matrimony with just the civil rites.

His words apparently were sufficiently effective, and the prompt and considerate intervention of one of Titta's friends, Mario Orlandi, must have been equally effective. At five in the afternoon everything was ready for our wedding at the Church of the Philippines in Verona. Since I'm of the Orthodox faith, as I've said, the rite was celebrated in a side chapel. There were six of us in all: the priest, who spoke such moving words that I cried, the sacristan, two witnesses, and Titta and I. We exchanged vows and swore eternal love. I was dressed in blue, with black lace over my head. I hadn't had time to buy a new dress. The ceremony did not take long. Once again I had been deprived of the joys and fantasies dearest to the female heart: the wedding preparations, the gifts, the flowers.

No preparations, no gifts, no flowers. Only a great love and an exalted simplicity. Immediately afterward I returned to the hotel and packed the trunk that would follow me to Buenos Aires. Titta accompanied me to Genoa, and the following morning, very sad and alone, I boarded the *Argentina*, headed for Buenos Aires.

PART 4

During that lonely and melancholy trip aboard the *Argentina* I came down with the flu when we crossed the Equator, and it was five days before I managed to recover. For that reason the performances of *Turandot* and *Norma* at the Colón in Buenos Aires are linked in my memory to the prolonged effort that it cost me to rise from my bed, in spite of a fever, and to arrive, by force of will, at the conclusion of the performance. The South American tour lasted until the middle of July and was a long period of torture for me because the public's enthusiasm could not compensate for my being away from Titta, the man whom I had married one afternoon three months earlier and whom I had had to abandon the day after the wedding.

I finally returned to Italy, to my husband, who in the meantime had furnished a cozy apartment above his firm's offices at 21 San Fermo, right behind the Arena. But the joy of living together was made bitter right from the very first days by many family troubles; troubles in which the motive of financial interest was fatally involved, which led, unfortunately, to interminable squabbles. I do not wish to linger, however, over this question, one that is too delicate and personal. In December of that same year, 1949, I opened, for the first time, the opera season at the San Carlo in Naples, with *Nabucco*; then I went to the Rome Opera for *Tristan* and at the same time accepted an offer for *Aida* in Brescia. I remember that Maestro Serafin didn't want me to submit to this *tour de force*, the more so as my *Aida* would be followed fifteen days later by that of Tebaldi's at La Scala. That coincidence, however, left me completely indifferent, and I saw no reason to withdraw from my contract with Brescia for such a futile reason. I therefore began shuttling—by train—between Brescia and the capital, and in exchange for this tremendous wear and tear I asked the Milanese theatrical agency for a single favor: to get me the costumes and wigs that I had already worn many times before for performances of *Aida* and that I usually rented from a Florentine tailor's shop. I received the most fulsome promises, of course, but at the dress rehearsal the costumes hadn't arrived. Mrs. Scalvini, however, whom I hadn't seen in a long time, was there. She wanted to know the reason for my obvious worry and guaranteed—she was taking the responsibility upon herself, she said—that I would have costumes. But two evenings later, when I arrived at the theater for the opening performance, I found a piece of silk the color of red brick, as long as my body, with a cut in the middle for the head and two seams at the sides. That is exactly how it was and I beg you not to think I'm exaggerating. And let's not talk about the wig, suitable at best for a baby. Furious—didn't I perhaps have reason to be?—I began yelling, and I screamed at Mrs. Scalvini, who just at that moment turned up in my dressing room, "What costumes have they given you? You've let them put one over on you!"

The deplorable incident didn't manage to compromise the performance because, as always happens, desperation suggested a superb idea to me. At the last moment—the performance was already a half hour late in starting—I remembered that the singer who was playing Amneris (I think it was Pirazzini) had her own costume as well as the theater's. I tried on the latter and fortunately it fit well enough. Fortunately, moreover, I'm a brunette, not a blonde. Because of that I was able that evening, by gathering my hair into a thick bun, to perform *Aida* without the traditional wig. But the surprises weren't over. Immediately after the famous aria "O patria mia," at the moment when the audience was about to give way to applause, a voice from the gallery ordered, in Brescian dialect, "Quiet, the aria isn't finished." There were several seconds of perplexity in the orchestra, enough time, you understand, to deprive me of my applause. But every time that I'm the victim of an injustice—by now I know it from experience—I'm rewarded at the end with a true, warm triumph: and that was the case on this occasion, too. Nevertheless, I returned to Rome very regretful that, in my stubbornness, I had refused to follow Serafin's advice.

After *Tristan* I sang *Norma* in Rome and *Aida* again, in Naples. Then, in the company of my very dear colleague Giulietta Simionato, I left for a series of performances in Mexico, and it was a trip full of vicissitudes that nearly cost Giulietta her life. It is an episode about the happy outcome of which I can now smile, but for a long time it came into my dreams like a terrible nightmare. We had arrived in New York, Simionato and I; the heat was awful, and we were exhausted from a stormy crossing. The plane for Mexico City that was supposed to leave in the evening was held up, so I invited my friend to be my guest at my parents' apartment. No one had told me that my mother was in the hospital (she had had a minor eye operation), and I was surprised to find the apartment empty when I arrived. I didn't have any time to think: Giulietta was dying of thirst and I hurriedly put down the suitcases and opened the refrigerator. I found a bottle of 7-Up and gave it to Giulietta. Scarcely had she gulped down half the liquid when she to had to throw up. She told me later that it had a strange taste: she thought it must have been kerosene. Worried and upset, I ran to the telephone and called my father at the pharmacy. He advised me to give Simionato some milk right away and to run to the hospital, when Simionato had calmed down, to ask my mother what infernal concoction she had put in the bottle. I went there and I can't forget with what disconcerting frankness my mother calmly answered, "It isn't kerosene, it's insecticide."

The hours that followed were among the most distressing of my life. Simionato continued to feel bad, and I had completely lost my head. At last I managed to track down my godfather, who, as I already had occasion to say, is the director of the Orthopedic Institute of New York, and I told him everything, asking him anxiously for advice. But instead of calming me down, his words increased my terror. I learned from him, in fact, that if a disaster occurred, I would be accused of having poisoned my Italian colleague, because when the incident took place there was no one at my house who could testify exactly how the events had unfolded. Just a few evenings ago, when we were seated together at the Biffi-Scala, I revealed to Giulietta the real nature of that "disinfectant." Until then I had never had the courage.

The season at Mexico City took place among many difficulties, also due to the terrible climate. I won't tell you about them, because if I lingered over every episode in my life I would fill two or three volumes.

Here I have to make a digression. At that time I never felt well: I continually felt the effects of influenza, I was nauseated, and I had pains in my bones. But as always, I continued to sing. Upon my return from Mexico I granted myself three weeks of rest and immediately accepted Maestro Cuccia's proposal that I take part in Rossini's comic opera *Il Turco in Italia*, an offer that particularly cheered me (I, too, certainly have the right to amuse myself once in a while) because it allowed me to get away from the theme, by then habitual, of the grand tragedies in music, to breathe the fresh air of a very comical Neapolitan adventure. While I was preparing in Rome, under the direction of Maestro Gavazzeni, I had the chance to become better acquainted with Luchino Visconti, who even before that had always paid me compliments, but whom I had never had the opportunity to get to know better. I remember my amazement at seeing a man of his distinction attentively observing almost all the rehearsals of *Turco*, which lasted a minimum of three or four hours and were repeated twice a day. Beginning then Luchino Visconti endeared himself to me with his limitless admiration and precious friendship, and our close collaboration in the last few years was born precisely out of that mutual esteem.

I was saying that I never felt well. My husband didn't know what to attribute my condition to, but he discovered it later when, unknown to me, he had a letter from my mother translated, as a consequence of which I was so upset that I had to take to my bed. He read it and found it full of recriminations, unjust accusations, and rash deductions. He couldn't control himself and replied to my mother on his own. He told her among other things that in order to marry me he had had to go against his family, that my happiness was his life's aim, and that therefore he would not allow my mother to do anything that would distress me. Another painful exchange of letters followed, and we ended up, unfortunately, breaking off relations.

I beg the readers' pardon for this long disgression, which has cost me great effort, and I take up my autobiography again. We are at the end of 1950. Among my engagements I had *Parsifal* at the Rome RAI, *Don Carlo* at Naples and Rome, and then, on January 15, 1951, my first *Traviata* in Rome. I sang *Parsifal* and at the same time prepared for *Don Carlo* under the direction of Maestro Serafin. But during the rehearsals my health worsened to the point where I couldn't even swallow a sip of water. Battista then refused to listen to my arguments and forced me to return to Verona, where as soon as we arrived I took to my bed with a case of jaundice. I was immobilized by that irksome illness, and I had plenty of time to reflect on my family woes and to conclude that I must watch out, first of all, for my health and my husband's peace of mind.

I was replaced for the performances at Naples and Rome, but I didn't want to give up *Traviata* as well. For that reason, on Epiphany, barely able to get to my feet (for more than a month I had been fed solely milk), I went to Florence and began studying. As God willed it, the dress rehearsal arrived and I had a tiff with Maestro Serafin, who scolded me for turning up at the theater with too modest an air, dressed casually, and in general for not behaving, in his opinion, like a prima donna. I told him that I preferred to have people like me for my simplicity: colleagues (a vain illusion), chorus members, orchestra players, and everyone who lives around the stage (that's not an illusion). It was, however, a tiff without consequences, and the *Traviata* went very well. Immediately afterward I opened the Palermo season with *Norma*, and there I received a phone call from the director of La Scala, Antonio Ghiringhelli.

He asked me to come to see him as soon as I returned to Milan, which I did. But he only had a proposal: that I "take over" Tebaldi's *Aidas*, because Renata was indisposed. The preceding April, on the occasion of the Fair, I had been offered *Aida* at La Scala, and after much persuasion on the part of the management, I decided to accept. But after those performances, as had happened to me other times, I learned nothing more, and other opportunities to cross the threshold of the greatest opera theater in the world didn't present themselves. For that reason I told Ghiringhelli clearly and directly that I considered myself a singer worthy of having her own operas on the schedules and not just to be used to "take over" operas already performed by others.

Then I went to Florence, for *Vespri Siciliani*. In the meantime Toscanini couldn't find a Lady Macbeth to suit him and had suggested my name for an audition. But when his daughter Wally asked a Milan theatrical agency for my address, she couldn't get it. She was told, moreover, that I was difficult, a hysteric or nearly one, and that I would never agree to be auditioned by Toscanini. In any event, Wally didn't give up and tracked me down another way. Toscanini—I recall this episode with infinite emotion, the more so as the great Maestro is dead—heard me and offered me the part in *Macbeth*, which was to be produced at Bussetto. But just then, as readers will recall, the first alarms about the Maestro's health were sounded, and he was obliged to give himself a little rest. And I lost the marvelous opportunity (which later turned out to be unique, unfortunately) and the greatly coveted, extraordinary privilege of being directed by him.

While I was singing *Vespri Siciliani* in Florence I at last had a visit that was decisive for my career: that of Ghiringhelli, who this time had come to offer me the opening of the 1951–52 Scala season in *Vespri*. My contract additionally called for *Norma*, *The Abduction from the Seraglio*, and some performances of *Traviata* that didn't take place, for reasons that I don't know or don't wish to discuss, because by now it isn't worth the trouble. I accepted with joy, it goes without saying, and while waiting for that longed-for goal, I took part, although reluctantly, in a series of performances in São Paulo and Rio de Janeiro. In São Paulo I was supposed to open the season with *Aida* and afterward sing *Traviata*. Then I was supposed to go to Rio, for *Norma*, *Tosca*, *Gioconda*, and *Traviata*. Nevertheless, a few days before leaving, I received the news from São Paulo that, yes, I would open the season with *Aida*, but that the "prima" of *Triavata* had been assigned to Tebaldi, while the second performance had been reserved for me. I assure you—and I beg you to believe me—that I didn't fret about that. On the contrary, I consented willingly to "take over" my colleague's *Traviata* two times.

I arrived in São Paulo with my legs swollen, as usual (I'll tell you later on the reasons for these persistent swellings), and in far from good health. For that reason, after the dress rehearsals of *Aida*, which went very well, I had to give up the "prima," to my great desolation, and I was compensated for it only by the great success I had in *Norma* in Rio de Janeiro. It was in Rio that the first clashes between Renata and me occurred. We hadn't met for a long time and were very happy to see each other (at least I sincerely was). I remember that we were always together, in Rio's merry restaurants: I, she, her mother, Battista, and Elena Nicolai and her husband. Then, one fine day, Barretto Pinto, the director of the Opera Theater (a rather odd man, but quite powerful in the financial and political fields, married to one of the wealthiest women in Brazil), invited the singers to take part in a benefit concert. I don't know—and still don't know—for whom or what that concert was organized; at any rate, we accepted, and Renata proposed—we were all in agreement with her—not to grant even a single encore. But when her turn came, she ended the "Ave Maria" from *Otello* halfway through because of applause and, to our great surprise, launched into an aria from *Andrea Chénier* and immediately afterward "Vissi d'arte" from *Tosca*.

I was very taken aback (I had prepared only my usual bravura piece, "Sempre libera" from *Traviata*), but I attached to Renata's action the same weight that one would give to a child's caprice. Only later, during the supper that followed the concert, I realized that my dear colleague and friend had changed in her attitude toward me, that she couldn't manage to hide a certain tinge of bitterness every time she had to address me. Then I remember that a short time before, when she entered the theater, she had passed by in front of me without a gesture of greeting; and that at *Norma*, on meeting me in the corridor at the end of the performance, she had said to me in a somewhat spiteful tone: "Brava, Callas," calling me "Callas" for the first time, rather than "Maria." It was a matter of shadings, it's true, but I was upset by it. Later—we were eating at a round table and Nicolai was also with us—Renata began speaking of her alleged failure in *Traviata* at La Scala, warning me of the difficulties that I, too, would meet, as it seemed to her, in Milan. I replied rather brightly, and I remember that Titta nudged me with his elbow to get me to end the discussion. But everything would have been left there, with that exchange of views, a rather animated one, true, if the *Tosca* incident had not occurred.

PART 5

After the benefit concert in Rio de Janeiro, Renata Tebaldi left for São Paulo, where she was to sing *Andrea Chénier*. I remained in Rio, waiting for the "prima" of *Tosca*. The discussion between Renata and me about La Scala had not left any traces: our relations had remained cordial, even if, perhaps, a bit less affectionate. But during my performance of *Tosca* a regrettable incident occurred. I had just finished the second-act aria when I heard someone cry out amid the applause the name of another singer, Elisabetta Barbato, and I perceived a certain dissension in a part of the audience. I managed to control myself, not to allow myself to be defeated by humiliation and panic, and at the end of the performance I had the comfort of a long, warm ovation. Nonetheless, on the next day the director of the Opera Theater, Barretto Pinto, of whom I've already had occasion to speak, summoned me to his office and without wasting words told me that I wouldn't be able to sing the subscription performances. In other words, I had been "protested," as they say in the theatrical parlance.

At first, because of the surprise, I couldn't manage to say even a single word; but then (I always rebel when I feel myself struck unjustly) I reacted very quickly. I yelled that my contract included, besides *Tosca* and *Gioconda*—subscription performances only—two non-subscription performances of *Traviata*, and that he would have to pay me for them, even if he prevented me from singing them. Barretto Pinto flew into a rage. "All right," he told me (he had no other way out), "go ahead and sing *Traviata*, but I warn you right now that no one will come to hear you." He was a bad prophet, because the theater was sold out at both performances. Nevertheless, he couldn't resign himself to the burning defeat and tried to throw various obstacles my way. I remember very well that when I went to him to collect my pay, he spoke these precise words to me: "With the catastrophe that you had, I shouldn't even pay you." At that point I could no longer see straight and blindly grabbed the first object on his desk within reach, to throw at his head. And if someone hadn't been quick enough to seize me by the arm and restrain me, I don't know what would have happened.

I've told about this unpleasant episode in my career because it's linked to other bitter developments as well. As I've told you, while I was singing *Tosca* in Rio de Janeiro, Renata was singing *Andrea Chénier* in São Paulo. Naturally, since I'd been "protested"—and in that way —I was curious to learn the name of the soprano who had taken over in *Tosca*. And I had the sorrow of finding out that it was Renata, the singer whom I had always considered more a very dear friend than a colleague. It was said in addition that Tebaldi had ordered a copy of the costumes I had worn in *Tosca* from the dressmaker's shop that had made them for me; not just that, but it was added that she had gone to try them on herself, and all that before leaving for São Paulo, that is, when no one could know that I would be "protested."

Even now, every time that I look back on these now distant facts, I repeat to myself that Renata cannot have wanted to so disrupt our good friendship, and that perhaps there is a painful and incomprehensible misunderstanding at the bottom of all of this. And even if the circumstances seemed unfavorable to her and those around her, I try to persuade myself that this is surely just a misunderstanding between us, and I continue to hope sincerely that it can be resolved someday.

After the unhappy interval in Rio, I returned to Italy. I was disappointed and hurt, but I needed all my energy and all my enthusiasm:

I was to open the La Scala season for the first time, and I thought I had never faced such a difficult test in all my life. But the welcome that the Milan public gave my *Vespri Siciliani*, under Maestro de Sabata's direction, was enough to remove doubts, and in the subsequent performances I was already sure of myself, proud of having conquered the most demanding audience in the world.

Afterwards I gave Rossini's *Armida* in Florence (I had to learn it in five days), closed the Rome season with *Puritani*, and then left for Mexico, where among other things I sang *Lucia*, a rather challenging opera that I wanted to "try out" abroad before including it in my repertory in Italy.

On returning from Mexico I sang *Gioconda* and *Traviata* at the Verona Arena and then, in September or October, went to London for several performances of *Norma*. It was my debut in England, and I remember that at the moment I stepped onto the stage, I thought that my heart had suddenly stopped beating. I had been preceeded in London by sensational publicity, and I was terrified by the idea of being unable to live up to expectations. It's always like that, for us artists: we labor for years to make ourselves known, and when fame finally follows our steps everywhere, we are condemned always to be worthy of it, to outdo ourselves so as not to disappoint the public, which expects wonders of its idols. And we, unfortunately, are only human, with the frailness of our nature. I, for instance, am considered a very sensitive actress; but that sensitivity complicates my already arduous work incredibly. When I sing, even if I seem calm, I suffer in the unbearable fear of not being able to give my best. Our voice is a mysterious instrument that often deals us sad surprises, and there's nothing we can do but turn to the Lord at the beginning of a performance and say to Him with humility, "We are in Thy hands."

I'm not superstitious, or perhaps I am, but in a way different from others: but I can never part with a little portrait in oil, attributed to Cignaroli, of the Madonnina. That little canvas, which was given to me by my husband on the occasion of my first *Gioconda* at Verona, accompanies me everywhere; I whine if I don't have it in my dressing room. Perhaps it's pure coincidence; however, twice I forgot to take it with me and in both cases I was obliged, not because of any fault of mine, to give up the performances. For that reason, last year, when I realized I'd forgotten the precious little portrait (I was in Vienna for

Lucia), I hurried to call one of my friends in Milan and begged her to come to Austria immediately to deliver the Madonnina to me.

Let's return to the "prima" of *Norma* at Covent Garden in London. In spite of my apprehensions, the performance went very well and I had a warm reception from the audience. I returned to Milan to open the 1952–53 Scala season with Verdi's *Macbeth*. But during the performance, immediately after the sleepwalking scene, I distinctly heard two or three whistles amid the applause. It wasn't the usual whistling done with the lips: it was quite obvious that the disrupter was using a real whistle. I felt rather bad, and the wonderful public, so impartial and generous, took up my defense, turning my success into a triumph. Nevertheless, the whistler didn't become discouraged and made his presence known to me at the performances of *Gioconda* and *Trovatore*. Since then he's never been missing when I sing at La Scala. By now I'm used to it: I'll say even more, I've almost become fond of it.

After finishing the *Trovatore* performances and a concert tour of various Italian cities, I sang Cherubini's *Medea* in Florence. As usual, I had had to study the score in eight days, and this time it was a challenging part with regard to interpretation, too: the enthusiasm that I provoked—it was a truly unforgettable performance—stupefied me and elated me.

In June I set out for London again, where the official ceremonies for the coronation of Elizabeth II were under way. I sang *Aida*, *Norma*, and *Trovatore*. Then I returned to Italy, and between the performances of *Aida* at the Verona Arena and those of *Norma* at Trieste, I could allow myself a bit of rest. But during the performances of *Norma* I had to shuttle frequently between Milan and Trieste: the new Scala season was approaching and the management, at a certain moment, had decided to replace *Mitridate* (which was supposed to be performed between *La Wally*, the season opener, and *Rigoletto*) with Cherubini's *Medea*. The opera was to be directed by Maestro Bernstein, but to my amazement, he showed himself reluctant to accept the assignment. I learned at last—and my amazement naturally diminished—that he had been advised by a group of "friends" who, to frighten him, had spoken to him at length of my difficult personality, my scenes, and so on. In any event, the management of La Scala made an appointment for me with Bernstein; and as soon as he heard me, he put any uncertainties aside.

At that time the newspapers were beginning to talk, in as veiled a way as possible, of an alleged rivalry between Tebaldi and me, and I remember that precisely on the occasion of *La Wally* I read in the columns of *L'Europeo* sage advice from a dear friend, the writer and music critic Emilio Radius. Why, said Radius, don't these two singers publicly shake hands in order to silence the gossip and eloquently demonstrate that there is no rancor between them? Since Rio de Janeiro I hadn't had further occasion to meet Renata, and Radius's words gave me the idea of going to hear *La Wally*, which was sung by her, and to salute her from a box. I thought to pay homage to her in that way and was convinced that the next day, at my *Medea*, Tebaldi would reciprocate. So I went to La Scala to applaud my fine colleague with warmth, as she certainly deserved; I smiled at her often, to make my intentions understood, and I expected a sign or a salute from her that would have authorized me to visit her in her dressing room. But that sign and that signal weren't forthcoming, and Renata wasn't at the "prima" of *Medea*. She was present, however, at the third (or fourth) performance of the opera, because my husband saw her enter the box where he was, just at the moment the curtain rose. Battista greeted her cordially, helped her remove her fur, and asked after her mother. There was a polite reply, but even today Titta is convinced that he wasn't recognized. In fact, as he told me, soon after my entrance Tebaldi rose to her feet, nervous and irritated, and hastily putting on her fur, left the box without saying good-bye, and slamming the door.

That season at La Scala marked two of my greatest successes: the first in *Medea* and the second in *Lucia*. Apropos of *Lucia* I remember that after the Sextet I made the tenor Giuseppe di Stefano go out by himself to receive the audience's applause. (He was still depressed by a not very happy performance of *Rigoletto* and needed some injections of enthusiasm.) I'm recalling that not to give myself any special credit, but because, as you know, I am constantly accused of never allowing my colleagues to share with me the joy of an ovation.

In October, after singing *Mefistofele* at Verona, I left for Chicago, where I was engaged for *Norma*, *Traviata*, and *Lucia*, and on my return I opened the 1954–55 Scala season with *La Vestale*, entrusting myself for the first time to Luchino Visconti's direction. Right after *Vestale* the schedule called for *Trovatore*, but the tenor, [Mario] del Monaco, suddenly refused to take part in the performance because, he said, he had had an attack of appendicitis. *Trovatore* was then replaced with

Rehearsing for *Tosca* (Athens, 1941). Callas was only seventeen,
but critics found her an already mature artist.

As the imperious Turandot (Buenos Aires, 1949). Callas sang this impossible role gloriously but was only too happy to drop it from her repertoire as soon as she could.

As Isolde in *Tristan und Isolde* (Venice, La Fenice, 1947). Such was Callas's musicianship that her sight-reading of Wagner's score persuaded the conductor, Tullio Serafin, that she knew the opera well.

Callas in the costume that she wore both as ▲ Leonora in *Il Trovatore* and Elena in *I Vespri Siciliani* in the early 1950s.

As Abigaille in *Nabucco* (Naples, 1949). Callas complained to her husband that the Naples audiences did not realize what stupendous performances she had given in this treacherous role, but succeeding generations of Callas's admirers have long since recognized the live recording of the December 20 performance as a classic.

As Elena in *I Vespri Siciliani*, with Boris Christoff and Eugene Conley (La Scala, 1951). This was Callas's first opening night at La Scala, an honor that the management bestowed on her belatedly and grudgingly.

As Euridice in Haydn's rarely heard *Orfeo ed Euridice*, with the Danish tenor Tyge Tygesen (Florence, 1951). This performance earned Callas her first mention in her hometown paper, *The New York Times*.

As Constanza in *Die Entführung aus dem Serail*
(La Scala, 1952). Callas found Mozart's music
vocally not very rewarding, and Constanza is
the only complete Mozart role that she ever
sang.

As Lady Macbeth in Verdi's *Macbeth* (La Scala,
1952). Malicious whistling from part of the
audience provoked an ovation after the Sleepwalking Scene.

As Leonora in *Il Trovatore* (La Scala, 1953). Critics marveled at the young singer's intelligence and technique.

Gioconda

In *La Gioconda* (La Scala, 1953). Callas rarely performed the role on the stage but made two brilliant recordings of it.

As Margherita in Boito's *Mefistofele* (Verona, 1954). These were Callas's last performances in the city where she had made her Italian debut and had met her husband, Giovanni Battista Meneghini.

As Gluck's Alceste (La Scala, 1954). Audiences were stunned by the newly slim Callas.

◄ As Lucia di Lammermoor (La Scala, 1954). Claudia Cassidy remarked that audiences' reactions to Callas's singing in the last act made one wonder just who was mad—Lucia or the public.

◀ As Giulia in Spontini's *La Vestale* (La Scala, 1954). One of several brilliant Visconti-Callas collaborations.

◀ A haunting memento of Callas as Giulia in *La Vestale*, revived at La Scala especially for her.

As Elisabetta in *Don Carlo* (La Scala, 1954). Surely this was an Elisabetta who would not allow Eboli to steal the show.

As Madama Butterfly in a studio portrait made in conjunction with the Angel recording (1955). Her performance of the role in Chicago the same year caused at least one patron to opine that with Callas in the cast even trashy operas acquired respectability.

Ettore Bastianini as the elder Germont and Callas as a despairing Violetta in *La Traviata* (La Scala, 1955). With Luchino Visconti as the production designer and Carlo Maria Giulini as the conductor, this *Traviata* quickly entered the annals of legendary performances. ▼

A trio of curtain calls, two (*above and left*) as Gluck's Alceste (La Scala, 1954), one (*below*) as Iphigénie in his *Iphigénie en Tauride* (La Scala, 1957). Callas always managed to make curtain calls seem an integral part of the performance.

As Amelia in *Un Ballo in Maschera* (La Scala, 1957). Callas's costumes were extravagant, and so was the critics' praise of her performance.

Tito Gobbi as Figaro and Callas as Rosina in *Il Barbiere di Siviglia* (La Scala, 1956). Callas made a delicious recording of the role, but her stage performances disappointed even her most ardent admirers. By all accounts, Callas's Rosina was a shrew, not a minx.

▼

In Giordano's *Fedora* (La Scala, 1956). The production was a big hit, but Callas dropped the role after six performances.

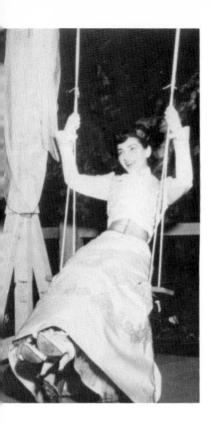

As Fiorilla in Rossini's *Il Turco in Italia* (La Scala, 1955). Callas enjoyed getting away from tragic roles once in a while, but comic roles were a risky undertaking: she had very little sense of humor. Franco Zeffirelli created funny business for her Fiorilla, however, and audiences loved her.

Nicola Rossi-Lemeni as Enrico
VIII and Callas in the title role of
Anna Bolena (La Scala, 1957).
Callas's Donizetti performances
created a Donizetti renaissance
from which audiences are still
profiting today.

◀ In *Iphigénie en Tauride* (La Scala,
1957). As happened all too often, Callas simply acted everyone else off the stage.

As Donizetti's Anna Bolena (La ▶
Scala, 1957). The role provided
Callas with one of the greatest
triumphs of her career.

Alfredo Kraus as Alfredo and Callas as Violetta in Act I of *La Traviata* (Lisbon, 1958). A live recording of the performance was a recent major addition to the Callas discography.

◄ As Amina in Bellini's *La Sonnambula* (La Scala, 1957). Amina was one of Callas's most delicate creations.

As Violetta in the last act of *La Traviata* (1958). Here Callas looks rather healthier than she normally allowed herself to appear in this scene.
▼

As Imogene in Bellini's *Il Pirata* (La ▶ Scala, 1958), partnered by Franco Corelli. This was Callas's last unqualified triumph at La Scala. In the Mad Scene she worked her familiar extraordinary wonders. When Rudolf Bing fired Callas from the Met, she gave concert performances of *Il Pirata* in Washington, D.C., and New York, and the press renewed its demands for Bing's decapitation.

As Tosca (Metropolitan Opera, 1958). Callas's second season at the Met finally proved to New York audiences that her renown was justified.

As Paolina in Donizetti's *Poliuto* (La Scala, 1960). Callas was never more gorgeous to behold, but almost everyone agreed that she had taken on a role that exposed her vocal faults more than it displayed her strengths.

As Cherubini's Medea (Covent Garden, 1959). This series of performances led Noel Coward to call Callas one of the few truly great artists he had ever seen.

Callas as Medea, with Giulietta Simionato as Neris (La Scala, 1961). A year later, when Callas said her farewell to La Scala in the same role, her voice sounded so ragged that even her most devoted fans cringed.

As Medea (La Scala, 1961). Her Jason was a young tenor ▶ just at the outset of his career—Jon Vickers.

Medea

▲
As Bellini's Norma (Paris, 1964). Zeffirelli, who staged the production, remarked that one can see many things in the theater in a lifetime, but that Callas as Norma was something very, very special.

As Norma (Paris, 1965). Callas thought that Zeffirelli had given Parisians one of the most beautiful productions mounted at the Opéra within living memory, but she found the performances a terrible ordeal and was humiliated when she had to drop out of one before the final act.

Tito Gobbi as Scarpia and Callas as Tosca (Covent Garden, 1964). Zeffirelli helped coax Callas back onto the operatic stage after a hiatus of over two years in order to realize one of his own long-standing dreams—a production of *Tosca* with Callas as the heroine.

As Tosca (Paris, 1965). Zeffirelli described her acting as so frighteningly real that he occasionally had to remind himself that he was witnessing only an imitation of life

Callas at the 1958 Paris "monster recital." The program included arias, duets, and the entire second act of *Tosca*.

A 1959 European recital, with Nicola Rescigno conducting. Recitals with orchestra did not highlight Callas's unique artistry as well as opera performances could, but for many audiences they were certainly preferable to nothing at all.

Callas during joint recitals with di
Stefano (1973–74). Audiences
generally found the performances
wrenching experiences, because
both in voice and demeanor Callas
projected uncertainty and fragility.

After a joint recital with di Stefano
in Dallas (1974). Callas pro-
grammed relatively little music for
these recitals because she knew that
there would be much applause.

After a joint recital with Giuseppe di Stefano in Paris (1973). By then audiences heard only occasional faint echoes of the voice that had taken Callas to the summit of the operatic world.

A rehearsal scene and two stills from Pasolini's film *Medea.* Callas had high hopes for her movie debut, but audiences were indifferent.

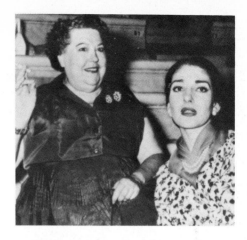

Callas and Elisabeth Schwarzkopf. By her own admission, Schwarzkopf eliminated Violetta in *La Traviata* from her repertoire after hearing Callas in the role.

Callas and her voice teacher, Elvira de Hidalgo (1960). Callas always maintained that de Hidalgo was responsible for everything good about her as an artist.

A dream photograph. Maestri Arturo Toscanini, Antonino Votto (back to camera), and Victor de Sabata with Callas during a rehearsal break (La Scala, 1954). Callas greatly regretted that Toscanini's plans to conduct her in Verdi's *Macbeth* never materialized.

Callas recording *La Gioconda* (La Scala, 1959). Rudolf Bing, then one of Callas's arch foes, attended one of the sessions but had to conceal himself in the darkened auditorium.

Callas recording *Carmen* (Paris, 1964). Callas complained that she had been "tortured" into making the recording, and perhaps by way of avenging herself, she insisted that the recording schedule revolve around her frequent trips to see Aristotle Onassis.

Master classes at the Juilliard School of Music (1971–72). Callas occasionally demonstrated specific passages,

With Luchino Visconti, who had never seriously considered staging opera until he saw Callas. She struck him as the greatest tragedienne since Duse, and for a while he gave up films in order to mount productions for her.

and the emotional force of her singing reduced audience members to tears.

Callas and Meneghini (Milan, 1957). None of Callas's acquaintances understood what she saw in him.

On stage or off, Callas's entrances were events. She claimed not to be aware of her charisma.

Callas as a model of studied elegance.
Gloves accented the beauty of her hands.

A pensive Callas. Francis Robinson thought that Callas's looks often reflected an exquisite melancholy.

At ease, studiedly so.

Callas looking out from her Paris apartment. Biographies and memoirs make it clear that the less said about the final years in Paris the better.

Andrea Chénier, and so I had to learn that opera in five days. In return, naturally, I was accused of having provoked the substitution myself. We went on with *Andrea Chénier*, and at the third-act aria the usual monotonous nuisances made themselves heard, as always. At the end of the performances of *Andrea Chénier* I myself proposed that Mario del Monaco, who was to leave for America, take a solo bow: first of all because he was the protagonist of the opera, and then because it was his last performance at La Scala for the year. Mario del Monaco has never spoken of that gesture of mine. Instead, an incredible story about my "kick in the shins" has been spread. As you know, according to that fantastic account, during the performance of *Norma* I allegedly gave him such a violent kick in the shins that it made him groan and limp, in order to prevent him from taking a curtain call with me!

It's better for me to continue my autobiography, which is now approaching the last chapter. We're at the end of 1955 and are preparing for the "prima" of *Traviata*. The rehearsals went on in an exhausting way, because of the listless collaboration of certain colleagues, especially the tenor, di Stefano, who was never punctual. In the evening, then, we waited for him for hours, because di Stefano—as he affirmed candidly—couldn't sing before midnight.

Mortally tired, we arrived at the "prima," and after going out in front of the curtain all together many, many times, I took a solo bow, at the invitation of Maestro Giulini and of Luchino Visconti. At that point di Stefano left, slamming his dressing room door. The following day he went to his Ravenna villa, and we, on the eve of the "seconda," were without a tenor. Fortunately, Giacinto Prandelli kindly agreed to "take over" the opera and we were able (no one is indispensable) to continue the performance.

I forgot to say that as *Traviata* approached, several anonymous letters (I received them, too; it is not, unfortunately, a privilege just of Tebaldi's) had forewarned me that I would be whistled. Instead, to my great surprise, no one caused any disruptions either at the "prima" or the "seconda," and I was particularly happy about that unexpected truce. But it was only a trick to make the snare more dangerous. In fact, when, at the third performance, right after the attack on "Gioir," I heard a kind of roar from the gallery, and—out of surprise—I was about to cut the note short, and my rebellion was such that it was felt, I think, even by the audience. That evening (there were also many critics in the theater who had been notified by anonymous letters and calls to come to hear me because "there would a chance to have some fun") it was I—I declare it openly—who demanded that none of my colleagues go out before the curtain with me. I wanted the audience to tell me its opinion clearly and straightforwardly, and the audience did so, with a generous rain of applause that extinguished my fury.

In September, after a period of rest, alternated with intense preparations for recordings, I sang two performances of *Lucia* in Berlin, heading then to Chicago, for the second time, to open the season: I had in my program *Puritani*, *Trovatore*, and *Butterfly*, the last of which I had never sung before then. During the final performance of *Butterfly* there occurred one of the most deplorable incidents of my career. The previous year, while I was in Chicago, legal action had been taken against me by Bagarozy, and in order not to be disturbed by my adversaries during performances, I had had a clause included in my contract according to which the theater management would have me protected from anyone and everyone, through the last of my performances. With the last performance of *Butterfly*, which was repeated a third time, as an exception, my season at Chicago was concluding. But while I was waving to the audience, bowing to the applause, in the wings someone was transacting—I don't have words to describe my disgust—my "delivery" to the process servers, i.e., to those who presented the summons.

Many of my readers will remember having seen in the newspapers the photograph of an incensed and enraged Callas who was threatening and demanding justice. I was not indignant at the poor process servers, who in the final analysis were carrying out orders they had received (in America a citation is not valid if the person who delivers it doesn't meet the addressee), but at those who had kept silent about the trap and ignobly betrayed me.

I returned to Italy and opened the Scala season for the fourth time, with *Norma*, and on that occasion had the usual accompaniment of nuisances and the usual discussions with my colleagues. One of them, a woman, more animated than the others, threw herself between my husband and Mario del Monaco, who didn't know to whom to pour out his blazing irritation for a summons that had arrived for him that very day.

In January 1956 La Scala revived *Traviata*, and at this point I should talk about the "drama of the turnips," but it's an old story by now. It's true, at the end of the performance I gathered up a bunch of turnips, mistaking them for flowers because of my nearsightedness. Some carrots fell from the gallery, rolling between the hands of Luchino Visconti, who was in the prompter's box and was dying of laughter. They were vegetables that were out of season, which for that reason couldn't have been purchased at a regular stall before the performance, but revealed a prearranged plan, careful preparation. Indeed, who goes to the theater with turnips in his pocket? However, those pitiful gestures always turn to the disadvantage of the person who performs them, or rather, the person who suggests them: and I have long since ceased to be grieved by that business. After the "drama of the turnips" I sang *Lucia* in Naples; I was again at La Scala, in *Il Barbiere* and in *Fedora*, and then at Vienna, in *Lucia*. At Vienna a certain colleague arranged the usual yelling against me. At the end of the opera I had only one wish: to get out of my costume, remove my makeup, and leave the theater. But Maestro von Karajan begged me to go before the curtain with him, because it is a custom in Vienna that the conductor take a solo curtain call at the end of the performance: and there was someone who disliked that. But in any event, one gets used to everything, and my colleagues' caprices no longer upset me.

But now, I say this with infinite tiredness, I had to begin again from the beginning, because the tangle of caprices, resentments, grudges, and rumors has become public property, to the point of impelling me to this open, frank, and painful confession. Last November, as you know, I went to New York to sing at the Metropolitan. I had heard Mr. Bing spoken of a great deal, and from what had been related to me, I was a little prejudiced against him. Instead I found in him a perfect gentleman, an exquisite and solicitous director. While I was preparing *Norma*, an article about me appeared in *Time* magazine that repeated a number of commonplaces that were for the most part figments of the imagination. I wanted to refute those reports; but I thought that time, as always, would be the best avenger. Instead, that article had the power to influence the American public unfavorably in its attitude toward me; it was picked up immediately by the Italian press and has become a weapon, in the hands of my enemies, for an absurd and unjust campaign against me.

And, unfortunately, I am now obliged to defend myself, to excuse myself for blows that I never dealt. It is not true that at the Metropolitan the turnips "encore" occurred: if I had received vegetables in homage in America, too, I would calmly tell you about it, as I did with regard to *Traviata*. It is not true that when interviewed by the *Time* correspondent, I told him: "Renata Tebaldi is not like Callas; she lacks backbone." That phrase, besides, was attributed—and for anyone who can read English there can be no doubt about it—not to me, but to a third party. Moreover, I don't understand why Renata is offended by those innocuous words. What should I say, then, about an article that treated topics that ought not even to be touched on, such as those concerning the relations between my mother and me?

And of the accusation, publicly tossed at me by Renata, of "lacking a heart"? I am only cheered that my colleague, in her letter to the editor of *Time*, finally decided to confess that she herself wanted to keep her distance from La Scala, whose atmosphere, she explained, is "stifling" for her. That sincerely cheers me, because until recently, among the other innumerable accusations, I was also assailed with this one: of having impeded, with my diabolical arts, Renata Tebaldi's return to the stage of the theater that has always loved her.

My story is finished. I have been sincere, perhaps even too much so. But there is only one truth, and it does not fear refutations. In a few days I'll sing at La Scala again, first in *Sonnambula*, then—for the Fair—in *Anna Bolena*, and finally, in *Iphigénie*. I know that my enemies are lying in wait for me; but I will fight, as much as is humanly possible, not to disappoint my public, which loves me and whose esteem and admiration I don't want to lose. "Watch out, Maria," my good friend, the celebrated critic Eugenio Gara, has often told me, "remember the Chinese proverb that says: 'He who rides the tiger can never dismount.'" No, dear Eugenio, don't be afraid: I'll do everything I can so as not to dismount my tiger.

From French Interviews, 1958–1969

We must not forget that the composer drew his inspiration from a script—a drama—and that the music sprang from every word of that drama. The notes weren't simply chosen as ornamentation. Every note and every phrase has a precise meaning, and it varies enormously, as in a conversation. Wouldn't it be horrible to hear someone express varied sentiments without ever changing the tone of voice? One must learn every musical role to perfection and perform it like Heifetz, Paderewski, and so many other great artists. We singers must modulate our phrases exactly as they do. If our voice cannot submit to the same discipline as instruments, we ought not to sing. I have that ability from nature. I have always had it. The audience should understand what work, what nervous tension, what fatigue, and what love go into every little seemingly unimportant word or note, not to mention the gestures and expressions that are an integral part of the role.

How can we attract young people to opera? By trying to attain the highest artistic standards. That implies hard work, sacrifice, anguish, many doubts about oneself, and the risk of not being understood at times.

I am not perfect. I don't pretend to be. My only desire is to fight for art, no matter what it costs me. Even the simplest melody can and must be sung with nobility. Have you noticed that even jazz singers have class, never vulgarity? Even they are sensitive to that necessity.

Arts, December 10, 1958

My whims? It's clear: everyone of us, the stage director, the orchestra conductor, I, we are always asked to do anything, in any way. If we refuse—not because of a whim, but because we cannot, we should not, or we can't manage it—others will immediately say: "Oh! Isn't he naughty, isn't he capricious! He refused to do it for me, me, when I was so nice!" And then the vicious circle begins: we can't do what other people would like to see us do. We have to know how to say no. Of course, afterward we take the consequences.

At the beginning, I didn't have stage fright. When we are young, we are owed everything. That's thoughtlessness: life has a duty to give us all the chances in the world! I wasn't afraid of anything. I couldn't have cared less. Now things are very different!

When I work on a character, I always ask myself: "If I were in her place, what would I do?" One must transform oneself while remaining oneself. From time to time I consult the historical context, but with prudence: when I played Anne Boleyn, for instance, I wanted to read books, collect information, and I realized that the real historical person had very little to do with the heroine of that opera! I think that it's instinct in the first place that points us in the right direction—the music suffices to explain everything. I'm certain that with sensibility one can discover the composer's world, the atmosphere of which he dreamed. Little by little, everything forms in our head, in our soul, so well that we already know, even before the first rehearsal, what we are going to give it. And then, when all the details have been worked out, there comes a moment when the mind stops and instinct takes the upper hand. Marvelous things happen on stage: one is in a second state, hypersensitive. The audience's slightest reaction affects us. At times one feels oneself to be *enormous*, larger than the theater. At other moments one is small, tiny, one feels ashamed, one would like to run away, one is terrified. And at those times the performance continues, one must sing, act, create.

In our profession you need lots of things: the physique, acting, diction (one must "speak" with the voice), respect for the music. People don't take the necessary time for that. They want to make money, sing high notes, impress the public, stun people with cheap effects. But that's no longer art.

I accept advice. I seek it. But my friends must not be too clumsy! I cannot be taken too abruptly, because then I become truly wild. But with kindness people can get anything from me, can make me foolish. I can't hate anyone, but I close myself off, go away, and forget. One must pay attention to our self-esteem. It's not arrogance, it's pride. People should wait for the proper moment to tell us the truth—which we often know very well. It's difficult, you know, to be famous and to retain the humility of a little school girl at the same time.

I very much like company, but not for too long. After two or three hours I get tired, I need to be by myself. My career has also led me to spend a lot of time alone. I like television, good films, Westerns, because that relaxes me. I also have a childish streak in me—I recognize that very well. I have stayed very young. My profession is very serious, but it's also good to amuse yourself from time to time. All our experiences aid our career. And then, I'm like everybody: I like to enjoy myself and see good shows, but not too depressing, not too dramatic. People are tired of those eternal tragedies!

I can be a great friend, but I don't turn up a lot. I rarely call people. I know my character very well and I also see my faults. If I criticize others, you can believe that I start by criticizing myself. I am very lucid. Yes, I have a poetic side that I carefully hide: I also have a little bit of a dreamy side, where everything is loyal, everything is beautiful and pure. But after forty one no longer has many illusions: one knows that that is nothing but a dream. You speak of will power? I think especially that I have managed to defend myself, for my career: in life you have to struggle, often very hard, in order to get something. People shouldn't reproach me for that.

"Three Days with Maria Callas," interview with Micheline Banzet, O.R.T.F., February 1965

When I was singing *Tristan* in Turin, Tullio Serafin heard me in *Norma* and said, "It's very good. You know the notes, the music very well. Now, would you like to forget the notes and *speak?*" And then, later, he gave me another piece of advice: "Yes, this music is very difficult, but don't become tense. Forget everything that you've learned at home. From now on you have an instrument at your disposal: serve it!" That was very good, very intelligent. Even today I still sometimes forget those recommendations.

What is my true tessitura? I'm a light soprano. My world is that of Rossini, Donizetti, and Bellini. That's the manner of expression that I feel the best, where I find myself most at ease. It is bel canto. I can tell you that *Tristan*, which seems so difficult, is much easier than *Norma*. And you know that Lilli Lehmann once declared: "I prefer five Brünnhildes to one Norma!"

Am I happy? Yes, without a doubt. I ought to think about that more often. Sometimes I don't realize it.

Conversation with Bernard Gavoty, O.R.T.F., May 18, 1965

I've started working again on my entire technique, like a beginner. With the teacher from my early period, my dear old Mlle. de Hidalgo. She's over eighty years old, unfortunately. She can't leave Milan. Now I have a teacher who comes from London. I've been working enormously hard for a year, many hours a day. I'll make my major comeback in *La Traviata*, next January, in Paris. It was announced that it would be in Dallas, in the Verdi *Requiem*, I know. But after seeing all the publicity I picked up my phone one night, and I told the director across the Atlantic what I thought. I detest it when people make publicity at my expense.

I have an obsession for perfection: if I allowed my instinct to work without reflection, I believe it would be creative. But at the same time my intelligence criticizes. And destroys. My last recording, for instance, had sent everyone at the studio into raptures—the artistic directors, the technicians, everyone. But I demolished it piece by piece, band by band: "There the recitative should be more intense. Here my intention doesn't succeed, there the cadence, there the cello." It's mad! I destroy myself.

When I open the newpaper and see my name there all by itself, without even the first name, I sometimes think that perhaps it's someone else with the same last name. Every time a taxi driver recognizes me it astonishes me. It irritates me. You know, I don't go out very much. I don't put myself on exhibit. I live in seclusion. I am wild. Very.

Elle, April 28, 1969

From an Interview with Kenneth Harris, 1970

KH: Turning from opera to film [Pier Paolo Pasolini's *Medea*] must have been a tremendous challenge.

MC: I enjoy challenge: here I have had two challenges. First, to express the passion and turbulence of this ancient legend in a way that makes sense to a modern cinema audience. Second, I had to learn to act in front of a camera, and act without singing. I do not sing in this film.

Acting in front of a camera is different from acting in the theater, especially in the presentation of opera. On the stage it is necessary to make gestures with the hands and arms and to assume expressions which can be seen at a great distance, at the back of the stalls and above in the gallery. When performing opera, singing while you act, the movements must be even more obvious because they must be exaggerated to make their full contribution to expression in that particular medium.

Again, the actor is frequently one of a huge group of people on the stage, many of whom are also simultaneously making movements. He must act so that he can be distinguished from the others. This does not mean that he should try to compete for the attention of the audience, you understand. Not at all. A great actor distinguishes himself by his mere presence, by the idiosyncracy of his gestures and the authority of his movements. The great actor does not have to dress differently from the rest: the public picks him out almost at once. But he, too, must act for an audience sitting at a distance from him. And for him, too, the cinema is different. The camera watches him from perhaps a few feet away. It can come if it wants to, and peer at him from a few inches.

Then, because in film you are speaking your love or your grief, which is natural, whereas singing about it is not, your gestures must be more natural, too. They must be more restrained. And because the microphone may be only a few inches from your lips—every whisper, every sigh, every murmur can be heard a hundred yards away—you must be subtle. But each gesture must be perfect, or as near as you can, because the mobility of the camera ensures that the person who dramatically ought to be in the eye of the audience is so: the audience have only to look at one person at a time, and they look hard. It is scrutiny. And you must not annoy the audience by doing things outside this tiny field of vision: you must not wave a hand where the camera cannot see it.

KH: Are you satisfied with how you have managed to adapt?

MC: I am never satisfied. At least, I am never satisfied with my work. I am personally incapable of enjoying what I have done well because I see so magnified the things I could have done better. But, yes, at any rate I have managed, as you say, to "adapt."

KH: What is your Medea about? In the Greek legend, she helps Jason to discover the Golden Fleece and then when, after ten years, Jason tires of her and decides to marry the King of Corinth's daughter, Medea revenges herself on him. Is that the theme of *your* Medea?

MC: Yes: that is the same Medea. But the film does not give the whole of the legend, and we have given our own rendering of it. If you come to see it, do not expect a film version of Cherubini's opera or the drama of Euripides.

KH: Does the role of Medea appeal to you?

MC: As a *role*, yes, very much. As a person, no. I understand the Medea whom I play, and I have compassion for her. She kills only because she is in despair. She kills her children because she feels she has no other choice, and because being a goddess she can remove them from this bitter and bloody world, and enable them to join her in everlasting life: she kills so they may live in peace and dignity. She know there will be no hope of that for them in this world, so she commits them to the next. She is fragile enough to be broken-hearted by Jason's treatment of her, but she is strong enough to deal with it as she feels she should.

Yes, the role appeals to me very much. And, after all, it is a great opportunity to make your debut in the world of film at the top: no aspiring film actress could have a better start. But if you mean does the woman Medea appeal to me, the answer is no. She can be a cruel woman, and I do not like cruelty, and I could never be cruel. No, I like the role, but I do not like Medea.

KH: Of all the roles you have played, which is the woman among them who most appeals to you?

MC: Bellini's Norma. When she finds herself in a terrible crisis of love, she chooses death rather than hurt the man she loves, even though he has betrayed her.

You must not think this is a film of bloodshed, hate, and fury. It is not a horror film. There are too many such films already. There is too much violence in too many movies, sometimes in theater production. I dislike violence, and I find it artistically inefficient. Where it is necessary to include the shedding of blood, the suggestion of the action is more moving than the exhibition of it. I always eliminated the knife when singing Lucia: I thought it was a useless and old-fashioned business, that the action could get in the way of the art, and realism interferes with the truth.

We have reduced the bloodshed in *Medea* to the minimum— Pasolini has the same attitude as I have in this matter. It is not only that we have tried to eliminate much of the violence: we have taken much of the sound and fury out of the original story, by what I would call significant silences. There are comparatively long passages in which no words are spoken.

KH: I imagine that one of the difficulties was that you had to learn your new job while actually doing it?

MC: Yes, but it is amazing what can sometimes be done by thinking about the problem in advance. Intuition and response to the actual experience of the problem are essential, and ultimately it is at that point that the artist solves the problem of his art. But you can think ahead. You can figure things out. Also, I am quick to learn. That is not a boast. Some great minds learn slowly—some inferior minds learn very quickly. It is a matter of what gear the machinery works in. I happen to learn quickly. When I made the film, the people I worked with said that I had adapted more effectively than they had expected. This was because I had anticipated the problem, and in applying the solution I had figured out to the actual situation. I had thought quickly.

Also, I was helped by the stimulus of living and performing in another world. The people I worked with were very kind and encouraging to me, and they were very gifted. I did not know how I would get on with Pasolini. He is an introvert, and I am an introvert, and we did not know each other before the film: I wondered if we would be like two Great Walls of China, facing each other, staring at each other, and saying nothing. But no. There was the maximum communication between us. We found we thought about the film, its problems and its theme, in the same way, along the same lines, and wanted to achieve the same objects. He is concerned only with the purity of the artistic product, and he will sacrifice everything to get it. He is not, as so many even gifted artists are, taken off his course by egotism of any kind, especially artistic egotism, which is the most insidious kind, because it masks self-will as a stubborn dedication to this or that artistic value. His eye is always on the *work* being produced, not on *his* way of producing it.

I am like that. I do not think: "How should Callas sing this, play that?" I think "How should this song best be sung? How should these words best be spoken?" and then work hard to try to do it. I got on with Pasolini because I listened to what he said, discussed it, and then when we agreed I did it.

I am a simplifier. Some people were born complicated, born to complicate. I was born simple, born to simplify. I like to reduce a problem to its elements, so I can see clearly what I have to do. Simplifying your problem is halfway to solving it. It is with life as it is with art. To simplify a problem is not to solve it, not even to make it easier, but it enables you to concentrate your energies on a real solution. Of course, if you are going to simplify, you must face up to what you find. Some people complicate in order to veil. If you are going to simplify, you must have courage.

Also, to simplify habitually, you need not only the right kind of mind, but the right kind of temperament. You must be cool, capable of being cool, and want to be cool. Many people *want* to raise the temperature. Always. It is as though they had a kind of low emotional blood pressure—they feel they cannot do anything, cannot exist, cannot function unless they work themselves up.

Before I did my screen test for Medea I invited Pasolini to dinner. I said: "If I do this film, and at any time my treatment of the role or my performance in general causes problems for you, do not go to anyone else—come right away and tell *me*. I shall try to do what you want. You are the director. I am the interpreter, and I shall try to make the role my own to give it back to the public. It is the public that must benefit from what I do. And you, for me as I make the film, must be the public. As I interpret the role for the public, you will be interpreting the public to me. We must therefore resolve all our problems."

So, if Pasolini and I had any difficulty about how something should be done, which was rare, we just sat down and talked about it. We sorted things out. It is not hard for intelligent people to overcome their difficulties if they act grown up and not like children. Intelligent people sometimes behave like children, and it is usually because they want to. Because they cannot unravel a situation, they regress.

KH: It's interesting to hear you say you are not temperamental because many people, as a result of reading about you in the newspapers, seem to have the impression that you are in fact a very temperamental person. Some years ago, in Rome, for instance, you sang the first act of *Norma* and refused to sing the rest.

MC: I am passionate, but about work, and about justice. I am a passionate artist and a passionate human being. I am impatient when I am asked to conform to standards of work and behavior which I know are inferior. You say that many people have this or that impression of me because of what they read in some newspaper: I think that is so. But I do not write in the newspapers. Much of what I read about myself in the newspapers is wrong.

Sometimes I do not recognize the woman who is written about in the newspapers.

KH: Could you tell me what happened at Rome?

MC: Well, if you wish. It was a great occasion. The President of Italy was to be there. Great preparations had been made. After the general rehearsal I became ill with bronchitis and laryngitis. I was in bed. I felt I could not sing. Incidentally the mezzo-soprano, Barbieri, fell ill also. The management came to see me. I said: "Do you have a substitute for me?" They said: "We do not substitute for Callas."

You know what is said on such occasions: people have come to hear you, tickets have been sold out—and it is true. There is a dilemma: if you do not sing, you disappoint; if you sing badly, you will also disappoint. Against my will and my judgment I gave in and sang. At once I knew my singing was not good. By the end of the first act I knew I could not finish the performance. My voice was becoming completely hoarse.

While I was still singing, two or three people, paid to do so, were hissing in the gallery. Some of them shouted: "You cost a million lire. Go back to Milan. You are not worth it." There was always a few people, committed to rival interests, who will hiss however you sing. It is when there is no hissing that I will worry: that would show they thought I was finished. Hissing from the gallery is a part of the scene; it is a hazard of the battlefield. Opera is a battlefield and it must be accepted. But that night I was without weapons. My weapons are my voice and my technique. That night fate had struck them from my hand. I was defenseless. If I did not retreat, then I would never recover them and be able to fight again.

So I told the manager: I could not continue to sing that night. He was very upset. He told me it would be very bad for the theater if I did not sing Act II. I told him that he must look after his theater: I must look after my throat. It was that simple.

Afterwards the management accused me of not being willing to accept a substitute. I have told you what I said about a substitute. There was a lawsuit. We fought twice, and I won twice. I had deceived nobody. I never do. I am a very simple woman, and I am a very moral woman. I do not mean that I claim to be a "good" woman, as the word is: that is for others to judge; but I am a moral woman in that I see clearly what is right and wrong for me, and I do not confuse them or evade them. When I say "yes," I mean "yes." I do not need to sign a contract if I agree to do a thing. In principle I do not like the idea of a contract, because a contract means your word is put into question.

KH: You sound very Victorian.

MC: Maybe I am Victorian. I believe in self-discipline and a degree of self-restraint. We live in such a complex, small, and intimate relationship, all of us in so-called civilized society, that we must not shock one another too much. We have to live with one another—we need to be a little, shall we say, strait-laced? The British have so far understood this more than most.

Speaking in general, I find society becoming too permissive. Today, young people too much criticize their parents. They do not realize that parents have something valuable the young ones do not have, a sense of values which may easily slip from their grasp and which it may be harder than they realize to recover.

KH: What do you think of the British as an opera audience?

MC: I could not wish to sing before a better audience than the one I associate with Covent Garden. But I ought to warn you that I may be prejudiced. I have had a love affair with London. It was in Covent Garden, 1952, that I sang Norma. Until then *Norma* had not been heard in London since Rosa Ponselle had sung it there in 1930. She was the greatest singer of her time; and the British are not easy to please; after all, immortal names are written on Covent Garden's walls. I was given a great reception. I was hailed as "the" new Norma. It was a tremendous compliment. Forgive me if I am prejudiced in favor of the British.

KH: What exactly were the people who hissed you in Rome trying to do?

MC: They were hired to try to destroy one reputation so that a rival one might more easily be created. Reputation is all-important in opera. My crowning year had been at La Scala in 1954. There I sang Medea, Lucia and Elizabeth de Valois. Success had not come easily or quickly. I had been singing major roles at 14—Tosca at 15—and was talked about as successful, in Italy and many other countries. I mentioned Covent Garden. In 1953, 1954, I had arrived, as they say, at the top. After that I had a great reputation.

Then, immediately, the agents who wished to bring up other singers and exploit them began to try to get me down. It has not only happened to me, you understand, it is a part of the struggle for survival in the field. So they put these people in the galleries, who hiss me, and applaud their agent's favorites. If they can they will create such an impression that it will be reported in the newspapers that "Callas is going down hill—they hissed her last night. X is rising like the sun—there was great applause for her."

You understand that: I am speaking at the moment of people who are paid to hiss—the claques. Others hiss who are not paid—with them it is a sincere expression of emotion. But I do not like that either. It hurts me to feel that when artists have risen to the top and are trying to interpret artistic masterpieces with everything they have they are not given the proper atmosphere to do their best. It seems not so much unfair as wrong, a cruel nonsense.

KH: You say opera is a battlefield. Why?

MC: Opera is a very artificial form of art. The people who perform it—singing, playing, or producing—must be very skilled. This makes them expensive. To produce opera is very, very expensive—great sums of money are necessary to have a chance of making it commercially viable, and they may be lost. It is a very expensive gamble. Not everybody cares to take it. There are more singers, players, producers, and theaters than money to finance them. Therefore there is great and fierce competition for what opportunities present themselves.

The impresarios, the managements, the backers of opera consequently tend to think in terms of deals. Package deals. The manager of a theater might say: "I want X to sing *La Traviata*." He goes to her agent. Her agent says: "Yes, you may have X to sing *La Traviata*, but only if you will take Z to sing Alfredo and Y to sing his father," plus agreement to the casting of several small parts as well. Maybe the manager does not want Z or Y; maybe he thinks they do not go well with X, or with somebody else he wishes to cast. Maybe he would like to give small parts to up-and-coming younger singers who deserve a chance. But if he wants X for *La Traviata*, he will have to take the rest as well.

I do not like these package deals. I want to sing only with those whom I think will make, with me, a proper production. I stand on my own merits, and I want always to work with people who are included on theirs. I do not want to horse-trade my way across the world of opera. I am concerned with art, not commerce. If I cannot sing what I want with whom I want, and with those and for those who want me for what I am, I do not sing at all in public.

I do not want this for myself, you understand. If it were what I wanted for myself, it would be easier to accept the deals and give in. I want it for my art and I want it for the opera—the best standards, the best work, the best company.

KH: Do you ever feel like giving up your work and taking things easy?

MC: Sometimes, often, even in the middle of a performance, I have said to myself: "You are no good. You can't take it. You must give it up. It is not worth the effort." But what is there in life if you do not work? If you do not work there is only sensations, and there are only a few sensations—you cannot live on them. You can only live on work, by work, through work.

What do you *do* if you do not work? I do not understand. Perhaps some people who do not work pass the time in talking of themselves. I do not want to talk about myself. I find me boring. It is what I do that interests me, not what I say. How can you exist if you do not do things, and how can you exist with self-respect if you do not do things as well as lies in you? And how can you achieve that if you do not work at it?

So, to live in a way you can tolerate for yourself you must work. Work very hard. I do not believe with Descartes: "I think: therefore I am." With me, it is "I *work*: therefore I am." . . .

KH: What is bel canto, exactly?

MC: Well may you ask. There is much confusion on this subject. Bel canto means, in Italian, "beautiful song." Some people, therefore, think bel canto means the aria in the opera, the song, the air, the lyric, as opposed to recitative, which is, so to speak, talking in song. Other people seem to think bel canto is a description of any beautiful singing. But the word means something quite special.

Bel canto really means a schooling of the voice so as to develop it as an instrument. . . . Bel canto is not everything, you understand. When you have mastered it, you must go on and learn to interpret the music, what weight to give your words, the pace, the feeling, the intensity. Mastery of bel canto does not make a great singer, but there is no great singer who has not mastered bel canto.

Elvira [de Hidalgo] developed my voice as a light voice. This was good. My range was on the short side then: some people said I was a mezzo-soprano, not a soprano. But I developed higher notes. Elvira taught me the low chest notes. It is not just a matter of what a teacher advises you to do, and trying to do it. It is an attitude, a relationship, help. . . .

KH: Do you think that music is the only thing that matters in life?

MC: No, not at all. Communication is the most important thing in life. It is what makes the human predicament bearable. And art is the most profound way in which one person can communicate with another. Music is the highest way of saying things. But it is not the only way. As for me, I could easily have moved into another field when I was young. And I would have worked at it.

KH: But don't you sometimes hanker to be, well, back on the battlefield?

MC: I am still on it. In many different ways. Life is a battlefield. . . . I do not ask for anything. I let things and people come to me. . . . Why not ask, you might ask. That is how I am, the basis of my nature.

Maybe it is because I do not want the risk of being refused. Maybe it is pride. But I do not want to ask. I do not want to command, I do not want to be able to command—in public or in private life. I let things come to me, and I do not complain if they go away again.

The Observer, February 8 and 15, 1970

As They Saw Her:
Essays and Appreciations

≡⋮≡⋮≡⋮≡⋮≡⋮≡⋮≡⋮≡⋮≡⋮≡⋮≡⋮≡⋮≡⋮≡⋮≡

Callas the Stylist   *by André Tubeuf*

The pictures testify that Maria Callas believed in her image. She must have carried it within herself for a long time, hidden at the bottom of the cocoon, and distinct, clear, and deliberate. All by herself. Mr. Meneghini offered her roses and paid for clothes, but her figure, her allure, her style—it was she herself who wanted them. That was her first metamorphosis, her only one perhaps, because this extraordinary artist did not metamorphose on the stage, not in the least. She appeared—and under Norma's mistletoe or La Sonnambula's wreath of flowers she had only to be what she had become—Maria Callas. In the same way in the film *Camille* it is not Marguerite Gautier who appears before us. It is Greta Garbo. She too must have believed in her image, when one knows what she was before she became Garbo. In the same way Callas herself, Callas alone was the Pygmalion of this Galatea, the voice already as much as the vision (before even having opened her mouth). Certain influences spurred her on and at times even directed her. Visconti, first of all, taught her expression. He awakened in her the consciousness of her face, that reverse mirror that may be consulted from within, good at depiction, and which obviates the necessity of a real mirror. From Visconti she learned the art of applying makeup from within. The singing, in the end, is nothing more than a verification. From [the director] Mme. Wallman, who blocks a scene the way one arranges a shop window, she learned display. She invested in it, sublimating her shopgirl background. The shopgirl was dead for a time in the sylphide: but when the sylphide was killed, the tubby and impressionable girl who consoled herself by being common while eating cakes came to life again in the slim and elegant woman who survived, Callas in Paris. That is the most celebrated image of the live Callas, unfortunately. Her only televised recital revealed her to the whole adoring world in that indecent short Paris dress with its pretentious train fit to reach beyond Elsa Maxwell and the gawkers at the entrance to Maxim's and impress the girl next door in Brooklyn in the 1930s. One can find worse things: a photo of Callas with Eliette von Karajan looking like a kept woman who has gone to the dressmaker's.

That is what Paris and idleness made of Callas's image: that other parvenue who existed, a little girl, in one of the two aspects of her dreams. The other was the artist. One finds it on the stage. The image is refined. It is enough that she sing: she is in her setting (which we do not see); she is natural, positioned, her eye dilates, her face composes itself, one hand, the palm toward the enemy (or toward the gods), clenches at her mouth, her other touches her shoulder and crumples her scarf, a thin arm is thrown across the heart as though to prevent something, or to quiet it, to stifle the voice, to excuse it in advance if it breaks in a cry or strangles. Visconti encouraged her in this same theater of poses, but heroically, old-fashioned in a Stendhalian way, like a Sanseverina in her wimples and laces. Visconti taught her to inhabit with brio and grace—that more natural truth—outfits and postures that she could not have been tempted to copy in town: Violetta in paste jewelry and black satin, with a bustle, Iphigenia under the crescent diadem, in the finery of a high-society woman. Visconti estranged Callas brilliantly. He repatriated her in her sole artistic milieu, Utopia: Tosca in her own theater. Nowhere did Callas expand her imagination and her verve, which were not made for the street, as much as in the scenes from La Sonnambula, infinitely remote from all possible reality, which bring much more to mind the image of the dancer she will never be, Taglioni, than they do the voice of the singer to whom she has been compared, Pasta. Yes, the photographs are essential. They show to what a brilliant extent Callas was the stylist for her own image: she exposes directly to the lens her silent-film poses, ports de bras (even immobile ones)—an entire choreography of the silent screen. Appearing and posing are the very acts of the actress who is only acting when appearing, only being when seeming, and at no other time. In her pose of actress, Callas is neither natural nor sincere, but she is complete, absolute, real, alive. The counter-proofs are striking: in those atrocious Paris years, a few disdainful and ascetic traces of her Norma aside, how many times we will see Violetta on the arm of a Douphol, a diva fallen and mundane, and at once demimondaine with the air of a dead person. Surprised bareheaded in the street, walking her dog and wearing shop-window clothes, she is pathetic.

Condemned to the artifice that expresses her—such is the lot of the child of the theater. She usurps identities. She is nothing without her greasepaint. The voice was all of Callas's personality. She could not remain someone without the singing, because she had neither the prodigious superiority complex that Patti's indisputable position as star of the era gave to her, nor the royal favor granted to Melba and Emma Eames, nor above all, in modern times, the culture, dynamism, and pragmatic intelligence of Mary Garden. It is not at all astounding that Callas's mute Medea did not burst through the screen as Garden's mute Thaïs did. Callas had to find and defend her difference all alone. She had a timbre. She dared a tone. A repertoire was able to come back to life—that is a historical fact. People have imitated her. That makes for genius, a place in civilization, a stele. But does it make for a style?

The first paradox. The woman who made the renaissance of Italian opera possible has nothing Italian about her. Neither vocal quality, nor birth, nor schooling. When it comes to vocal quality, Callas has neither reliability nor luminescence of sound, nor sonorous directness of emission, but instead a veil, fog, flashes of lightning, and opacity. Nothing Latin, nothing liquid. By birth and education she is uprooted, a daughter of Greece and America. Born an American, Ponselle put down all her roots in the Italian milieu; Callas, her antennae, her ears. The very nature of the voice says enough. The second paradox. The person who resurrected styles had no vocal models. Her childhood could not have done other than to take Lily Pons for the allegory of Europe conquering America, the legitimate incarnation of Lucia, La Sonnambula, Gilda, Rosina. No other models. Callas did not listen to Lilli Lehmann's recordings in order to convince herself that the technical prowess of a Callas is possible at all times. Did she listen only to those of Muzio, who in several ways also foreshadows her, and above all in that manner of transforming weaknesses of the voice into confessions of the soul?

And of living models? Mme. de Hidalgo was able to equip her pupil from head to toe, but the fact that she sang Rosina before Callas ought not to mislead us. The influence is nil. She taught her embellishments and inculcated in her the philosophy of agility. But Callas owes to her teacher nothing of what makes her Callas: the instrumental perfection of the legato, which seems to be traced by an agile viola, and which the words illuminate and animate without, however, disturbing it; nor the impalpable rubato that carries the syllables the way a dancer carries her arms, linking them like movements, in accordance with an agogic of languor, which is like the energy of morbidezza; nor the elegiac luster of her descending scales. One need only listen to Elvira de Hildalgo. The old records may deceive one about the timbre, but they do not deceive about the singing. She could not communicate a style to Callas. She had none. She did not have even an idea of style. One cannot begin to place Callas in the proper perspective without noting right off that this person who resurrected a heritage was born without patrimony and outside a tradition. There was no tradition of bel canto. A tradition, by definition, is something conveyed from one person to another, and without interruption. And it is fortunate: in this way Callas was able to reinvent bel canto in terms of modern sensibilities. Without roots, without masters, without models, without anything to imitate or admire, whom could she continue or revive? That fire from the heavens was indeed, in our century, an irruption.

We note, moreover, that this same vocal versatility that occasioned the first break for Callas's career is in essence the absence of style. What is style? Obvious unity of behavior. With Callas, the vocal corset of *I Puritani* could be unlaced sufficiently to accomodate the bellows of an Isolde, or rather Isotta. When used, such an operation has something of the irreversible about it. The voice does not come back from the vehemence of Isolde to feverish and more fragile effusions, to the vocal dishevelment of the madwomen of the 1830s. Callas was the theater, the battlefield, of quite another kind of irreversibility. It is the immensity of Isolde's vision, once lived, which came to expand, larger than life, the somewhat narrow field of the soul where Elvira's delirium plays. Until then, Donizetti's and Bellini's madwomen had had blond and sparkling voices—Toti, Lily. How could they have ventured to resuscitate the bloody queens—Boleyn, Stuart, Tudor? Here are the stormy sky, clouds, the rumbling elements, the imminence, an entire theater of the fantastic. Here one notes the prodigious new fact: the return to an out-of-date repertoire, but with the curiosities, the nuances, the experience of modern curiosity. Not from having read Freud, thank God, but from having heard Wagner. Made for Isolde, Callas's voice did not harden, nor did it skip over (as the verismo singers did in their Normas) the passages in *I Puritani* calling for agility. It illuminated them and made them palpable, dramatically alive. A stunning correct use of anachronism. From the first developments of her career on, Callas alternated *La Vestale* and *La Sonnambula* as though they were of the same format, or simply of the same style. A simple confusion of usage, a much noted phenomenon. It conceals another one, remarkable in another way. From her Medea on—a pivotal role, at once epic and elegiac, marble and melodrama—Callas would bring to characters born of the conventions of three-quarters of a century of opera, from Alceste to Anna Boleyn and Lady Macbeth, the energy of sentiments, the variety of timbres, the instrumental coloration and nearly the *orchestration* inspired by the company of the music of the three-quarters of a century that follow, from Wagner to verismo. The multicolored palette, the genius of the miniaturizing inflection (a simple stroke of instrumentation, as in Mozart's concertos of 1784), the immediacy of the emotional modulation, of the expressive suggestion, the seemingly spontaneous mimetics of the mood and state of soul (the voice, that reverse mirror), Callas found them, *alte Weise*, on the terrace of the third act of *Tristan*. She owes her musical imagination to the orchestra of the end of the nineteenth century. It is not in singing that one should seek her masters and models. It is in instruments. In the detail of her Traviata, of her Sonnambula, of her Norma, look for the sudden color and presence of the oboe, or flute, or even clarinet—under the conductive legato, that outline of the viola d'amore. There is a color of the voice just as there is a color of the eyes, and with some people one is worth a thousand. With Callas the color is veiled, lunar, opalescent, iridescent. She sought her additional tints in the sharp-filled orchestra of *Don Carlos*, in the flat-filled orchestra of *Aida*, in the lively variegation of *Tosca*, which is like a Gustave Moreau that dances for real. To a music that one believed outdated, Callas brought this sensibility of timbre and inflection polished in later eras. This Norma hears in her clearing what the clarinet inspired Brahms with in a forest and what one knows the English horn inspired Wagner with by the sea. Callas managed to be born without a singer's roots. She was born a German musician. Her destiny as an artist was immediate exile, isolation, anachronism.

How did it come about then, that she was able to dictate a style, and even to be a style, that absolute exception who continued no one and whom no one has followed? One need do no more than go back, in another way, after her, to a repertoire that she did not make fashionable, but that her stamp alone later sufficed to consecrate. Vanishing too soon from the stage, she was not a fashion there, but rather, a furor. And since the stage has been empty, a cult. The mayfly left a few of her ashes on the roles that she touched, revived, branded.

If there is style, it is by virtue of records. It is time that the ecstatic hagiography of those who once touched the hem of her costume and who act as though their own lives and the face of our civilization were altered by that calm down a little. What made Callas is the record. Not in the first, obvious sense, where it is the record that keeps her present and active. It made her immortal; that is a truism. Rather, in her lifetime it had made her known, internationally known, the queen of a theater that no one had occupied before her and that no one has since, a theater without images, vaster than the world, more populous, and more confined than solitude—the theater of performance. The mature record gave her that, beginning in the 1950s, in place of those trivial and overheated scenes where she had done nothing more than pass by, where very few of those who saw her understood (heard) her, and where abuse and vegetables were hurled at her. It is in a profound, magical, nearly initiatory sense that the phonograph record made Callas. It forced her to be herself. It obliged her to become what she was aspiring confusedly to be: an arresting presence in invisibility itself, someone to whom one listens better, someone whose words matter, someone who reveals to us not a forgotten repertoire, but new possibilities for our ears. An intelligibility. The record, theater minus the visual, requires more infinitesimal and immediate accuracy of inflection, the illuminating textuality of the word, and it justifies them afterward, in reflective hearings. Records that allowed Callas to be simultaneously the champion of immediacy, urgency, and the first-degree absolute of emotional presence, and (along with Schwarzkopf) of the second-degree absolute, a singer to whom one returns and whom one studies. Thanks to records, our ear has been made a microscope. The challenge is for it to see what it hears. Callas, like Schwarzkopf, and for the same reasons, justified that microscope. With the exactitude of a nearsighted person and the freedom of a sleepwalker, she was what Schwarzkopf was with eyes open (and making us see those open eyes clearly): literal, attentive to punctuation, to the accent marked, seer of implicit legato, an exactitude that is *at the same time*, as with Leibniz, an invention. But if the Callas miracle is more astonishing than that of Schwarzkopf, it is because the latter's roles, deliberately literary—up to the lied, which for her was another repertoire of roles—in effect offered texts, and beyond the great communicated text, a school of attention and inflection. Callas made intelligence live in the roles which one thought one could do without, which seemed alive through the emotion or the vignette, but insignificant as far as the words. Her recitative disabused us of that right away!

Her visible theater, without which she could not have made a scandal—her only real scandal as an artist—opening our eyes to what is in our ears, has disappeared. Her footlights are extinguished. Farewell to that ascendency, to those poses. There remains, on records, that extreme mobility of voice that is something quite other than agility. One should recall, then (or learn), that she hardly moved on the stage. Her verve, her vivacity were purely musical, and in no way theatrical. By abolishing the theater and its ostensible movements, records liberated and magnified that pure mobility; it made of it a Racinean truth, complex in meaning, pure in accent. Callas put all of herself into those words. Her words sang for her. Two peculiar corollaries result. The first: those who did not see her on the stage know her better, by knowing her without her veil—and except for Violetta and Amina, her stage images all obscure the entirely sufficient truth of her singing. The second: Visconti, the director, thanks to his operatic culture, was able to direct the emotions of this pure genius at investing in the individual shiver a voice that can be like gooseflesh or like a blush. A pure director of actors, like Chéreau, would not have been able to do anything with her. One can take Callas or leave her. She had nothing to learn.

If there was a Pygmalion, it was Walter Legge, who converted an artist who had nothing to learn into one who makes her most lasting contribution of genius: making communication intimate, *the optical quality of the sound*, the novel perspective of the record, blind and in relief. Callas's mise en scène is her singing; her theater, the record; her audience, the year 2000; her style, intelligibility.

A Voice for Reconstructing the Theater   *by Guy Coutance*

First of all, what one must try to recover and to describe is the sense of expectation. A sense of expectation, first of all anxious, as on the eve of a trip to a foreign country that will reveal no end of other landscapes. Then the irresistible and tremendous expectation when the overture quickens the tempo, cavalcading over fast rhythms and strong beats. The waiting at last nearly at an end when the tenor finishes his aria and the march of the Druids begins. Is she going to appear? All at once the large midnight-blue cloak comes into view above the scenery: it reveals at last la Divina.

The entire beginning of the first act of *Norma*—the overture, the chorus of priests, Oroveso, Pollione—is nothing but an enormous period of waiting—for Maria Callas. In that waiting there was not only all the mystery of being, all the mystery of singing, but also the mystery of that phenomenon that it is difficult to summarize: the performance. Finally, she was there. Our eyes could devour her. And then began another mystery: that of a presence.

For a long time after those years 1964 and 1965, which are now entering into legend, I wondered about what that presence consisted of, where its secret lay. I think that it can now be said that contrary to a personal annexation, it was the space of the opera that was entirely taken over; that opera, in some way the genre itself, was incarnated. The modern mise en scène was born, in this mid-twentieth century, of two particular and distinct trajectories: the revelation of a space, that of Wieland Wagner, and the revelation of a body and of a presence, those of Maria Callas. The two meet. Opera is nothing without the miracle and the mystery of the voice, just as the dramatic theater is nothing without the actor's body. And the whole art of opera consists of the art of the presence sublimated by the voice. In this sense, the task of the stage director is this wedding, simultaneously impalpable and rigorous, of a style, a space, and voices.

Before Maria Callas discovered this secret, what did one see on the stage? A flat world in two senses. In the first sense, in that of the stage itself, because nothing lived in its depths. Painted flats, a limited sky, ranks of choristers at the proscenium, soloists directly in front of the footlights: in its static quality nothing could make one suspect what one of the sources of opera's magic is: its explosion of shot arrows that rests on the core of the orchestra pit in order then to spread and extend toward the distance, the flies, the wings—those successive planes that the acoustico-dramatic architecture is responsible for suggesting. In the other sense, that of the auditorium, the same flatness existed, formed partially by the lines of spectators frozen into a bourgeois conformity, having nothing at all to do with an operatic theater. In the nineteenth century there also radiated waves of force resting equally near that secret and magic zone located at the juncture of the footlights and the pit. In the cinema, with the first frames of *Senso* in 1955, Visconti's intuition found in a flash this universe of particular radiations made up of mixed particles of the political, the social, and the artistic, and which made that auditorium space vibrate with the same intensity as that of the stage. But it was above all through voices, through the transmission of the direct and *immediate* energy of Maria Callas's voice that this combined space of the auditorium and stage was going to open up again in the two senses.

And it was nothing more, finally, no matter what voice! I mean no matter what sonorous emission. All the others before originated in nothing more than a perpetual and uniform stream and volume, which had a very quick tendency to level them, differentiated in that case only by the phenomenon of the quantitative.

With Maria Callas we hear a "distinctive" voice for the first time. The organ is not there exclusively to link together neutral decibels, but to project the colors, cries, moans, mottled effects, explosions that form the different shores of Medea, Gioconda, Santuzza, Elvira, or Lady Macbeth. And all at once the voice fills and justifies the opera entirely. The lost secret is refound, and the privileged space vibrates anew, like an invisible atom that will not cease emitting energy.

It could be Norma whose head is buried in those of her children in the third act; whether it be, also in the third act, Violetta slapped with the money and collapsing at the footlights under the weight of her pain and humiliation; it could be Tosca doubled up with suffering and supplication when the trap door at her feet opens to the cries of Mario being tortured; it could be that dazzling somnambulist, a white angel who at the crowning display piece is going to irradiate this very center of the theater space by the rockets and flashes of her voice, each time the very heart of the opera begins to beat and accelerates to the rhythm of the singing that fills that body.

People have spoken of the bullfight, of the circus. This was both less and more than that. Before becoming a social event that sublimated it, the electric and passionate atmosphere of the audience was what opera has always been made for. And through the mystery of the human voice and the total gift of that presence, one found again the magic, the mysterious accord between a breath and a public that beat in the veins of the Greek tragedienne.

The Gesture Woven by the Voice

Memory, often hazy and confused, contradicts itself here to cause images to arise that are blazing, precise, and that time does not alter. And yet in each of them the mystery of that presence is born, expands, and dissolves again. Why that unfeignedly weary, lingering gait in the first act of *Norma*, which serves as support for the diaphanous and sublime cantilena, for the gestures of the goddess? And why, to the contrary, in the second act, that vivacity and that modernity in the movements, that familiarity in the smiles that contrast all the more so with the explosive and concentrated outburst of the "Non tremare" to Pollione? Why that unbearable fixity of motionlessness wherein the glint of the dagger joins with that of the gaze before the "Son miei figli" of murder averted explodes? Then, in the last act, the extraordinary nobility of the silhouette, lengthened by the large red cloak, the final desperate violence of the duet with the lover, and the humility of kneeling at the father's feet, where the hands wring, supplicating, clutching at Oroveso's arms and tunic? All these "whys" find no rational explanation. There is nothing more than the evidence. Before that the great breaking-open had taken place. The impalpable "Son io" of a voice drawn out to the limits of the audible then reveals to us the process that could well be the very essence of the magician. With a very slow gesture of the arms, the singer has raised her two hands in order to remove the goddess's wreath. She lets it slide to the ground. Maria Callas rests for a moment as though suspended by an invisible thread over a precipice. Perfect balance creates the pathway, that narrow passage between divinity and humanity. The grand priestess is no more, only a woman, a mother who implores her father to save her children. And that immense presence, which until then overshadowed the entire opera from its beginning, now is reversed when the prima donna becomes that nothing, that dizzying cavity inside which all the music is engulfed. It expands to the point where everything topples over and converges near the hard diamond that glows at the footlights: partners, sets, the chorus, curtain, flies. The grand Wagnerian dream, the alchemical transformation of the goddess into simple mortal: Maria Callas assumes it alone and takes charge of the heritage. At her spot the density is such that it approaches the power of the galaxies that turn and command the world's order. The desire to respond to that singing, to those infinite radiations at last launches the "mise en scène," the putting into order or the putting into orbit of this *entirety* that was formerly separated and is now unified: *opera*. Thanks to Maria Callas, as of twenty years ago stage direction and production found its dawn.

Singing Rediscovered   *by Sergio Segalini*

In the beginning was the void. All was dust, death, and desolation. That is how we would like to begin our article on Maria Callas, who, in the space of a few years in Italy, was to wage a fierce battle for the renascence of an art that one thought dead. "Opera is a dying man who is having his final convulsions," she was to assert during one of her rare interviews. Perhaps she did not even realize herself that thanks to her, all was going to revive, spring up again, re-emerge out of the original void. For it is true that in the days following World War I, opera was dead. Since Alban Berg's *Lulu* and *Wozzeck*, which had breathed new life into the lyric art and assured the continuity of its language, it had been a void. For the first time since the *Dafnes*, *Euridices*, and *Orfeos* of the eighteenth century, opera was stagnating. What was being created, for people still were creating occasionally, did no more than continue a largely outmoded esthetic that had had its day. Puccini remained the master for some, the Vienna School or Debussy for others. The repertoire was reduced to great masterpieces of dying romanticism and of verismo. Verdi, of course (*Otello*, *La Traviata*, *Rigoletto*: not *Macbeth*, *Simon Boccanegra*, *I Vespri Siciliani*, *Don Carlos*!), Wagner, and Bizet's *Carmen*. Buffo operas by Rossini and Donizetti (*The Barber of Seville*, *Don Pasquale*), disfigured by a simple concern for theatrical effect. Bellini's *Norma* was sung by Wagnerian sopranos. Even Mozart was a rarity (*The Abduction from the Seraglio* would not be given its first performance at La Scala until 1952! And with Callas, as a matter of fact!). Handel and Gluck were no more than names. And Callas came. With her cultural message, her will for innovation, her desire to return to the sources.

In Search of Lost Singing

Verdi said: "Ritorniamo all'antico e sarà un progresso." Unconsciously, Callas made this declaration of principles her own and set off in pursuit of a lost language. For before life could be returned to opera, composers, the press, the public, the theater directors had to awaken to a historical past they did not even suspect existed. And the world had to understand (before it was too late!) what the word opera meant in all its fullness. Return life to opera! A difficult task for a young girl to whom nature had not been very kind, a Greek living in America. And for whom nothing presented itself under the most favorable circumstances. A tyrannical mother, the delicate situation of an immigrant, an automobile accident, the declaration of war. It was not until later, in Greece, that Callas would have all the chances: she would be able to work with Elvira de Hidalgo, a celebrated Spanish coloratura of the period between the wars, certain of whose 78's give us a pale reflection of "Una voce poco fa" or "Ombre légère." With Hidalgo, Callas learned the great technique of romantic bel canto, which, since the García sisters (the divine Maria Malibran and divine Pauline Viardot), had been perpetuated in Spain through numerous voices, such as Mercedes Capsir or Maria Barrientos, Marisa Galvary or Huguet de Arnold. Thanks to Hidalgo, Callas learned what Bellini's melodic line is, Rossini's *staccato*, Donizetti's ecstatic cantilena with its chain of explosions in the cabalettas. Nothing terribly original so far, if Callas had not possessed, from the beginning, a large dramatic soprano voice (which made certain teachers think that they were in the presence of a mezzo soprano!).

In order to emphasize her vocal gifts at that period, Callas sang with ease Rezia's great scene in Weber's *Oberon* and the "Habanera" from *Carmen*. The miracle would be that this great voice, large and powerful (which was simultaneously that of a Brünnhilde and a Turandot, of an Isolde and a Kundry) would learn little by little to grow lighter, more flexible, until it was able at the same time to absorb Proch's "Variations" and reach E *in alt* with the same facility in the roulades as a Lily Pons or an Adelina Patti. Actually, the evolution of the repertoire at the end of the nineteenth century had brought the bel canto scores in line with the taste of Victorian salons, lightening the emission, changing the timbre, diminishing the volume to a sort of singing that contained more fin-de-siècle coquetry and disfigured the original spirit of the works.

That was how Patti sang. Joan Sutherland would sing that way again, but in a much less pronounced fashion. Now Callas had learned to restore to bel canto her power of emission, her breadth of timbre, her dramatic profundity. But how to do that in Greece during the war? In order to be able to sing, she accepted *Fidelio* and *Suor Angelica*, and *Tosca*. In the United States she was later offered *Turandot* but said no to the Met, which wanted to have her appear in *Fidelio* in English(!) and particularly *Madame Butterfly*. How could this healthy young woman be credible as Puccini's fragile geisha? She said no. For, as we shall see, with Callas, everything would go hand in hand: the concern for musical truth and the concern for theatrical truth. To be extraordinarily, entirely, totally, definitively true. To be honest with the composers she serves, to be credible in the roles she tackles. A difficult task for anyone. But not for Callas, who knew without doubt from the start what she was going to become.

This battle that she was going to mount for the renewal of opera would be long, hard, arduous, and would lead to the exhaustion of her strength and to a premature death. Of course, at the beginning no one wanted to believe in the miracle. And besides, who really knew our musical past? Engaged in 1947 for *La Gioconda* at the Arena of Verona, Callas at that time confronted the routine of provincial Italian theaters with Wagner, with the Puccini of *Turandot* and *Tosca*, and with the Verdi of *Aida*. The theater managers, on hearing the fullness of the voice and on seeing the singer's flourishing appearance, could not imagine the unprecedented material that Callas carried in it. But she met

Serafin, the same Serafin who had worked with Rosa Ponselle. That same Rosa Ponselle whom Callas had heard on the American radio in *Carmen*, and certain accents of whose Norma she would keep (listen to their common sonorities in "Sediziose voci"!). Serafin understood everything, made her work on diction and expression, and had her appear in Bellini's *I Puritani*.

A Brünnhilde singing Elvira! That was the revolution in the Italian theaters. Yet before her Lilli Lehmann had been Constanza in *The Abduction from the Seraglio* and Brünnhilde in *Götterdämmerung*! Well then? But Callas, unlike her illustrious predecessor, grasped at once all the uniqueness of Bellinian singing, which had nothing to do with the expressionism of Wagnerian heroines. Later, when the May Music Festival in Florence would offer her in the first twentieth-century revival of Rossini's *Armida*, a critic would write: "I had the impression of hearing Rossini for the first time. Better yet, I realized what Stendhal and other chroniclers of the nineteenth century meant when they spoke of Malibran and Pasta." There again, Callas dazzled, astonished, provoked endless discussions, but did not yet make the importance of her revolution understood. She would finally do so by tackling a work of the repertoire that everyone knew by heart: *Lucia di Lammermoor*. For up until then her revolution had not been perceived except by certain specialists; a few less than scrupulous critics had even gone so far as to write that in the last analysis "this Greek woman did not wish to risk the current repertoire, for fear she might be judged"! Of course, how could one find points of reference with *I Vespri Siciliani* and Haydn's *Orfeo ed Euridice* (which she literally created!), *Armida*, or *Macbeth*, which no one else knew! But with *Lucia*! What shrill, piercing, nasal sopranos with a whitish timbre and plaintive sound had masked the true visage of that dramatic Donizetti heroine! One had to recover the correct expression for Donizetti, who had written his *Lucia* for the *coloratura drammatico* voice typical of his age. Of course, the celebrated voices had each introduced their own variations: Lucia's entrance aria and the "Mad Scene" had been conceived for that. But from there to make of Lucia a sister of Lakmé or Philine. When Callas sang Lucia for the first time at Milan's La Scala, under the direction of von Karajan, in the audience was Toti dal Monte, Toscanini's celebrated Lucia, whom the illustrious maestro had used even in Germany, during La Scala's historic tour in the 1930s. At the conclusion of the performance, tears in her eyes, Toti went to Maria's dressing room and confessed to her with honesty and frankness that she had realized that evening that she had never understood anything of the role. Supreme lucidity and touching modesty from a genuine artist. Later, Callas and von Karajan, in their turn, would leave for Berlin and Vienna to perform the new Lucia in the footsteps of Toscanini, that Toscanini whom von Karajan had in fact heard conduct *Lucia*, when he was a young man seated in the top gallery of the Vienna Opera.

To establish a new way of singing *Lucia* was also to open wide the doors to other works by Donizetti. For by hearing Callas in *Lucia*, everyone became aware that Donizetti was not a composer of the second order whose music had been a simple pretext for roulades, but rather the indispensable link in the history of romanticism, ideally conjoining Rossini and Verdi. The triumph of that *Lucia* permitted Callas to revive *Anna Bolena* and then *Poliuto*. There too, after hearing her in *Anna Bolena*, certain illustrious pens wrote: "Callas is sublime in *Anna*, but can the opera live without her? Doubtless not." Now it has conquered, and *Anna Bolena* has entered the repertoire. No one has equaled Callas in the role, of course, but *Bolena* lives. Just as subsequently *Roberto Devereux, Maria Stuarda, Lucrezia Borgia, Caterina Cornaro* could live. Sometimes one thinks with nostalgia and regret about the extent to which Callas had elevated those roles. Others before her had sung those rarities: Beniamino Gigli and Iva Pacetti had tried to give *Il Pirata* another chance; Esther Mazzoleni, *Medea*; Giacomo Lauri-Volpi, *Poliuto*. But their attempts remained short-lived, because, to judge by all the evidence, they were not able to discover the exact spirit of that music. With Callas the kick-off had been made. In *Lucia* and *Bolena* she had said everything: all one had to do was to follow her. And she had said it with a voice that was not one of the most pleasant to listen to, with its inequality of registers (quite characteristic of technique in the nineteenth century), her stridency, her metallic sound, her harshness. To the fundamentally beautiful, round, ample, sensual, and limited verismo voice Callas opposed an instrument of diverse sonorities, spontaneous pulsations, and infinite coloration.

A Voice and a Body in the Service of Singing

Her other revolution would be to demonstrate that opera needs not beautiful voices, but voices capable of serving a composer, a text, and an expression. "Could one say 'Serpenti venite a me' in *Medea* with a velvety voice?" she would say. And in making her voice, rebellious by nature, an instrument of extraordinary docility, Callas would invent different colors for each heroine. For Norma the priestess, Gluckian declamation mixes with the ecstatic cantilena typical of Bellini and the tragic fury of neoclassicism; Amina the somnambulist will have the accents of a sylphide, of a water sprite, an unreal creature at the midpoint of dream and the subconscious. Her singing would be the reflection of the legendary dancing of Taglioni. The two universes that Callas succeeded in creating with these two Bellini heroines are perhaps the most profound examples of this diversity of approach and of this quite specific individuality of each heroine she tackled.

Rediscovering a forgotten repertoire, linking herself to the genuine roots of singing, adapting her instrument to the various exigencies of a role—all that was already a great deal, and Callas did not cease demonstrating it as well with Mozart (her Constanza in the *Abduction*!), with Spontini (her *Vestale*!!), with Cherubini (her *Medea*!!!) and with Gluck (*Alceste* and *Iphigénie en Tauride*), in more of the specifically bel canto repertoire. But not without difficulty. For how could one manage to make the real meaning of bel canto understood? Everyone had confused that expression with "beautiful voice" and had believed that that simply signified "beautiful singing," confusing in that way beauty of singing and beauty of voice. Think what a revolution that could provoke in 1950, when only yesterday a singer of the stature of Anja Silja (she was called "the German Callas" with good reason!) declared of her Marie in *Wozzeck*: "One needs bel canto in Berg, because if one looks at the music carefully, one sees that Puccini is not far away"! To say that thirty years after the Callas revolution!

In order to make her revolution even more true and more striking, Callas would even dare to do what no one until then had done. In the space of a few months she lost sixty-five pounds, and the awkward and clumsy actress became a woman of astonishing beauty, with a royal bearing and perfectly controlled gestures. For Callas thought, and rightly so, that in order to save opera she also had to make it credible to an entire generation that, thanks to the movies, thanks to television, demanded a much more coherent, much closer vision of the desires of the contemporary world. She who had known how to make each of her heroines vocally credible, putting them entirely in their correct musical context, wanted to make then scenically credible. She would never sing Mimi on the stage. And for Violetta she would metamorphose under Luchino Visconti's skilled hands into a new Eleonora Duse. Thin, beautiful, proud, her Violetta would even have the colors of death in her voice in the last act, which would not fail to provoke from her detractors the fateful reaction: "Callas gets tired by the end of the evening"! And on the stage she would be the equal of Greta Garbo's Camille or Sarah Bernhardt's Marguerite Gauthier. "The greatest actress that the twentieth century has seen since Duse," wrote Visconti, who for Callas would leave the movies and do his first opera productions: *La Vestale, Traviata, Sonnambula, Anna Bolena, Iphigénie.*

In 1955, with the Visconti-Giulini *Traviata* at La Scala, Callas was at her vocal and dramatic summit. That year the opera turned an essential page in its history: leaving the limited cult of aficionados, it again became that popular art one imagines it to have been in the nineteenth century. The international intelligentsia studied the phenomenon, the press took possession of the celebrity, movie and theater directors invaded the opera houses. And at the same time, the most refractory theater (New York's Met) tackled a different repertoire. Rudolf Bing asked Callas to create *Macbeth* in New York. In 1960 he was even ready to revive Bellini's *La Straniera* for her. Everything was in motion. The triumphs became greater and greater and the message more and more obvious. The conservatives reacted more and more badly. In 1957, for Visconti, Callas the Greek would even agree to don costumes inspired by Tiepolo for an *Iphigénie* shifted entirely to the eighteenth century. Callas the Greek renounced ancient Greek tragedy! But it was necessary, because opera needed to find new keys for reading. A part of the public, twenty-five years afterward, apparently had not yet understood this revolution, such an essential one. When in 1965, with a final *Tosca* at Covent Garden in London, she left the stage forever, everyone spoke of the shortness of her career. It had begun in 1939, however! People would then invoke her reducing diet, her social life, her liaison with Onassis. It was nevertheless easy to observe from close up the chronology of her performances. Could the voice last indefinitely when alternating verismo with bel canto, neoclassical declamation and Verdian expressionism? Even in her concert programs Callas went from "In questa reggia" from *Turandot* (written for a Nilsson) to the "madness" of *Hamlet* (written for a Lily Pons). And each time with a different voice, a different style, a different sound. For Callas did not do as her illustrious predecessors had, or as those no less illustrious singers who have succeeded her and who have the deplorable habit of adapting the music to the possibilities of their voice. Callas bent her voice to the needs of the music. And she *was* Medea and Violetta, Norma and Amina, Fiorilla and Armida, Anna Bolena and Amelia, Imogene and Alcestes, Tosca and Butterfly, Maddalena and Turandot, Elvira and Lady Macbeth, Euridice and Elena, body and soul, with a sense of professionalism, a scrupulousness, a meticulousness that have not been equaled. Let us recall, in closing, the last *Medea* that she gave at La Scala in Milan, in 1962. At the moment of the famous phrase "Ho dato tutto a te," Maria moved directly forward on the stage and sang that avowal, her eyes fixed on the audience, instead of addressing herself to Jason.

Yes, she gave everything to her public, and especially to that of La Scala. Could her revolution have made any sense in any other place? She gave *us* everything, made us understand everything, told us everything. Happy are those who knew how to listen.

The Triple Revolution   *by Jean Lacouture*

Who has not "knocked" Callas? Read if anything the Milan press after her first *Aida* (1948), the Rome newspapers the day after the scandal of *Norma*, the majority of the Paris critics of the 1958 recitals. The unanimous adulation of today is far distant: these are nothing but denunciations of an "exacerbated dramaticism," of "improper" hoarseness, and "excessive" stridency, then of the fatigue of an "overworked" voice. In short, a decline before maturity. And I am delighted today not to have found a forum at that time where I could have commented on that production of *Norma* at the Opera. Would I too not have believed it necessary to qualify my admiration with mockery of a certain already perceptible wavering in the middle register?

The young people who are discovering today—say in the last fifteen or twenty years—the intoxication of the opera house, that universe studded with suspect truths and true lies, are indignant at our shamefulness in receiving Maria Callas. If, the Florentines and Londoners excepted, Callas's audiences were so beneath the chance that was offered them, so pitifully blind and deaf, it is because the entire revolutionary enterprise is naturally rejected by those who have sampled the delights of the "ancien régime." We lived, it is true, in another golden age, peopled with gods named Beniamino Gigli, Tito Schipa, Gino Bechi, Toti dal Monte, Maria Caniglia, and finally, Tebaldi. Divine voices drugged us with verismo and overexcited emotion. People who have not heard Gigli in *La Bohème*, Ferrucio Tagliavini in Cilea's *L'Arlesiana*, or Lina Pagliughi in *Lucia* do not know what a certain form of ecstasy is. The timbre, the panache, and a dramaticism of the first degree intoxicated us: opera was a paradise bathed in notes that were strangely independent of the dramatic action that had once served as a pretext for them. And we, the devout, the obsessed, confederates in a secret lay order, we would go around masked, too happy over the strangeness of the rite and heedless of the delicious absurdity of singing cut off from its roots.

It is this reign of an insulating unreality that made of opera a world apart, a vast but closed sect, that Maria Callas came to abolish, opening another era, one in which opera is of life and in life. She very carefully shattered the windows where an art of artifice languished, and we, lashed by the wind, did not understand what was happening and what was the breath of truth. The passage from verismo to the true.

The first revolution: the irruption of opera into current events, into public discussion. As late as the mid-1950s the lyric theater was a private domain, scarcely less so than those of drugs, of bullfighting, of cockfights. Was I going to say, at a dinner in town, that my most precious dream was to get a folding chair in order to go hear Björling in *Il Trovatore* at Parma? What an unwashed country bumpkin! A tenor would not know how to be anything other than a fat Toulousian with an accent reeking of garlic, a female singer, a grotesque character for one of Labiche's vaudevilles or René Clair's films. Suddenly, one January morning in 1958, at the office of *Le Monde* where I was on duty, I was brought a dispatch from the newspaper's Rome correspondent, and those few lines that the editor-in-chief had decided to print on page one turned the hierarchry of genres upside down and at one fell swoop, wrenching opera out of its ghetto. That the news was about a scandal in the first place changes nothing in the matter. For Maria Callas's sudden silence at the Rome Opera at the beginning of the second act of *Norma* that January 2, 1958, would not have made any noise, if one may so express it, if that mute woman had not had a voice so great that in two or three years she had achieved the stature of a mythical figure of the modern world, the equal of a film star or a champion cyclist.

Who would have thought five years earlier that the breaking-off of a performance in Rome, even if in the presence of Mr. Gronchi, the President of the Republic, could have found the slightest place in a French newspaper?

Now it was *Le Monde*, the first page of *Le Monde*, reserved for the greatest political news, the death of academicians, and the awarding of Nobel prizes. Stupefaction: opera, by the roundabout means of a loss of voice, was granted all at once the honors of the mighty press! I was present at the thing, fascinated, feeling the walls collapse around me, savoring it like a discharge from prison. Opera had been made an event and thing of life.

Is it not ridiculous, you will say, to speak in the first place of Callas's silence and of an incident deplorable on all points that does less service to her memory than the Verona *Gioconda* or the Covent Garden *La Traviata*? Certainly. But it was there all the same that the phenomenon of society broke out in all its virulence. Dating from that 2nd of January, the singer was no longer just the renovator of modern opera; she entered into the life of everyone, into the common language. She became a legend, an absolute reference. Several months later, Prince Sihanouk, the Cambodian chief of state, whom I interviewed for *Le Monde*, did his best to demonstrate to me the world importance of the People's Republic of China, and in order to do that, exclaimed, "In short, China is like Callas . . ." Could one imagine, several years earlier, a chief of state pleading for the recognition of the USSR and declaring that "the Soviet Union is like Amelita Galli-Curci"?

Fine. So much for achieving stature in our consciousness and in the media. But so what? An eccentric endowed with several talents could do it by bold strokes of defiance to which, her fame achieved, people wished to reduce her legend. It is on a plane other than one of stature and the mythification of the character that Callas's second revolution operates: that of the use and employment of the voice.

Pardon me for going back thirty or forty years. The world of opera, overflowing with vocal riches, was the most compartmentalized in the world. Everyone had his own domain, his own field. Light, lyric, and dramatic sopranos, coloraturas, mezzos, altos, contraltos—the boundaries were well marked according to tessitura, defined by tradition more than by the composers or even by the great teachers of singing. On the one hand, there were the Rosinas, Manons, Micaelas, Violettas, Mimis, Lakmés, Lucias, Gildas—and on the other, the Normas, Alcestes, Aidas, Giocondas. Not to mention, of course, the Wagnerian universe into which hardly anyone ventured except the specialists with metallic voices.

And then at the end of the 1940s there appeared a singer who, after having achieved in a few months a sort of glory by incarnating in turn Isolde and Brünnhilde, Turandot and Abigaille from *Nabucco*, the most dramatic and vocally heavy roles for a voice, included in her first recital the aria from *I Puritani* in which but a short time before coloraturas had won renown (for an Isolde the very idea of tackling this aria would have made her faint from fear). Could one even imagine Germaine Lublin or Gina Cigna singing, even in recital, the "Bell Song"?

But soon, Maria Callas did even more to break down the barriers that isolated the characters and currents of the opera stage from one another, barriers that had them in a suffocating stranglehold. In October and November 1951, in Rome, she alternated performances of *Il Turco in Italia* and *Parsifal*. Now the extreme comic and vocal lightness of Rossini and the extreme gravity of late Wagner—she was Lily Pons and Kirsten Flagstad simultaneously! And a few months later, in Florence, she risked singing in succession in a recital "Ombra leggiera" from *Dinorah* and "Casta diva," Proch's *Variations*, and "O patria mia" from *Aida*. All the conventions were forgotten, all the barriers broken.

Truth or madness? Maria Callas wanted to demonstrate that the art of singing is one, that it is at the service of the dramatic action, and that, no more than Anna Magnani or Madeleine Renaud could have locked herself into one kind of role, a singer could not tolerate being the prisoner of a narrow repertoire. Who could doubt that this type of attitude, in broadening prodigiously her dramatic and musical field, contributed to the shortening of that incomparable career? The greatest operatic tragediennes of the last century, from Pasta to Malibran, risked broadening their repertoire to infinity, from Donna Anna to Norma and from Semiramide to Rosina. But the repertoire of that time did not include Brünnhilde, Isolde, or Turandot. The taste for challenge, Callas's revolutionary passion, the concern for going the limit led her to suicidal experiences. In his lovely book *Images of a Voice*

(Editions Francis Van de Velde) Sergio Segalini speaks of a "flagrant desire for self-destruction." Should we regret that? Immoderation was part of her genius. Would a reasonable Callas, prudent with her talent, a good manager of her art, have turned opera upside down? And would she so shatter us with her singing of Violetta's "Addio del passato"?

For it is there, of course, that Callas's real revolution lies: the reinvention of tragedy within opera, the synthesis of the dramatic action and the sung expression, that manifest evidence that the problem is not the one that Richard Strauss posed (text or music first?) but rather the obvious indivisibility of one and the other, not the preexistence of singing for all expression, but rather the necessity of singing in order *to achieve* the expression.

On the stage—and even in recital—Callas, by her comportment, swept away the very idea of formulating the question as Strauss had. In Lady Macbeth, in Tosca, in Violetta, often at the limit of *parlando*, she rose to the most lyrical singing by any imperceptible progression, imposing the idea that no other means of expression could be natural without being trivial.

But what can be said here that has not already been said a hundred times? "The greatest tragedienne since Duse," her director Luchino Visconti said. To be the most illustrious voice of the century and to tackle the cinema, deprived of music. She had to do that, to go as far as the renunciation of her vocal gifts in order to proclaim her place in the world of tragedy.

The End of a Dream *by Yves Saint-Laurent*

And suddenly, rising from the depths, a fiery, low-pitched, high-pitched, strident, supernatural, baroque voice, a voice without any equal, tried to combat death. A miraculous voice, that of a genius, with its oddness, its defects, its blackouts, and prodigious flights that took our breath away, its trills, its vocalises, its gusts of warmth, its stridencies, and its irritations that rushed forth in flashes of lightning, in a cataclysm, in orgasms. A valiant siren cutting through the ocean's swell whose magnetism made those who heard her dash themselves on the reefs of her modulations and her resonances.

Diva of divas, empress, queen, goddess, sorceress, hard-working magician, in short, divine. Devastator, explosive, nightingale, turtle-

Yves Saint-Laurent sketch
for a dress for Callas.

dove. She passed through the century like a great solitary eagle whose outspread wings have concealed from us forever those who will outlive her.

Rainbow of light, Niagara Falls, underwater breeze, abysses of a bottomless shaft to the chasms of an infernal forge, cascades of crystal, gauze sash unrolled under the breath of dawn, entrails of the earth, viscera of the Minotaur, torrents of honey, swamps, quicksand where one sinks, where one forgets oneself to the point of vanishing. You spin a long spider web of threads, of braids, of bows, of straps in which we become entangled. Ghost of Duse and Malibran, draped in Rachel's robe, you stumble over Sarah Bernhardt and you come rocketing to us in spite of your fears, pure as a carbuncle, Nereid, Morgana, Armida, Melpomene, monster of the theater, outside of us. You extended the magic circle of your arms and the crowd killed itself. You sang and we did not know that that apotheosis masked the cataclysm. Everything melted, everything toppled over, everything was dying of love. Everything was going to die.

Unreal, vaporous, invisible threads, you wanted to make us believe in your weakness. And if you slipped, it was in order to take flight, a rocket, a firework, inferno of blast furnaces. Your heavy mantles of tragedy were lighter than the wings of the dragonfly. You glided, you capered about, you galloped, you attained unexplored heights, virgin summits that you passed over smoothly, with a casual air, in order to fly even higher, even farther, and to penetrate the eternal system of the planets and the stars.

You no longer sing, but you will always be there. Your voice broke on the reefs. You have left, eternal eclipse. You preferred to leave. You had a foreboding of the drama.

A somber odor of rot was already worming its way through the pilasters and the doors of the boxes. What does it matter that from now on, after the three knocks, it is no longer you who commands the show. It is on your legend that the heavy purple curtain covered with glory comes down. You took away everything with you. Deprived of its enchantress, the red and gold pit functions no longer. Gone forever the magic spells, the charms, the fascination, the trap doors, the wonders, the fugues. That hideous crowd that pushes, gets in a tangle, congregates in the sleep of the void, invades your palaces, soils them, blackens them, demolishes them, destroys them. You would not have been able to bear it!

But you too have abandoned me! You too were no more than a dream! But through that of others it is always your voice that I hear! Those overwhelming gold-fringed curtains, those shadowed ground-floor boxes, those loges, those galleries, those balconies, those rows of plush seats, those arc lights, those spotlights, those marble stairs, they are YOU!

It is always you, your head bristling with the laurels of glory, in a volcanic eruption of vivats and bravos, the clicking of photographers, the thunderous adoration of crowds of slaves, your wake strewn with hearts in a trance.

Through the world, suspended above the walls of the long, dusty tunnels of the wings, your trains, your mantles, your furs, your ermine pelisses, your togas, your peplos, your stars, your veils, your crinolines, your bustles, those are your radiant clothes!

Piled high in the wicker baskets of triumphal tours, your shawls, your laces, your tulle, your mantillas, your wigs, your headdresses, your fans, your gloves, your jewels, your pins, your hooks, your crowns, your diadems, your tiaras, your palms, Tosca's dagger, they are also YOU! Eternal, immortal, glorified by the colossal garland of red roses of all the operas in the world.

Crown of bereavement, crown of farewell, funereal crown, the death of your voice. The death of a dream! I know very well that it exists, the dream! Of course, it's a passing dream! It slipped between my fingers. It is fragile! And your voice in its crystal goblet could not resist those who thought to become intoxicated with champagne when it was the magic potion that led to the height of the most subtle dreams. Their coarse, clumsy hands broke the goblet! Your voice evaporated. It fled this impure, debased, putrefied air that was going to suffocate it, petrify it, degrade it!

The gods were bored. They remembered their Voice. The Enchantress has returned to the Olympian summits, where, sovereign, imperious, proud, she can only blossom, shine forth, blaze in the ethereal and grandiose atmosphere of eternity. For us, unfortunately, she is no more. It is night. You did not give us much time, but enough for us to be tormented by regret. And this sudden silence is so terrible, so despairingly empty, so tragically disquieting that I cannot help thinking that the death of your voice was a fateful omen. It was the sign. The premonitory sign of the twilight in which we were going to be swallowed up. It was the end of the world of which you were the last fête, the last jewel, the final flame.

Your voice revived everything. I was confident, full or ardor, of promise. Happy, I was carefree, I loved. It galvanized, energized, magnified my love. Its harmonies merged with mine and prevented me from hearing the menacing rumbling of destruction that was beginning to well up. My bedazzled eyes did not yet see that deep erosion that was beginning to spread its poison, insert its worms, its parasites, multiplying its microbes!

The Opéra. The old Opéra. The sad, brutalized, battered Opéra, surrounded on all sides, I suffer with you. I dream of that time back then. How proud you were when you received her! How you vibrated! How you battled to recover your splendor, your prestige, your glory! You thrust out your chest. You pulled in your stomach. You had a slightly roguish air of satisfaction. You swaggered. You puffed yourself up. Your fat carcass was imposing. You bustled about. You ran everywhere. You gave orders. Lots of orders. A director of a model hotel who receives a queen!

It is the Queen of Sheba who is arriving! It is the Empress of China and of all the Russias! It is the Queen of Spain! Keep the senior lady-in-waiting in readiness! It is Cleopatra! It is Aida. Double the trumpets. Redouble the fanfares! It is all the queens and all the empresses at once!

Who could have resisted that voice! Hypnotized, my ship sailed straight to crash on Lorelei's reefs! I was in love!

This evening, you are going to sing.

This evening, you will sing.

This evening, you are singing.

Remembering Callas: Recollections by Fellow Artists

≡═✕═≡═✕═≡═✕═≡═✕═≡═✕═≡═✕═≡═✕═≡═✕═≡═✕═≡═✕═≡═✕═≡

Noel Coward

Nov. 4, 1956

On Saturday afternoon I went to Bing's box to hear Callas sing *Norma* at the Met. She was fighting a bad cold and all hell was apparently breaking loose backstage, but she completely captured me. True, her high notes were a bit scratchy but she is a fine singer, beautifully controlled and in technical command of every phrase. She is also an artist: she did some superb bits of acting which only Mary Garden could have equalled. . . . At the very end Callas got an ovation the like of which I have seldom heard. She is a perfectionist and a stylist and it was fascinating to see how her quality triumphed with that vast, prejudiced, over-knowledgeable audience.

June 28, 1959

On Monday I took Graham [Payn] to *Medea* at Covent Garden and we were both overwhelmed by Maria Callas, who was completely and absolutely superb. The opera is not really up to much and should have been by Strauss, but she makes up for everything. She is one of the few really great artists that I have ever seen in my life.

The Noel Coward Diaries, edited by Graham Payn and Sheridan Morley
(Boston: Little, Brown, 1982)

Plácido Domingo

I met Maria Callas through a friend of my wife's who worked for Angel Records; we were thinking then of recording *Traviata* together. Of course, we spoke a great deal, but I realized then that Maria was her own worst enemy: she did not in fact want to sing anymore after having been so great. Nevertheless, if in 1970 I had been in the position that I am now, perhaps I could have managed to persuade her.

Later I asked her many times, "Maria, why don't we sing *Cavalleria Rusticana*, for instance?" People even dreamed of giving it at Covent Garden. But every time she found a pretext for shying away: "No, I must sing *Norma* or *Traviata* this year." But I knew well, and she did too, that unlike *Cavalleria*, those roles were no longer for her.

We continued to see each other, we were good friends, and we often had dinner together. But it became very difficult to communicate, because she lived from then on in another world, one from which opera was banished. When she stopped singing, she thought that everything was finished in that domain, that there were no longer any stage directors, any conductors, and especially singers. She had drawn a line through her career and avoided discussing that period, and it was almost impossible to talk about music with her.

I believe that Maria allowed herself to die of sadness. One really can die if one wants, even without suicide, by abandoning life. Just like that.

As for her voice, of which people have spoken a great deal, it was not "beautiful" in the current meaning—but the most beautiful voices are not necessarily the most touching ones. It was fascinating, in its timbre in the first place, but also because of the way she used it, bringing each note of the music to life.

In the Hamburg concert that was shown on television, for example, in *Don Carlos*, even during the orchestral introduction, she *is* already Elisabetta, in the first notes. And, from the way that she feels that introduction, whose music is inscribed on her face even before she sings, one can already understand everything. And every note that she then sings is thus transfigured, as though brought by a breath of wind coming from afar, from deep down inside her.

In thinking about Maria Callas, I in fact have only one regret:

that of having been too late to know the experience of singing with her.

"Singing after Callas" (Remarks collected by Isabelle Patriot),
L'Avant-scène, October 1982

Tito Gobbi

It was on this tour [to South America in 1951] that I sang for the first time with Maria Callas, who was to become the greatest of all my colleagues. Tilde and I had already heard her once in *La Gioconda*, with which she had made her first impact on the Italian audience. Now I sang with her myself in *La Traviata*.

Looking back, I cannot believe that anyone else in the whole history of the work ever sang that first act as she sang it then. Later perhaps she looked the part more convincingly, later she may have added certain refinements to her characterization of the role, but I find it impossible to describe the electrifying brilliance of the coloratura, the beauty, the sheer magic of that sound which she poured out then. And with it—perfect diction, color, inflection, and above all feeling. It was something one hears only once in a lifetime. Indeed, one is fortunate to hear it once!

In 1953 I joined her in the recording of *Lucia* under Serafin in Florence and then, later the same year, came the first recording of *Tosca* under De Sabata. This was the beginning of a long professional association in both recording and stage work, an association so complete in its integration and understanding that I think I may claim the right as well as the privilege to write at some length about what was one of the most amazing appearances in all opera.

I think of Maria—and I venture to believe that she thought of me too—as a friend as well as colleague; and, as far as one can say one understands a fellow-artist, I came to understand something of her. First and foremost she was a diva, in the sense that she was set apart: not just in the top rank but beyond even that—something unique. This meant that people demanded the impossible of her, so that she forever carried the burden of having to reaffirm her supremacy or else be regarded (by herself as well as by others) as in some sense failing. Such a unique position creates a great loneliness and a sense of responsibility so crushing in its weight that it is almost more than a human being can bear.

For a singer this striving for eternal perfection is particularly cruel, for the singer—unlike every other musical peformer—is his or her own instrument. If the singer is sick, so is the voice. If the singer is under a great strain, so is the voice. If the singer is shaking with terror, only the most reliable technique will save the voice from doing the same.

Self-appointed critics tend to say: "If you have a good, well-trained voice you should be able to sing well." But it really is not so simple as that. There are so many other factors, particularly in the case of an opera singer who has to act as well as sing. And it is not acting in the sense of straight stage acting. All must be contained within the musical form. You cannot pause on a word for added dramatic effect. The music does not allow you to declaim, "To be"—pause for effect with hand on brow—"or not to be." The integration of acting and singing must be absolute. In Callas this integration became nothing short of miraculous. Her musical and dramatic instincts were faultless, and her dedication to her art was total. In consequence she did not suffer fools gladly, particularly in her earlier, less patient days, and I am bound to say—why should she? For she never demanded from anyone else a standard for which she was not herself prepared to strive.

It would be absurd to pretend there were not times when she behaved badly—when she was, as people loved to say of her, highly temperamental. Sometimes she was undoubtedly in the wrong, sometimes the stories were complete invention, and sometimes she was fully justified in her reaction—as on the much-publicized and photographed occasion in Chicago when some fellow without even the manners to take off his hat tried to serve a writ on her as she came from the stage. She was perfectly justified in thrusting him from her path with words of furious contempt. How dared this oaf lay a hand on someone who had just given 99 percent of everything she had and was in her effort to serve her art and her public? Suppose she did owe money—the matter could have waited for a couple of hours. To attack any artist at such a time is contemptible.

My own single serious brush with Maria also occurred in Chicago, in 1954, and perhaps deserves a full account since I can personally vouch for the truth of it. I also give it as an illustration of what sometimes happened in the highly charged atmosphere in which this controversial figure moved. It was during a performance of *Traviata*. The second act, with its superb duets between Violetta and the elder Germont, had gone splendidly; she had left the stage, the short scene between Alfredo and me had taken place, and I had sung my final aria which practically closes the act. Then, as the curtain fell, something went wrong with the mechanism so that one half of the curtain came down while the other remained up and then vice versa, all to the amusement of the audience. As the technicians struggled to sort things out people back-stage were saying desperately: "Go out and take another call, Mr. Gobbi, until we get this damned thing right."

I looked around, inquiring once or twice for Maria and the tenor to join me, but was forced to take several solo calls—to considerable applause. Out of the corner of my eye I saw Maria's husband, Battista Meneghini, go off in the direction of her dressing room and presently she joined me for the last call and, the curtain having decided to behave by now, we went off to our respective dressing rooms.

As the interval lengthened out extraordinarily someone came to me to tell me that Madame Callas was very angry with me and wanted to see me in her dressing room. I went along there, passing Meneghini in the doorway.

"They tell me you are angry with me, Maria," I said. "What is the matter?"

"Shut the door," she ordered, as though I were a servant. And then: "You must understand that I will not allow anyone to interfere with the success of *my Traviata*. If you ever do such a thing again I will ruin your career."

As will be imagined, I took a deep breath at this. Then I replied very calmly: "You were right to suggest that we close the door. Now —first I have always understood that it was Verdi's *Traviata*. As for what happened with the curtain, I did what seemed best at the time, with no thought of harming my colleagues. Your saying you will ruin my career is just a piece of nonsense. It is true you are a power in the opera world, but I also have some power and don't forget that I arrived on the scene ten years before you did. I give you three minutes now to go on the stage and continue the performance. Otherwise I go out and explain to the audience exactly what happened—and you know I will do it."

I left her then. Two minutes later she passed my door on her way to the stage.

The third act went beautifully and just before the last act I went onto the stage to check the layout, as I usually do. Only the work light was on and suddenly from the shadowed bed a rather subdued voice said in Venetian dialect: *"Tito, s'i tu rabià?"* ("Tito, are you angry with me?")

"Oh, Maria," I replied. "Are you already there?"

"Yes. Are you still angry with me?"

"No, Maria, I'm not angry," I said more or less truthfully, for there was something so silly and childlike and touching about this tentatively offered little olive branch that it would have taken a harder man than I am to reject it. "We all have our nervous explosions at times. Now forget about it."

I never had any real trouble with her again, and in later years there were times when she would not take on certain engagements unless she had my support.

This is a rather extreme case of temperamental behavior, but when I told her that we all have our nervous explosions it was true. I can myself recall a few times when I kicked things around the dressing room. I hope those occasions will never be chronicled but, if they are, may they be recorded with a little charity.

On the subject of Maria's total dedication to her art, of which I have spoken, there were some interesting personal results, none more so than the dramatic change she made in what might be called her public image. It was, I remember, during the 1953 recording of *Lucia* in Florence, when we were all lunching together, that Maestro Serafin ventured to tell Maria she ate too much and was allowing her weight to become a problem. She protested that when she ate well she sang well and, anyway, she was not *so* heavy.

With a lack of gallantry which surprises me now, I remarked that there was a weighing machine just outside the restaurant door and suggested she should put the matter to the test. We went there together and, after the shock of reading what the machine recorded, she gave me her handbag and her coat and kicked off her shoes. All the palliatives that most of us have tried in our time! The result was still somewhat dismaying, and she became rather silent. In one's middle twenties— which was all she was then—it is not pleasant to have to face the hard facts of excessive overweight.

I saw her only briefly later that year, when we recorded *Tosca*. In the following year, when we were to record again, I was coming from the theater one morning when a voice called: "Tito!" And I turned to see a lovely, tall young woman in a long coat. She flung open the coat and demanded: "What do you think of me now?" And I realized that it was Maria, completely transformed.

"Maria," I said with all my heart, "you—look—beautiful."

At which she gave me a smiling, sidelong glance from those lovely long eyes of hers and said, with an enchanting touch of coquetry: "Tito, are you courting me?"

"Of course!" I replied. "May I join the queue, Maria?"

To myself I said: "She is really awakened now; she knows she is a woman and a beautiful one at that."

I think it was her absolute determination to channel everything into becoming a world star which had induced her to make that dramatic change, and for good or ill it made her a world figure overnight. Now she was not only supremely gifted both musically and dramatically— she was a beauty too. And her awareness of this invested with fresh magic every role she undertook. What it eventually did to her vocal and nervous stamina I am not prepared to say. I only assert that she blossomed into an artist unique in her generation and outstanding in the whole range of vocal history.

Later when we frequently partnered each other in *Tosca* we worked marvelously together, deeply respecting and considering each other for the sake of the performance. During the rehearsals we would study and arrange everything together. Then at the performance we threw our-selves into an exciting adventure, in the absolute certainty that each of us would complete successfully any sudden change. This bold and inebriating freedom gave us moments of supreme excitement rarely experienced on stage. We were never Callas and Gobbi. We *were* Tosca and Scarpia. In some indefinable way we would sense exactly what the other was going to do and even if—as is bound to happen from time to time—something went wrong we would not only work it into the action so that no one guessed there was an emergency, we would even sometimes turn it to an advantage.

I remember once, in the second act of *Tosca*, at the moment when Cavaradossi is dragged away with Tosca clinging to him, one of the men (as the action demands) pushed her away and, as she staggered back, she either forgot or did not notice that there was a small step behind her and she fell heavily. From the other side of the stage I asked her with my eyes, "Are you hurt?" and with an answering glance she was able to reassure me. But, realizing what a fine piece of stage "business" we could make of this, I went over to her and disdainfully extended my left hand to her. Immediately, also realizing what could be done, she almost clawed her way up my arm on the pleading word, "Salvatelo!" ("Save him!") To which I replied ironically, "Io?—Voi!" ("I—No, you!") and let go of her, whereupon she dropped back despairingly on the ground with such apparent helplessness and pathos that a slight gasp of indignant sympathy ran through the house. She needed no instructions, no hint of what was in my mind theatrically speaking. She *knew* and made the perfect completion of what I had started.

With Maria it was not performing but living. Today I could not say with certainty what happened here or there, at a rehearsal or a performance, so intense was our commitment. But on one occasion at Covent Garden—I think it was at a dress rehearsal before an audience—I suddenly realized that, when she had backed against Scarpia's desk, her head hanging backward, she had put her wig in the flame of one of the candles and smoke was beginning to rise from the back of her head. I went over and took hold of her, putting my hand on the back of her head as though to draw her into an unwanted embrace, and managed to put out the smoldering curls.

Fully confident and relying on me, she never made a false movement. We simply went on acting and singing. She waited for my help and just whispered, "*Grazie, Tito*," when the chance came. *That* was Callas.

On another occasion, in Paris in 1958, we were invited to take part in a big gala. We were to do the second act of *Tosca* with only one rehearsal. When we arrived for the rehearsal we found no one in charge or with the remotest idea about what was to be done, and the actors for the minor roles were wandering about aimlessly, most of them loaded with irrelevant theatrical props. There was a good deal of talking and no action: whether from inefficiency or sabotage I am not quite sure.

Suddenly Maria stood up and demanded silence and everyone's attention. She flatly declared that the performance must take place and that, in view of the total lack of organization and co-operation, she had arrived at a final decision. Then she turned to me and said: "Tito, please will you be the producer and try to organize this performance? And from this moment everybody will obey you!"

So authoritative was she that no one queried this decision and, although I had not had any real experience of producing, it never occurred to me to refuse her request. Everything went smoothly from that moment. Everyone obeyed my direction, including Maria herself. At that time she had not yet become a great Tosca of her later years and when in the stabbing scene she raised her hand menacingly with the knife I said: "No, no Maria! If you lifted the knife as high as that I would be able to see what was coming and would take evasive action."

She accepted my instruction like the humblest member of the cast; and her perfect example of professionalism and dedication to the work at hand made everyone else give to me the unquestioned obedience they would have given to the most experienced producer. And that was Callas.

In contrast, I remember one day in New York she was alone and I asked her to join us for dinner. She gladly accepted and played like a young girl with Cecilia, but when we took her later to the hotel lift she suddenly turned to us and said: "I feel so lonely. I haven't even my little dog with me here. Wouldn't you like to offer me just another ice cream?" And that was Maria.

Again, much later—indeed, as late as October 1967, when she was virtually in retirement—Tilde and I were celebrating my birthday in London with a small group of friends at the Savoy Grill when suddenly Maria appeared smiling in the doorway, her beautiful eyes shining. As she made her way toward our table she said, without raising her voice but with that effortless projection of words which was one of her great gifts: "Tito, I remembered it was your birthday today. I have just flown over from Paris to wish you a happy birthday. May I join the party?"

It can be imagined with what delight we welcomed her. The next morning I wanted to send her flowers but the hotel staff informed me that she had already left for Paris. She had truly come just for my birthday. And that was Maria.

When in January 1964 she made her great comeback in *Tosca* at Covent Garden (after two or three years of semi-retirement) it was an event of worldwide interest. It is impossible to describe the sensation it caused and, to a creature of Maria's sensibility, it must have been sheer torture. I suppose there are few more appalling ordeals than to make a stage comeback when you are headline news; far worse than any debut. Mercilessly caught in the crossfire of public searchlights, you hang there suspended for all to observe and criticize. Triumph or crucifixion? You are battling for the one, but fate may deal you the other.

Everyone at the Royal Opera House was frantically afraid that she would cancel at the last moment. Sander Gorlinsky, her manager, had no time for anything else. The strictest orders were given that no one should be admitted at any rehearsal and the only reports issued were brief ones to the effect that everything was going well.

One charming incident in connection with this secrecy is worth recording. Maria stayed away from a rehearsal of Act II one day because of a slight cold, and John Copley stood in for her. On this occasion it so happened that a distinguished titled lady came to the box office to pick up her tickets and, realizing that a rehearsal was in progress, she implored Sergeant Martin to allow her just one glimpse of the diva: if he would just open the door a single crack . . . The poor man, with all the solemn authority for which he is famed, explained that he simply could not do so, not even for such a distinguished lady. Well, would he just for one moment open the little window connected with the house so that she might at least hear a note or two from that famous voice?

With this request Sergeant Martin complied and at that moment John Copley, lying in my arms with beard and glasses, let out an excruciating shriek: "Ah piu' non posso, ah che orrore."

"Ah, the unmistakable voice!" whispered the delighted lady to Sergeant Martin. "Thank you, thank you." And she went away quite satisfied.

But there were not many of these lighter moments for any of us as the first night drew near. To some extent David Webster had put Maria in my care—to coax, to reassure, to support her insofar as one colleague can support another; and never, I think, did I prize a trust more highly. We worked very hard, since Maria was always a tremendously disciplined artist, but after the long rehearsals she would phone me at great length to discuss our parts and go over them all again. At the dress rehearsal, looking a mere girl in the beautiful pale pink dress which Zeffirelli had decreed for her, she was scared to death but sang resolutely and acted superbly. The clicking of cameras backstage made the place sound like an office with twenty typists and, in the atmosphere of nervous tension, even David Webster must, I feel sure, have had some difficulty in maintaining his slight customary smile.

January 21, 1964. Here is Tilde's description of that never-to-be-forgotten night, written in her diary next morning.

"What a night! A beautiful performance, though for the first time in my life I heard the 'Vissi d'arte' go without applause." (My own view is that the audience was too spellbound by the drama to interrupt with ill-timed applause.) "The second act was unbelievable: two giants, and they bowed to one another before the curtain like two gallant opponents. The stage was invaded after the endless ovation. I have seen for myself the self-controlled English people go mad, take off their coats, scarves, or whatever and wave them in enthusiasm. Tito was great and it was wonderful to see the perfect reactions of the two of them. Maria certainly gave a big shake-up to the character of Tosca, making her much more human and extrovert. But this can be done *only by her.* Others who would try to imitate—beware!"

In spite of her tremendous, unparalleled triumph she remained desperately nervous. On each day of performance she would phone me to say she could not sing—she had no voice left, or else she must change everything in the second act. I would be half an hour on the telephone consoling the poor girl and encouraging her. "All right," I would say, "you don't sing. It is enough for you to appear. You just act and I'll do the singing. . . . All right, you change whatever you want. You know we understand each other—" and so on.

In the evening she would come by my dressing room before going onstage and I would take her to the wings, holding her icy hand and whispering encouragement while rivulets of perspiration would be running down her neck and the edge of her dress. Yet when she came off stage after her exquisitely sung duet with Cioni she would clasp my hand and wish me luck and stand there waiting until my first phrase had been sung. Indeed, there was something utterly touching in the way she would show endearing flashes of concern for others however deeply absorbed she might be in her own ordeal. When Cecilia arrived in London it was Maria, not I, who said to her: "Tonight your father and I are going to sing for you."

We gave six performances in London and we repeated the same team-up in Paris and New York. I doubt if anyone who was present at those performances will ever forget them. I know I never shall—not only for the artistic peak which they reached but for the extraordinary rapport and understanding between us.

Probably millions of words have been written about La Callas, and quite a few about the vulnerable, lonely, elusive creature who was Maria. There is little I can add. She shone for all too brief a while in the world of opera, like a vivid flame attracting the attention of the whole world, and she had a strange magic which was all her own.

I always thought she was immortal—and *she is*.

My Life (Garden City, N.Y.: Doubleday, 1980)

George London

When I learned upon my arrival in New York, early this fall, that I would sing Scarpia in Callas' Tosca, I must admit I had a few forebodings. So much had been printed about this "stormy" star that I was prepared for almost anything. ("Look, she can't do more than actually kill you in the second act," my wife Nora said to me calmly. "What are you worried about?")

The first rehearsal assured me. Here was a trouper, a fanatic worker, a stickler for detail. Remembering my first season at the Met, and the forlornness one can feel, I crossed the stage before curtain time and, knocking at Mme. Callas' dressing room, said a quick "*in bocca di lupo*" (the Italian version of "good luck" or "*Halls und Beinbruch*"). Miss Callas took my hand in both of hers and seemed deeply moved. She later told me that this insignificant courtesy had meant a great deal to her.

Callas and I also sang a scene from the second act of *Tosca* on the first Metropolitan Opera broadcast of the Ed Sullivan Show. Again, she was a most co-operative colleague. At one point, during dress rehearsal, after she had "murdered" me, I fell too close to the desk and she couldn't pass to cross the stage and pick up the two candelabra which Tosca places next to the dead Scarpia. Callas laughingly stopped and announced to the director, "There just are too many legs around here." We all had a good laugh; I fell thereafter so that she and her long train could pass, and that was that. Yet, the day after the broadcast many newspapers reported that Mme. Callas and I had had a tiff during our rehearsal. I tried to tell my friends this was just not so. But, I finally gave up. For I realized that Callas, the prima donna reincarnate, fires not only the imagination of her audiences but also of the press. They want her to be "tempestuous" and "fiery," and that is the way it is going to be. And I believe this is a good thing. It brings back a long lost atmosphere of operatic excitement. There is nothing that can fire operagoers—and send them to opera box offices—so surely as the desire to see a genuine member of that sublime species, the prima donna.

"Prima Donnas I Have Sung Against," *High Fidelity Magazine*, March 1957

Janine Reiss

My encounter with Maria Callas began with a telephone call from Michel Glotz, who told me that Callas had just arrived in Paris, that she needed a teacher to help her practice the French opera arias that she was to record for a record that, moreover, was followed by a second—*Callas in Paris*—that I was that teacher, and that she would come the following day at six P.M. to have her first lesson. I hesitated a bit, at once incredulous and staggered. And the following day exactly at six P.M. my doorbell rang: I saw a tall, very beautiful, very elegant woman enter. It was Maria Callas.

She told me immediately, "For this record I need someone who can teach me this whole repertoire, someone who is very strict, who will not let me get away with anything. Let's begin with *The Pearl Fishers*." She handed me the score that she had brought. I sat down at the piano and played the short introduction that precedes the first recitative. At that moment she turned toward me, stopped me, and asked, "Do you have a voice?" I mumbled, "Listen, Madame, yes, I have a voice, but . . ." "Then sing *The Pearl Fishers* for me." And so, before Maria Callas, I sang *The Pearl Fishers*! But at the moment when the cadenza arrived, she again turned to me, "Stop, please, because before hearing you sing, I would like to have you explain to me how that cadenza is constructed, rhythmically and harmonically, because one can only sing a cadenza well if one knows exactly how it was written." Then I said to myself, "So Callas is Callas! This isn't a woman who has a yacht, who has a Rolls, etc., this is the woman who has reinvented music *because she reads it*, that is to say she goes to the source of what is written, forgetting what one calls tradition."

What I realized in working with her was that Callas's career and her glory were based almost exclusively on her work. Her musical art was made out of instinct, that's surely true, but also very much out of experience—and it is astonishing, moreover, that all the singers who have used Callas for inspiration have sought to imitate her solely on the vocal level but not on the musical level. Her only secret was to return ceaselessly to the source of the music, to be respectful, beyond the limits of possibility, to the composers' wishes. Incessantly, while we were working together, she would say to me: "Is that good like that? Do you feel that that's right? Do you think that I rest too long here, that I rest long enough there? Do you think one could set off this phrase?" Or, with determination, "One cannot shorten this phrase, and too bad if one has to die when one sings it."

I was, moreover, immediately struck by her fantastic musicality and that sense of phrasing that gave all its expression to the text. One has heard voices intrinsically more "beautiful" than that of Maria Callas, but perhaps never as expressive. Because of that poetry of singing carried to the extreme of her musical *and* dramatic resources. Because of the timbre, too, which was a reflection of her soul, by which she knew how to give her voice all the colors possible in order to express love, gentleness, hatred, passion, despair: all the mirrors of the soul.

It serves no purpose to have a Stradivarius in the throat if one does not know how to play it. And she told me often, "At bottom, I have no recourse against my vocal difficulties, because I have never really exercised my voice." But she had practiced singing. That is to say she practiced her music like a pianist, like a violinist: she read it, then sang it, since her instrument was her voice, while seeking the phrasing, the colors, while seeking also to match the color of her voice to the modulation of the orchestra, to make it glow with all the feelings that she wished to embody. She did not say to herself, "My C is a little flat, my F is a little nasal, my E is a little too far back." She said to herself, "That does not correspond to the feeling that I want to express." And in that way she succeeded in placing her voice as she wanted. It is quite obvious, too, that when she was physiologically diminished, she no longer had the resources that a singer possessing a solid technique would have had. She used her voice like an instrument that would have no limit: she used it like everything she did in her life, with passion.

The spirit of singing, an astonishing woman of class, a shattering tragedienne, and beyond all that an exceptional musician, in all her body and in all her soul, Maria Callas was for me the living confirmation of what I have dedicated my life to.

"At the Source of Singing" (Remarks collected by Alain Duault),
L'Avant-scène, October 1982

Joan Sutherland and Richard Bonynge

I stood and watched Callas through my own special peephole [at Covent Garden in 1953] and was astonished at the impact both Maria and Stignani made. I remember how Callas worked, she was always indefatigable. You couldn't fault her. The impact of *Norma* and her *Aida* and *Il Trovatore* made me wonder if I had the audacity to continue. I wanted to, but I really thought ten times about it after I saw those performances. . . .

I used to think my large voice was incapable of singing those roles. Callas showed me this was not so. She sang them and this fact indicated that I could too. . . .

She gave me the inspiration to join her at the beginning of my career and she never failed to encourage what I tried to do.

Brian Adams, *La Stupenda: A Biography of Joan Sutherland* (London and Melbourne:
Hutchinson, 1981)

Had she since thought about the Callas Norma in her own preparation for the role? The answer was immediate, emphatic. "Oh, of course! She was unforgettable. When I began working on it, I thought of nothing else. I couldn't even conceive of any other way of doing it." "Callas was phenomenal in the role," said Bonynge, "though she did bend it considerably to suit her own voice and talents. I think I saw her do it eleven times in all. Really, you New Yorkers can have no idea of what that woman's voice was like, because you heard her only later in her career. But those first London Normas! It was before she lost all the weight, you know. The sheer *size* of the voice, and what she could do with it! When she sang with Stignani, the Adalgisa, you couldn't tell which was which sometimes. She had such a beautifully rich and dark quality at the bottom of the voice, and yet the high notes were all there, too."

"The Pinnacle," *Opera News*, April 4, 1970

ROBERT JACOBSON: Was it the presence of Maria Callas that made you decide to go more in the direction of bel canto?

RICHARD BONYNGE: In many ways, yes.

JOAN SUTHERLAND: [Vittorio] Gui and [Tullio] Serafin had already started her in that big revival.

RJ: Did that start you too, in a way?

JS: Oh sure, it sparked the whole musical field.

RB: When we first came from Australia, we heard some of Callas's *Puritani* on 78s in '49 or '50. That really got to us. And Joan sang *Norma* with her. We went to her every rehearsal, every performance, and one learned an immense lot from her. Very, very great.

RJ: London heard some of her greatest performances.

RB: You see, up until '52, '53, beginning of '54 were her greatest successes. We were there all that time. When she sang *Aida*, the London press was very snide, very rude about her. The *Trovatore* was something! We should hear it like that today! She was always nervous in Act I, but once that was over, fantastic!

JS: Wear and tear, but oh, the tension! She was obviously well trained and well taught and had fabulous directors. She soaked up everything.

RB: But before she slimmed down, I mean this was such a colossal voice. It just sort of poured out of her, the way Flagstad's did. . . .Callas had a huge voice. When she and Stignani sang *Norma*, at the bottom of the range you could barely tell who was who.

RJ: An extended dramatic voice.

RB: Oh, it was colossal! And she took the big sound right up to the top.

JS: Callas was a fantastic example to a singer in how she was prepared to work. There was almost *too* much rehearsal—she was *too* willing. Years ago in Dallas, we rehearsed all day, and at quarter to eleven I told Larry Kelly I was tired and going home. He said, "Maria rehearsed until four in the morning." I told him it was great for her but not for me—and that she wasn't singing too well now anyhow.

Conversation Piece, *Opera News*, December 4, 1982

The Callas Debate, 1969

Originally published, in Italian, in *Radiocorriere TV* (November 30, 1969). English translation, by Madeleine Fagandini, first published in *Opera* (September–October 1970).

Those taking part in the discussion are:

Fedele D'Amico (chairman): musicologist, composer and critic of *L'Espresso*.

Rodolfo Celletti: author, musicologist, editor of *Le Grandi Voci* and contributor to the Bulletin of the Instituto di Studi Verdiani.

Eugenio Gara: journalist and critic. Has contributed many articles to *Musica d'Oggi, Le grande voci*.

Giorgio Gualerzi: critic and musicologist, regular contributor to *Opera*, the Verdi Bulletin, etc.

Luchino Visconti: producer of opera at La Scala, Covent Garden, etc.

Gianandrea Gavazzeni: conductor and musicologist.

Guerzoni: I wish first of all to thank the participants to our discussion. We have asked them to discuss a subject which has been debated among the readers of *Radiocorriere* in our column "Open Letters to the Editor."

The first of these letters referred to the radio series "The World of Opera." Our correspondent wondered whether the series might not have been entitled "The World of Callas" since, in his opinion, each programme seemed to find a reason for praising this singer at the expense of all others.

The correspondence grew in volume—the letters published are only a small sample—until we were obliged to call a halt. But since the argument had become somewhat heated, we felt the need to provide the opportunity not so much for a further debate as for a statement of views on the part of persons professionally involved in the subject, persons who would therefore be able to give our readers a helpful commentary on the points at issue.

They are: Rodolfo Celletti, Eugenio Gara, Gianandrea Gavazzeni, Giorgio Gualerzi and Luchino Visconti. In the chair, Fedele D'Amico.

D'Amico: I have read some of these letters to the *Radiocorriere TV*—those published and a few more. Perhaps to some people they may have given the impression of presumption and prejudice, but I am not of that opinion. Certainly some of the views expressed were extreme, but even these point to a real interest in a subject which deserves it. The feelings generated are evidently authentic.

Obviously, some of the letters degenerate into little more than a sporting contest—the usual Callas *versus* Tebaldi match! What should really matter after all is what an artist is, and not any one artist's victory or defeat in a championship. It would not be a bad thing to realise once and for all that Maria Callas's existence does not prejudice Tebaldi's, or vice versa.

However, such arguments have always arisen, and simply indicate that the persons in dispute have caused feelings to run deep and passionate. I myself cannot find anything wrong in this, just as I find nothing wrong in the tendency to transform the object of one's admiration into something mythical. Legend is always quick to flower around any artist of great personality; it is one of the ways in which the public acknowledges certain qualities. Any damage this veneration may entail is never lethal.

There is only one point upon which we should be absolutely categorical. Certain people have attributed Callas's ascendancy to organized publicity, implying by this that she is little better than certain film stars whose physical rather than professional qualities have enabled businessmen to transform them into lucrative properties! This is absolutely false. Callas's success, both public and critical, preceded by many years the time when she and her private life became of interest to the tabloids.

Her first major success dates back to 1947: *La Gioconda* in Verona. In 1947 Callas was totally unknown and enjoyed no unwarranted assistance. There were people in the musical world who had taken her seriously, and had pointed her out to those concerned. I believe that Tullio Serafin played a leading part in this process. But Maestro Serafin was neither a businessman nor a press agent. He was simply doing his job as a conductor and, if he came across a singer he thought worth bringing on to the stage, he would recommend her. That was all.

The myth was born several years later, after Callas had been around a long time and had already triumphed in Rome, Naples, at the Scala and so on. For one thing, in the early years, Callas's appearance was far from attractive—hardly that of a "cover-girl." The beautiful Callas was born later, and only then did the tabloids sit up and take notice.

I repeat, this is the only point which does not admit of discussion. Callas's success was *not* engineered. For the rest, we shall try to take into account all the arguments raised in the letters to *Radiocorriere TV*. Of course we shall consider them from our own points of view. These will not necessarily be better than those of our readers, but they will be different. As Dr. Guerzoni has already pointed out, our various points of departure are those of professional contact with the world of opera. We are musical historians, critics, producers, conductors. We are therefore obliged to go further than the immediate impression, legitimate though it may be. We must attempt to analyse, understand and make sense of the phenomenon we have been asked to discuss. And this we shall try to do.

Before we enter upon a technical or artistic discussion, there is one fact which should be noted. Not since the time of Alfred de Musset, Théophile Gautier and Heine has a singer aroused such interest, not only in the musical world but in the whole world of art. Only exceptionally since then has anything comparable been known.

We have observed that certain of Callas's interpretations, such as her Medea, have caused reactions outside the world of music. When she sang this part in Rome, the music critic, Guido Pannain, wrote an unfavourable review. There sprang to her defence two of the most important names in Italian culture: Mario Praz, a literary man and art expert, interested and well-informed in many subjects but not particularly in music, and Ettore Paratore, the classical philologist. The ensuing debate was heated and protracted. Another instance is the highly elaborate essay by René Leibowitz in *Les Temps Modernes*, the magazine edited by Sartre. Leibowitz is indeed a musician and musicologist, but one who always deals with major subjects; he was the first to write a book on Schoenberg. The mere fact that a review edited by Sartre could have considered printing an entirely serious article on a prima donna is astonishing.

Such events seem to prove that Callas is a new phenomenon, and that the myth of her personality—whatever degradation it may have suffered—is not an empty one: it is founded on something very real.

What is this reality? Our contributors will try to explain it. Not by arguing amongst themselves, but rather by each tackling a different aspect, trying to answer a different question, even if to some extent they discuss these questions among themselves. We shall consider the case of Maria Callas as an historical event, as though it were something that had happened a hundred years ago. We can do this for two reasons: first, because for some years now Callas has not appeared on the stage (although no one can be quite certain that she will not return), and secondly, because her work has had such repercussions on the world of opera that it is already possible to hazard a first judgement.

We shall start, therefore, with the subject that seems, by its nature, to underlie all other subjects: her voice, her vocal technique. I would like Rodolfo Celletti to speak on this since, as everyone knows, he is a great expert on such matters.

Celletti: In judging a singer's vocal qualities there are certain fixed parameters. One begins with timbre, proceeding thence to volume. These two qualities are mainly a matter of natural gift. One then passes on to examine technique, or technique allied to the inherent natural gifts: range, control, flexibility, agility. But the natural parameters are timbre and volume.

Now, the timbre of Callas's voice, considered purely as sound, was essentially ugly: it was a thin sound, which gave the impression of dryness, of aridity. It lacked those elements which, in singer's jargon, are described as velvet and varnish. In compensation, her timbre was incisive; I would say this metallic edge in her voice took the place of the varnish. Furthermore, her voice was penetrating. The volume as such was average: neither small nor powerful. But the penetration, allied to this incisive quality (which could border on the ugly because it frequently contained an element of harshness) ensured that her voice could be clearly heard anywhere in the auditorium.

In certain areas of her range her voice also possessed a guttural quality. This would occur in the most delicate and troublesome areas of a soprano's voice—for instance where the lower and middle registers merge, between G and A. I would go so far as to say that here her voice had such resonances as to make one think at times of a ventriloquist. At least that was the impression it would give me; or else the voice could sound as though it were resonating in a rubber tube. This would especially occur when she was forcing a little. There was another troublesome spot—as with so many sopranos—and that was between the middle and upper registers. Here, too, around treble F and G, there was often something in the sound itself which was not quite right, as if the voice were not functioning properly

I myself tried questioning her teacher, Elvira de Hidalgo, on this point, though to no avail (she was indeed extremely reticent on the subject), but it struck me that right from the start Callas's voice must have been already a bit forced. I mean it had not been subjected from the outset to technically correct training, so that certain negative consequences appeared—among them the troublesome areas of which we have already spoken. And further, right from the beginning of her career, whenever Callas had to sustain a note for any length of time, the voice would begin to develop a slight wobble. This was particularly noticeable in the very high notes. D, E and especially E flat.

At this point I must repeat that Callas's voice was certainly ugly in natural quality; and yet I really believe that part of her appeal was precisely due to this fact. Why? Because, for all its natural lack of varnish, velvet and richness, this voice could acquire such distinctive colours and timbre as to be unforgettable. Once heard it was immediately recognizable anywhere. This is an enormous advantage in terms of a theatrical career. Perhaps the general public does not realise how great is the attraction of a highly characteristic and individual timbre; but it is a fact that the most successful singers are precisely those of whom, as soon as they open their mouths, even a nonspecialist can say: that is Schipa, that is Caruso, that is Titta Ruffo.

As for technique: what does technique imply? Range, flexibility, lightness, agility, and—most important—the singer's capacity to emit, at will, sounds of different colours: now strong, now slender, now dark, now light. This control is the equivalent of a painter's palette. In any form of interpretation this ability is fundamental because it enables the singer to colour both music and words.

In the matter of range, Callas had no fears. Judging by the operas in her repertory, she could go from A natural below the stave to E flat above it.

D'Amico: In fact, two and a half octaves.

Gara: She could even reach the high F—as in Rossini's *Armida*, for example.

Celletti: Exactly, even F. In the middle and lower range one could detect the timbre of a mezzo, that is to say, rather dark tones. Higher up, in the very high notes, she had none of the usual characteristics of the so-called *soprano leggero*, and this was one of her outstanding innovations. Because for a long time—I don't know for how long, perhaps Gara can say better than I can—we have been used to hearing these top notes, from C up to F . . . In Callas's own time there was a French singer who could reach G, wasn't there, Gualerzi?

Gualerzi: Indeed! Mado Robin could reach G, and perhaps even higher.

Celletti: These very high notes hold a great fascination for the public. The general public doesn't know whether it's an E, an F, or a G; but it does realize the note is extremely difficult to reach, that it has broken a sound barrier. Now we were used to hearing these notes produced with a soft attack, and with a very pure, flute-like timbre. Well, of course, when she wanted to, Callas too could produce this quality, but always with far greater power than the traditional *soprano leggero*—and furthermore with a penetration and timbre that these sopranos never possessed. With the traditional light soprano, these notes were always plaintive and essentially instrumental: they could be taken to be produced by a flute, for example. Callas's very high notes, on the other hand, even though less sweet and inclined to oscillate, had a more human quality. One heard more voice and less instrument. Then she would attack these notes with more vehemence and power—quite differently therefore, from the very delicate, cautious, "white" approach of the light soprano. In other words Callas attacked these notes with the vigour of a dramatic soprano. The only difference was that when a dramatic soprano reached C, it was just about the most she could do, and even then she would light a candle to her patron saint for having made it! With Tebaldi, for instance, well, she'd be lighting candles for a B natural—and even sometimes for a B flat!

But let's get back to technique. Whenever Callas had to prepare an opera that either was no longer being performed, or was performed in a style very different from that of its time of composition (for twenty years I've heard *Norma* sung as if it were *La Gioconda* or *Cavalleria Rusticana*), she would virtually start to learn to sing all over again, in order to produce a voice that was consonant with that opera. Thus we have heard her produce the so-called "singing in the mask": that is when the sound is projected, as far as possible, from the area between the forehead, the cheekbones and the nasal cavities (without however producing a nasal tone); whereas sopranos of the *verismo* school, used to singing Puccini, Mascagni, Giordano, Leoncavallo, where the music requires more sensual singing, tended to project their voices rather from the lower cavities. This production in the mask, applied to both the middle and upper ranges, has been somewhat like the discovery of America in the world of the soprano. Certainly it is used by good singers even in our times, but not with the rigorous technical perseverance shown by Callas.

What was the outcome of this method? It was that Callas made good those sounds that did not lie easily in her voice; furthermore she achieved a lightness of production that was to be invaluable in passages requiring agility, in *mezzo-forte* passages and in *mezza-voce*. But Callas introduced other innovations too. The light sopranos we have been talking about not only limited themselves in the highest register to a very small volume but had another characteristic, which was formed more or less at the time of Bellini and Donizetti. The roulades and trills were soft and melancholy, always somewhere between *mezzo-forte* and *piano*. Callas, once she had mastered the technique—the true technique of singers around the beginning of the 19th century—what did she do? She restored to the trill the penetrating power of Rossini's time. Rossini did not like his coloratura parts to be sung with tiny, soft voices; he wanted voices that were full, vigorous, incisive. Maria Callas has shown us what he meant, and *Armida* was probably the finest example of her ability in this field. Then she did much the same thing in *Norma*. Here, there are certain powerful coloratura passages to which Callas was able to bring great expressive significance, although treating them simply as brilliant roulades, precisely because of the vehemence of her attack and the incisiveness of her tone. At the same time, whenever she needed to, she could produce exactly the soft, languid, elegiac agility required in florid *mezza-voce* passages. And we must not forget that she could tackle the whole gamut of ornamentation: staccato, trills, half-trills, gruppetti, scales, etc. Where did she yield to the usual type of light soprano? Well, her florid passages were a little slower. However, since it is thought that in the 19th century tempos were generally slower than nowadays, I do not know whether this slightly slower florid style was an advantage or a disadvantage. Another thing: in these soft passages, Callas seemed to use another voice altogether, because it acquired a great sweetness. Whether in her florid singing or in her *canto spianato*, that is, in long held notes without ornamentation, her *mezza-voce* could achieve such moving sweetness that the sound seemed to come from on high . . . I don't know, it seemed to come as if from the skylight of La Scala.

D'Amico: I think we can already draw certain conclusions from what Celletti has said. First of all, the essential virtue of Callas's technique consists of supreme mastery of an extraordinarily rich range of tone colour (that is, the fusion of dynamic range and timbre). And such mastery means total freedom of choice in its use: not being a slave of one's abilities, but rather being able to use them at will as a means to an end.

I think also that in certain aspects Celletti has endorsed the reference that early critics of Callas—Gara and Teodoro Celli, for instance—have made to the technique of the 1830s and 1840s, especially that of singers like Pasta or Malibran. And I'd like to ask a question here. Celletti explained that certain of Callas's qualities were brought about through playing on a voice which by nature was far from perfect. What were Pasta's or Malibran's voices like? Were they imperfect too?

Celletti: I would turn this question over to Gara. That's his forte!

D'Amico: Let's do that. In any case I want Gara now to take up the second point of our discussion, into which this question should easily fit. The point is this: having established the characteristics and technique of Callas's voice, what use did she make of them? In a word, wherein lay her interpretative qualities?

Gara: Today everyone talks of revolution. But between 1950 and 1960, such was her interpretative genius that Callas brought something that looked very much like revolution to the somewhat academic world of melodrama. We are still feeling the effects of it today. Probably only Chaliapin, at the beginning of the century, caused a similar seismic shock. This kind of vocal and artistic earthquake is not difficult to describe: it consists simply of the total illumination of the character portrayed. To use typographical terms, it has always been the habit of the great majority of singers to alternate between roman and italics—that is, to rely on a certain number of key effects in particular scenes: the big scene, this irresistible aria, that brilliant high note. The reminiscences of past impresarios, such as Monaldi, tell us of tenors singing "in their slippers" for almost the entire opera, only to pull out all the stops at the supreme moment. Callas certainly reversed this conception in favour of a totally conceived dramatic interpretation—with all the risks inherent in this approach. In her own words, at the expense of producing a sound less than pure, less than beautiful in the superficial sense of the word: "I have no intention of adjusting the score for the convenience of my voice."

As Celletti has noted, much has been said about her voice, and no doubt the discussion will continue. Certainly no one could in honesty deny the harsh or "squashed" sounds (especially, as has been said, in the G-A region, just above the change of register), nor the wobble on very high notes. These and others were precisely the accusations made at the time against Pasta and Malibran, two geniuses of song (as they were then called), sublime yet vocally imperfect. Both were brought to trial in their day, as authoritative witnesses tell us; Verdi's own crude and at the same time enthusiastic pronouncements on Malibran testify to this. Yet few singers have made history in the annals of opera as these two did.

Let us be quite clear about it, a voice—I mean the quality, the physical beauty of the sound—is certainly important. Yet it is difficult to forget what Wagner wrote to Wilhelmine Schroeder-Devrient, the great Leonora of *Fidelio*, who enchanted Goethe in his old age. Wagner wrote: "Because we have celebrated you as a singer, I have often been asked whether your voice was really exceptional—the question implying that this was the essential point. I have always been irritated by having to answer. If I were to be asked the question today I would give roughly this reply: no, she had no voice; but she knew so well how to handle her breathing and thereby to create, with so marvellous a musicianship, the true soul of a woman, that one thought no longer of singing nor of voice." So Wagner wrote of Schroeder-Devrient, and so with a little updating to fit the times, we could write of Callas, who clearly belongs to the same family and has trod the same ideal paths.

In certain of her interpretations, as in *Médée* and Macbeth, the sinister and immeasurably human power of her declamation remains an unrivalled and perhaps unattainable model of acting in music. At her best, Callas was never simply great here and there, at one or other point in an opera, in act one, or three, or five. Her greatness lay always in the musical and dramatic manner in which she made her roles come to life. A Callas interpretation has to be accepted or rejected; it can please or displease, but never in parts; it is a whole. And this explains the arguments, the love and the hatred that she has aroused. A whole turmoil which has at any rate, if nothing else, stirred the stagnant waters of the lyric theatre. It is only in the total picture of the role, in the grand tragic breadth of the character, that the vocal blemishes disappear which her enemies never tire of enumerating.

Her secret is in her ability to transfer to the musical plane the suffering of the character she plays, the nostalgic longing for lost happiness, the anxious fluctuation between hope and despair, between pride and supplication, between irony and generosity, which in the end dissolves into a superhuman inner pain. The most diverse and opposite of sentiments, cruel deceptions, ambitious desires, burning tenderness, grievous sacrifices, all the torments of the heart, acquire, in her singing, that mysterious truth, I would like to say, that psychological sonority, which is the primary attraction of opera. It is the point at which research ends and poetry takes wing.

D'Amico: To be specific, therefore, Callas's "faults" were in the voice and not in the singer; they are so to speak, faults of departure but not of arrival. This, if I am not mistaken, is precisely Celletti's distinction between the natural quality of the voice and the technique. And we may also apply the same conclusions to Gara's mention of Schroeder-Devrient. In that letter referred to by Gara, Wagner did not certainly mean to imply that Schroeder-Devrient was voiceless, nor that she was capable only of singing his music. The triumphal period of her career was in fact pre-Wagnerian, and comprised mainly the operas of Rossini, Bellini and Donizetti. It is clear that Schroeder-Devrient truly "sang" these operas; she acted them with her voice.

Celletti: She was always criticized, specially for the higher register. But even so, she had a great success.

D'Amico: Exactly. And talking of "faults," let us not forget that these—that is, the limitations of the vocal mechanism—have always constituted throughout musical history a powerful stimulus toward invention. We have only to think of instrumental music—music which has not only created for itself a specific style that cannot be reduced to that of vocal music, but has also at a certain point in its development founded in theory the idea of music as an autonomous art: that is, without reference to words or dramatic action. Now instrumental music would never have been born at all if the instruments had been capable of perfectly imitating the human voice, as was their original aspiration.

Precisely because of their imperfection, causing them to imitate "singing" by inappropriate means, the notion of stylization became necessary, thus bringing about an altogether new style. Think of the harpsichord, and even the piano, instruments incapable of sustaining a note at the same dynamic level as that of its attack: this alone forced composers to invent a whole series of expedients, a different kind of phrasing, in short a number of styles which have literally nothing in common with vocal styles.

Mutatis mutandis, Maria Callas has done precisely the same thing. If she had been born with an immaculate, velvety, perfect voice, Callas would have simply wallowed in it, as Antonio Baldini (author of *Italia sottovoce*) would have said, as if in a bathtub. No doubt she would have succeeded as a singer, perhaps even been quite spectacular, but only as many (or perhaps few) others have been. She was in fact forced to become what she is precisely because of those natural imperfections of her "instrument." Her achievement has thus a considerable critical and cultural significance. This does not mean that in achieving these results she was aware of all the implications, or that she had digested historical or aesthetic tracts to guide her. Artists are capable of reaching certain goals simply by instinct.

Celletti: What you have just said about voices that are born beautiful or that sink back into their own bathtubs is so true that there was a theory about them as far back as the 17th century. One of the first French theoreticians of singing, Bénigne de Bacilly, divided voices into two categories: the beautiful ones and the good ones. The good voices are those which, without any special natural gifts, are nevertheless capable, thanks to technique, of expressing all that a performance requires. On the other hand the naturally beautiful voices, content to wallow in their own beauty, rarely produce anything of significance and are often boring.

There is something else I wanted to say—also to clarify better my own point of view in relation to something D'Amico has just said—and it is this. Even if, when passing from one register to another, Callas produced an unpleasant sound, the technique she used for these transitions was perfect. Finally, as Gara has said, Callas would totally involve herself in the character of the part she was playing, both dramatically and vocally. From the point of view of voice, she could allow herself to do this by virtue of her technique. Her ability to manoeuvre her *mezza voce* was such that she could achieve dramatic effects even within a limited volume. In this way dramatic continuity was maintained while her vocal energy was spared. If she had tried to sing *Norma* forte from beginning to end, Callas would probably never have reached the end of the opera.

Gara: I would also just like to say that I agree totally with D'Amico when he says that Callas never read all that stuff that we would like to imagine she did. This did not prevent me, for example, from writing, on the occasion of her Medea (that very frightening Medea) that perhaps without Freud and without Kafka that particular Medea would not have materialized . . .

D'Amico: Some things are just in the air.

Gara: Certainly, they're in the air, they are of the time. Indeed Callas is entirely of her time. This to me is most important. I believe that the hankering after departed singers—past, or just old, as the case may be—is utterly stupid. All we ever seem to do is to look back all the time. Now when we do this—we ourselves, personally, in our own life span—we are looking back to our youth and that is all. But interpretation in art must always be in tune with its own time. There are elements in the air which determine these revelatory interpretations: interpretations that reveal something true for that particular time.

D'Amico: Without a doubt. And I would like to note here that Callas achieved this result, not only, as is generally allowed, in the operas of the early 19th century, but also in much more modern works. For example, in *Tosca*. I heard her sing *Tosca* in Paris, in one of her last appearances, produced by Zeffirelli, and I don't know whether she always performed it in that way. At all events, the generally accepted truculent interpretation was nowhere to be found. Callas made Tosca an essentially fragile woman: nervous, restless, perhaps a trifle hysterical. And this led perfectly to the murder of Scarpia: it was the typical violent gesture of a weak personality, in escaping forwards. She established the character from her very first bars in the opera, from the off-stage "Mario, Mario!" The stage direction says: "Tosca enters with a certain violence"; but the music of the orchestra is sensually calm and lyrical, so that the "violence" must be resolved—apart from movement—in brief declamatory passages which Callas produced with a quality of controlled, disguised anxiety, as if with a pallor in the voice. It was one of the most unforgettable experiences I have ever had in a theatre. "Vissi d'arte," a noted platform for so many trumpetings, was significantly muted and interwoven with a thousand subtleties of shading. Perhaps, because her voice was no longer at its freshest, Callas was making a virtue out of necessity. But what virtue! Puccini wanted to cut this famous aria because, he said, it held up the action. He couldn't do it because any soprano leaving it out would have been lynched. Well, I believe that if only he had heard it, in Paris, sung with that modest voice which, while maintaining a pure melodic line, formulated a true dramatic argument, Puccini himself would have become reconciled to his aria. Similarly we have heard many other operas become reconciled with themselves when sung by Callas.

Let's go back to the point that Gara made: Callas creates real people. And here I would like to expand on what Celletti only briefly mentioned. She creates them not only through her singing, but through the complete fusion of singing and acting. The comparison that Gara made with Chaliapin is most apposite, because here too the singer was identified with the actor and vice versa. Above all I would say that Callas belongs to that rare species of actors—rare even in the straight theatre—who manage to appear physically different according to the character they are playing. Mostly, with others, it is only the expression that changes. But there are some who contrive to make you believe that they are tall or short, as the case may be. The actor Petrolini was one; Callas is another. I remember when this thought first occurred to me; it was when I had the occasion to see her, within a short space of time, in three different operas. In the 1954–55 season at the Scala, when Visconti did his first opera productions, Callas appeared in all three of them. Her Giulia in *La Vestale*, her Amina in *La Sonnambula*, and her Violetta were three completely different people, in every sense of the word, right from their first entry. I am sure that on this point of the fusion of vocal and dramatic interpretation both Visconti and Gavazzeni, who have worked many times with her, will be able to tell us much. How was the aim achieved? It is our point number three: how did Callas work, and how did one work with Callas?

Visconti: I could choose several examples of how Callas worked; but the first one that springs to mind is *Anna Bolena*, which Gavazzeni and I mounted together. Callas was working on the musical side of the part, under the assistant musical director Antonio Tonini, who was in charge of the singers, and of Gavazzeni himself. It was an intensive, and daily, occupation. I was always there; I didn't miss a single second of it. Not only because the work in itself was fascinating, but also because I was able at the same time to clarify my ideas about the visual characterization of the part. In opera, you see, the stage characterization is the natural outcome of the musical one. First they worked in a rehearsal room, and then, gradually, on the stage for 20 days, if I'm not mistaken. When my scenic rehearsals began, Gavazzeni in his turn attended the whole time, and each time we would discuss details afterwards. In this way we reached our goal. And I don't think Callas has ever taken on a role without a similar amount of work and care. It may seem obvious with an opera like *Anna Bolena*: it was entirely new to her (as well as to the public). But take *La Traviata*, for instance. When she did it at La Scala, it was just the same. I don't know how many times she had sung the part before, but when she came to do it at La Scala, under Giulini, the whole of the musical preparation started all over again, as if it was something new. She would work every morning, for at least a couple of hours, and then continue in the rehearsal room in the afternoon, and so on.

Gavazzeni: Visconti has mentioned *Anna Bolena*. Whenever I hear talk of the relation between production and musical direction, I always think of this particular instance. It was without a doubt the high spot of the whole of my career in the theatre: a complete realization of what I have always felt should be the ideal collaboration between stage and music, between producer and conductor. And into this ideal the personality of Callas fits exactly. What Visconti has said is true: he came to all our rehearsals, to familiarize himself with the musical interpretation; I went to all his stage rehearsals, which were of enormous importance to me at every point. They brought confirmation, or alteration as the case might be, to my musical design; indeed, to the whole development through which any design must go when preparing an opera.

I'm glad Visconti also mentioned Tonini. The work of an assistant conductor at the birth of an opera production is almost unknown to the public and generally ignored by the critics, but it can be of cardinal importance, both in a positive and in a negative sense. In our case it was most decidedly positive, and should not be overlooked. The technical preparation which went on between Tonini and Callas was intense, and I only entered into it at a later stage.

D'Amico: Collaboration between musical director and producer is something no one nowadays would argue with, or at least it would be very difficult to do so. But this collaboration can be viewed in a different light and measure. The extreme view is that the actor or singer is no more than a puppet to be mechanically manipulated by the conductor and the producer. But actors and singers are human beings, and he who directs them must not only take their individual qualities and characteristics into consideration, but may even have to find ways—within well defined lines—of unleashing those qualities. But to what extent? Obviously this is not the place to pose this question in general: we are here to discuss a specific case. I should like to ask Visconti: what degree of freedom did Callas have in your productions?

Visconti: A circumscribed freedom. A freedom to operate within a general framework, but nevertheless a considerable freedom. I don't believe anyone can "manoeuvre" someone like Callas without allowing her particular engine a greater number of revolutions than could be foreseen at rehearsals. I've always given her certain guide-lines within which to work, certain objectives; but within those lines I've always allowed her to do what she wanted. A simple example is *La Traviata*, Act 1, the moment when Violetta hears Alfredo's voice. I would tell her: run downstage to the window, but *how* you run is up to you. And she would find her own way of doing it. Not only that, but once found, she would always execute the action in exactly the same way. Callas, you see, is one of those artists who, having once worked out and perfected a detail, don't keep changing it; they have no need to search for something different every time.

Another example is the opening of Gluck's *Iphigénie en Tauride*. Callas would enter, walk up a very high staircase, suspended almost in mid-air; then she'd come tearing down again, during the famous storm, get to the footlights and begin to sing. All *I* had told her was to go up to the top of the steps, stand there in the wind, and come down again to the downstage position in time for the first note. That's all. I gave her no timings. But Maria has timing in her blood; it is absolutely instinctive. And you know how short-sighted she is! In the dark, those steps were marked only with white lines, but that was enough for her: she didn't need anything else! Standing there in the wings I'd die a thousand deaths seeing her run like that, trailing 25 yards of cloak, with a wind-machine on her, back, up the staircase and down again, with split-second timing, *and* with enough breath left to start *fortissimo* dead on cue. You can only allow such things when you've got someone you know you can absolutely trust, because you know her sense of timing, her musical instinct and her ability as a dramatic and tragic actress. I'm certainly not saying you should use this method with every artist; but we are talking of Callas, and I would defy anyone to direct her differently. There are some directors, especially German ones—and great ones too—who I believe would have some difficulty in keeping control over a Callas.

Gavazzeni: Visconti has said that once Callas perfected a detail she would always reproduce it exactly, and he also mentioned her instinct. I should like to recall one of those many occasions on which she would use this instinct, when need be, to improvise. It was actually at the first night of *Anna Bolena* that a potentially disastrous incident occurred, which only her theatrical talent was able to overcome. Having reached the end of the final aria, Anna Bolena was to have been encircled—according to Visconti's instructions—by a silent chorus of hooded extras who were to engulf her, so to speak, in their circle and conduct her to her death. It was a most beautiful effect, which at rehearsal had made a great impression. And it wasn't an effect for its own sake: it was a true conclusion to the inner drama of the character. Well, because of an oversight on the part of one of the assistant stage managers, the chorus of extras did not appear, and Callas found herself unexpectedly alone. Yet she didn't panic. On the spot she improvised a series of movements, perfectly in harmony with the personality of the character she had evolved up till then; she then turned and disappeared upstage. No one in the audience had the least suspicion that there was anything amiss—and remember, this was the finale of the opera!

D'Amico: So: Callas obeys, but also invents; she performs exactly as rehearsed, but also improvises. All this at the level, let us say, of great art. But before concluding this particular chapter, I would like to ask Visconti and Gavazzeni a more ordinary question—a backstage type of question. The public generally imagines a prima donna, especially a great one, to be arrogant, selfish, uninterested in anything not directly concerned with her own personal success, while at the same time intent on sparing herself to the utmost, never giving anything; and would more than ever expect such an attitude from Callas, the most prima donna of prima donnas for decades.

Visconti: It's difficult to imagine anything further from the truth. I have worked for years with actors, in the theatre and the cinema; with dancers and with singers. I can only say that Maria is possibly the most disciplined and professional material I have ever had occasion to handle. Not only does she never ask for rehearsals to be cut down; she actually asks for more, and works at them with the same intensity from beginning to end, giving everything she's got, singing always at full voice—even when the producer himself suggests she shouldn't tire herself out and need only indicate the vocal line. She's so involved in the total outcome of a production that she gets irritated when a colleague is late. If being a prima donna means anything different from that, then Callas is no prima donna.

Gavazzeni: Even with the preliminary rehearsals, which don't have so rigorous a timetable as the general ones, she was always the first to arrive and the last to leave. I remember this particularly when we did *Il Turco in Italia*, in Rome in 1950. We were all new to the opera. How often, when rehearsals were over and everyone else was going home, she would ask me to stay on and work a bit longer. I wouldn't like to say that Callas is alone in this. Over the last 30 years we've seen many operatic singers who have shown great professional discipline, and who have ignored the "big star" attitude so favoured in the past. Callas certainly is one such artist. The society figure, the side of her that interests the magazines, has nothing to do with the person we have known at work, but unfortunately too many people believe the two to be one and the same.

D'Amico: I have never myself been a producer, a conductor, or even an assistant, but I too can testify to this. In May or June of 1962 they were going to resume performances at the Scala of *Médée*, which had been interrupted the previous December when Callas had to have an operation. I happened to be in Milan when they were rehearsing: the only rehearsal, I think it was, just to refresh their memory. I slipped into the theatre to have a look. It was one o'clock in the afternoon, and a sirocco was blowing in the streets as though it were Rome. Inside the theatre no one—singers, chorus, orchestra—felt like working. Even Schippers, usually so excited and worked up, was half asleep. But Maria was there. She was wearing a cardigan and the simplest skirt in the world, but it was enough for her to open her mouth for me to see the legendary crimson mane and the diabolical witch's train take shape before my eyes. And that's not all. She would give her colleagues their cues, urge the chorus on, stop the orchestra with a: "Please, maestro, once again!" Not for nothing have we already drawn a parallel with Chaliapin. I'm told he used to do just the same whenever necessary.

And so we come to point number four. What have been the consequences of Callas's advent on the world of opera? Gualerzi.

Gualerzi: I take my cue from the point that Gara made when he said that Callas created real characters; Visconti and Gavazzeni have explained how she did this; Celletti has made the distinction between beautiful and good voices. All this is very important because those of the public and critics who have identified the creation of a character with the vocal quality suited to that character have found the key to the entire Callas myth. Especially if we draw a comparison with Tebaldi; and if I refer to this contrived dualism it is because it can serve to bring a very important factor into focus when assessing the reactions of operatic audiences.

This factor has to do with the interest in, the attraction to, the irresistible fascination of the sensuous element in the voice, as emphasised by the persistent Tebaldi-Callas comparison. But the most valid proof of the Callas myth, projected into the future, lies in my opinion in the hypothetical, if paradoxical, reference to the past (and this is apart from any historical considerations of repertory). We are led to conclude that while Callas, with her personality, would at all times have been Callas, Tebaldi could easily have been some other singer blessed with an equally beautiful voice. I must add, however—and I underline this as a positive fact—that I have the impression that we are moving towards a definite improvement in this respect. There would appear to be a growing awareness—and this has clearly emerged from the majority of the letters published in *Radiocorriere TV*—that Callas really is an historical figure. In other words, just as 40 years ago between Gigli and Pertile the great majority of the public was for the sensuous element as represented by the wonderful voice of Gigli, while today Pertile is more in favour, so equally I believe that a similar situation is arising with Callas, who stands to Tebaldi as Pertile does to Gigli.

Celletti: Sorry to interrupt, Gualerzi, but you said that 30 or 40 years ago Callas would always have been Callas, while any other beautiful voice could have taken the place of Tebaldi. I would say exactly the opposite: that 30 years ago Tebaldi would always have been Tebaldi, a sort of Muzio . . .

Gualerzi: There, I didn't mention Muzio . . .

Celletti: . . . not so musical. But Callas would not have been Callas at all. She would probably have been a singer of secondary roles, because in my view, there was not then the necessary climate for reviving those operas which revealed her greatness.

Gualerzi: Yes, yes, I understand, but I . . .

Celletti: Just a moment. Let's remember that after all Lady Macbeth, Armida, Medea, Norma, the pillars that sustain the temple of Callas, were nowhere to be seen 40 years ago, or were not understood by the public. You know very well that at the beginning of the century *Médée* was occasionally sung by Mazzoleni, who had a peach of a voice. Well, yes, they clapped her, but that was about it. There were not the cultural and historical demands which have enabled us today to say: at last I've heard Cherubini's *Médée* as I've always imagined it should be.

Gualerzi: Certainly; I'm afraid you misunderstood me. I only wanted to say that, had such a climate existed 40 years ago (had what Gara has described been "in the air"), a personality such as that of Callas would have imposed itself regardless, while Tebaldi could easily have been replaced by an equally beautiful voice. So I agree with you. I agree with the importance of the second component of the myth: that is the revival by Callas of a certain kind of repertory, thanks to which there has arisen a whole nucleus of singers and interpreters clearly inspired by her example. In this respect, Callas is in the tradition of other great operatic personalities like Caruso, Titta Ruffo, Chaliapin, all of whom in their time created a race of followers. But whereas Caruso and Titta Ruffo (Chaliapin is really a case apart) limited themselves to creating new vocal followers and not necessarily with positive results—in fact frequently with negative ones—Callas has gone further. She can be said to have created great singers and notable interpreters, though always within that particular repertory which has thus in due course become more appreciated.

We know well who those singers are: from Gencer right up to Scotto (in certain phrases, certain moments of *Lucia*) and to Suliotis (certain utterances in the lower register). Finally there is Caballé, where the "Callas factor" is to be found above all in the implications of a particular repertory, still further enlarged from that of Callas herself. And when Giuseppe Pugliese states that it is to Callas that we owe "the acceptance, thanks to intelligence, sensibility, and exceptional art and technique, of an ugly voice, of ugly sounds," even in this partially negative key we come to appreciate Callas. I do not think it is in any sense derogatory to our singer to maintain that technically someone could be her superior. In that same way, if 80 years ago the advent of Bellincioni caused a revolution in the world of opera, and if then certain singers undoubtedly superior vocally and technically, like Pandolfini, Canetti, Storchio and Farneti, followed in her footsteps, this does not alter the fact that it is Bellincioni who was the fountainhead in the history of vocal interpretation. Similarly with Callas today. But when it comes to determining her precise influence on the evolution of opera, there is a further important fact to be considered: the progressive disappearance, caused by her arrival on the scene, of the *soprano leggero*. It is no coincidence that operas like *Rigoletto*, *Sonnambula*, *Puritani*, are sung nowadays by light lyric sopranos, to such an extent that today, in Italy, the real *soprano leggero* has virtually disappeared.

Gara: The last point, a very true one, is further proof of the current return to the past, to the time when the *soprano leggero* had not yet emerged beside and in competition with the dramatic soprano. Yet another indication of the historical importance of Callas.

D'Amico: I would add that the return to the past, to this particular period, has brought about a very important discovery: the true significance of the coloratura. For the pure *soprano leggero* vocal embellishments are simply a matter of technical virtuosity; and the public, steeped in Wagnerian, romantic and even pre-romantic ideas, consider them to be just that. But in the 18th century, as later in Rossini, coloratura passages could well mean ecstasy, lyrical rapture, fury; in other words, they were vehicles for dramatic expression. Even an operatic reformer like Algarotti defended them as such; as Gara put it, the *soprano leggero* was born later. So one of Callas's "historical" merits has been in knowing how to use her incisive voice (as Celletti has described it), a voice capable of an agility quite different from that of the *soprano leggero*, so that she was able to bring to these passages an expressive meaning, drawing a real phrasing from their inner essence. I had indeed read the music and the musical literature of the period, and I had certainly studied Rossini's serious operas; but it was not until I heard Callas in Rossini's

Armida in Florence in 1952 that I really understood the true coloratura style of the golden age.

Gavazzeni: That is a very true observation, and I can confirm it with a personal experience of my own. Fifteen years ago in Rome, when I conducted *Lucia* with Callas, I noticed during rehearsals certain unexpectedly expressive qualities in her coloratura passages. I even tried to capture these in the orchestral echoes of the same phrases. Callas's intuition in this was an invaluable stimulus to me also for the future: certainly from then on, my interpretation of *Lucia* was not the same as before. And if it was so for me, it was so for others also. Sometimes the understanding between conductor and singer can bring about results of this kind, as long as the conductor is not one of those who have the truth in their pocket and have already made up their minds about everything before they begin.

Gualerzi: To sum up: there is today recognition of the "Callas event": not as a matter of unanimous approval, because there is still considerable opposition, but as material for discussion on the part of all those engaged in opera and also those only marginally involved in the subject as a social phenomenon. There is then the matter of followers, which is so important in the creation of an operatic myth. There is also the highly personal, unmistakably individual voice, as Celletti has so rightly described it. Add to this the outward projection of those artistic elements and you have, together with those sociological elements which transcend the immediate circle of the lyric theatre, all the necessary components for the making of the Callas myth.

Gara: Just so. But allow me a postscript on the subject of Pertile. Andrea Della Corte, the eminent critic who died about a year ago, once asked Serafin for his opinion of Pertile's "ugly voice," that ugly voice which even Toscanini preferred to all others and which was later to conquer half the world. Serafin replied: "I haven't really had occasion to notice. I never actually noticed that Pertile even had a voice. I don't know why, but evening after evening I have only heard the voices of Faust and Lohengrin, of Des Grieux and Edgardo, and so on. I've heard as many voices as there are parts in his repertory." We could well say the same of Callas. What she did with *Sonnambula* was not the same as what she did with *Anna Bolena*. It was something quite different, another voice. The heavenly, tender tones of her *Sonnambula*, or her *Lucia*, for instance, were not to be found in her *Anna Bolena*.

Celletti: A postscript from me too. Gualerzi said the *soprano leggero* is disappearing. I quite agree. It is the direct result of Callas performing certain coloratura parts with a robust voice. But I should like the dramatic soprano to go too. By dramatic soprano I mean the type (and perhaps with any luck she is really on the way out!) that has so afflicted our ears in the operas of Verdi and in some of Puccini's too: the blown-out middle registers, the coarse lower ones, the top notes always at full blast, the vulgar declamation. And notice the misunderstandings that arise. Montserrat Caballé is for me the singer closest to the type that should replace the traditional dramatic soprano. When I hear it said that Caballé lacks dramatic bite, I can agree, but only up to a point. I feel we are too used to a type of dramatic soprano that is a mixture of Gioconda, Santuzza and Aida; and I just don't believe that this is the true Verdian style. And to come back to Callas. I have heard her also in operas for which she won't particularly go down in history— operas like *Fedora* and *Andrea Chénier*. But even in these, and in *Il Trovatore* (which she used to sing very well, even if it wasn't one of her landmarks), Callas brought great refinement of style, waging a constant battle against bad taste at all levels—the vulgar middle notes, the top notes blasted off indiscriminately just as they come—like village hurrahs. In short I would say that, just as Callas has initiated the disappearance of the *soprano leggero*, so has she rung the first death knell of the traditional dramatic soprano.

D'Amico: I should like to add a postscript on the matter of sensuousness. I have a lot of sympathy for what is known as sensuousness, and should often be called simply lyricism. Wagner, the 19th century and many illustrious spirits of that century considered 18th century *opera seria*, and also *bel canto*, purely sensuous. In truth, they were not: they were, the *opera seria*, the music, *bel canto*, an exaltation of lyrical values. The dramatic concepts were entrusted to the text; the lyrical elements to the music. Hence my veneration for Beniamino Gigli: and one of the few points on which I disagree with my friend Celletti. I greatly admired Gigli, always or nearly always; and in purely lyrical passages I found him incomparable, unique, irreplaceable. So the equation Pertile-Gigli, Callas-Tebaldi leaves me perplexed, indeed hostile.

But perhaps this observation is only of marginal importance. What follows, however, despite appearances, definitely is not. A few days ago, at a conference organized in Rome by the German Historical

Institute on Verdi and Wagner, reference was inevitably made to the recent Karajan *Ring* cycle in Salzburg. As we all know, this was based on the elimination of all vocal violence and strain, on a much more intimate vocal style than long tradition has hitherto dictated, and therefore one richer in detail and shading. It was Celletti himself who spoke of this, and of course he made a point of drawing the analogy with tendencies increasingly evident in the practice of singers of the front rank. Could we say that Karajan went to Callas's school? Personally, I don't think it's necessary to take such a drastic view. As we have already said, certain things are in the air. As for Wagner, it will be observed that, while Karajan was opening in Salzburg with *Die Walküre*, Leibowitz was writing an essay, to be published later in the *Nuova Rivista Musicale Italiana*, in which he advocated much the same ideas. A not too dissimilar style (imposed by the production rather than the musical direction), admittedly with singers not of Salzburg or Bayreuth standards, was to inspire the 1968 *Tristan* at Spoleto, mounted by Gian-Carlo Menotti.

True, Callas came long before all this; she embodied certain needs of the age, perhaps before anyone else. Without question she was neither the first nor the only singer in the history of opera to demand, as her first aim, the creation of a character rather than a sequence of big moments. But she was certainly unique in her way of creating characters, and this because of a technique and an interpretative attitude that have truly revolutionized the operatic scene. She resolutely avoided the only existing alternatives—abstract virtuosity or the vulgar histrionics offered by the Gioconda-Santuzza-Aida cocktail by means of which, as Celletti says, a Verdi style was supposedly arrived at; she re-discovered a Bellini and Donizetti far more worthy of attention than anything then in circulation—not to mention *Médée*. All this and more have caused immeasurable repercussions.

The enumeration of her followers is of little importance; so are comparisons between the level of some of her interpretations and those of other singers who have followed her; some of these may well be better than her, but without her would never have become what they are. What really matters above all else and can, I think, conclude our dialogue, are two things that her advent has brought about. First and foremost, the repertory. A whole range of operas, considered up till now to be dead or unperformable, has been rehabilitated by her example;

and I *mean* a whole range of operas, not just those particular ones that she herself has sung. In the second place, she has renewed our way of listening to opera: that is to say, our demands and the means of satisfying those demands, *i.e.* the performers. This is, in our opinion, the historical Callas; others may, if they so wish, prefer their own mythical image.

"*I am going . . .*
to meet our hellcat . . ."

From the Francis Robinson Collection

≡⋮≡⋮≡⋮≡⋮≡⋮≡⋮≡⋮≡⋮≡⋮≡⋮≡⋮≡⋮≡⋮≡⋮≡⋮≡

The Francis Robinson Collection of Theatre, Music, and Dance is housed in the Special Collections at the Vanderbilt University Library. It includes books, recordings, correspondence, photographs, artwork, posters, clippings, publicity material, programs, catalogs, artifacts, and Robinson's own writings. Robinson began collecting as a boy and continued while working at the Ryman Auditorium in Nashville during his college years, as a newspaperman on the *Nashville Banner*, as a scriptwriter and producer at WSM in Nashville, as a theatrical press agent, and most particularly during his thirty-two-year administrative career with the Metropolitan Opera.

From Robinson's Letters to His Mother

≡ *October 1954*

I am going out to Chicago tomorrow for the opening of the new Lyric Theater, my friend Rescigno conducting, and the American debut of Maria Callas. I'll be at the Drake, fly back Tuesday morning.

≡ *November 4, 1955*

I am flying out to Chicago Tuesday with Mr. Bing. He hopes to sign Callas—again. (See last week's LIFE.) We had a contract with her which she never honored.

≡ *October 12, 1956*

I am going to Jimmy's party tonight, to meet our hellcat (Callas) in the morning. The day with Miss Farrar was so lovely. A different type prima donna.

≡ *October 25, 1956*

You don't subscribe to TIME any more, do you. Well you must go out and buy a copy. Callas has the cover of the current issue—and the piece! Among other things, she told her mother she could starve. I must say, touch wood, she has been a perfect lady with us—so far.

≡ *November 21, 1956*

It will be a turkeyless Thanksgiving for me tomorrow. I had an invitation but Callas is singing and I never leave the theatre when she is in it. Too much can happen!

≡ *January 22, 1958*

Callas arrives tomorrow. As Othello said, "Farewell the tranquil mind."

≡ *May 17, 1958*

No letter here, the first lapse, and I'm afraid that there's no mail tomorrow. As Callas said about the big shiny black funeral coach type limousines we met her with at the airport and a party after opening night, I have become "habituated." So I'll drop you a line.

≡ *November 6, 1958*

What was that quote of Ike's that there had not been a day when some crisis had not landed on his desk? Mine is no exception. I am sure you have seen the latest. She is a great artist but I sometimes fear quite insane.

≡ *November 20, 1958*

Several rich experiences since I last wrote you to counteract some of the hell we have been getting on Callas.

≡ *December 12, 1958*

Your letter yesterday sheer delight. And I devoured all enclosures. I hadn't seen the local coverage on Callas although the young man on the *Tennessean* who interviewed me in October telephoned me the night it happened. I am only now coming from under the strain. One of the doormen at my apartment said, "Mr. Robinson, I haven't seen you smile for two weeks." Funny, I didn't know anyone ever noticed.

Among the other enclosures I should have mentioned the one on the Greek queen. Princess Sophie was here the other night and Mrs. Belmont elected me to be her—if I were younger I would say beau but now that I am of age I suppose I should say equerry. It was the night of the Ricordi function and when they asked for seats there was no room in the boxes which was all right with them. They wanted to come incognito anyway. So at the second act I picked them up and escorted them to Mrs. Belmont's table where on the other side was Ambassador Lodge.

At the next intermission I asked if she would like to go backstage. I wanted to present her to her countryman Nick Moscona. You should have seen his face, totally unprepared. She asked how long he had been at the Met and he said, "Since two years before you were born." She is a lovely girl. When I presented her to Tebaldi, the latter in her old blue wrapper, the diva curtsied. This was a triumph for me because the queen had snubbed Callas on the West Coast to Callas' intense annoyance. I think I know why. The poor Greeks of Detroit had planned a great fete for Callas when she was there and she stood them up, going on to Chicago. You don't do that to people who put themselves out for you.

≡ *October 29, 1959*

Callas never looked out more fearlessly nor beguilingly than her face in the clipping. But it is her silence that I remember most. Sometimes it is wistful to the point of making me sad—but if it doesn't make her sad I hope the gift never deserts her. I might wish some of the others of us had learned it so young and apparently so well.

≡ *[1960?]*

And the Callas review. I told Mr. Bing that whatever we now had was a complete example of what *not* to do. [My Daughter, Maria Callas] is a terrible book. The old woman [Evangelia Callas] lays it all on a fall Callas had on her head at the age of five!

≡ *August 5, 1966*

Thanks for the clippings although I wish Betty Beale would have let Paris rest. There is an NBC documentary to be run the night after we open to advertise our shame. Roberta Peters was unwise enough to say in an interview with them that Callas had organized the demonstration against us. In the first place it isn't true (Callas would be in position to sue) and if it were she still shouldn't say it. I have tried to get them to cut it and Bing got *her* to ask them. I don't know.

≣ September 13, 1968

Last night was the annual fall dinner at the Opera Club. Mr. Bing didn't go, I am sure to avoid making a speech, and I had to oblige. They don't get easier. Mr. George Moore also spoke and he is bringing Callas, or at least she is a guest in his box, at the opening Monday. She it out of favor with Onassis and seems at the moment to be a ship without a sail.

≣ October 18, 1968

Plenty of excitement re the wedding [of Jacqueline Kennedy and Aristotle Onassis]. Our phones have been buzzing, papers as far away as Chicago and London, wanting to know how to get in touch with Callas! I hear she gave an interview to *Women's Wear Daily*, "First I lost my weight, then I lost my voice, and now I have lost Onassis!"

Correspondence with Alfred Lunt

Alfred Lunt to Robinson

≣ November 12, 1956

I'm dying to hear about Callas and all the goings on—sounds like the old days according to Noel [Coward]—who called up yesterday— He'd seen the Saturday matinee—Admires her as an actress, not so mad about her voice and says she looks so much like Valentina at times—she delighted him—

Robinson to Lunt

≣ November 17, 1956

I am sorry I missed your calls and would have loved to see you before you took off. Yes, Mr. Coward has been in three times since the season opened, a record for him, I would say. He did a murderous impersonation of Tommy Schippers, the little conductor, at a supper after one performance. "And your entrance, dear boy," he said. "It had all the spontaneity of eight weeks rehearsal!"

I wish you could see Callas in action.

Martha Graham to Robinson

≡ *November 11, 1956*

It is a late letter of gratitude for a special evening you gave me—that tardiness I cannot go into—but none of the radiance has dimmed for me—

First I had never been to a Metropolitan opening night and it is an excitement special to itself—I had never, of course, heard *Norma* —nor Callas—She is for me exciting and deeply moving—Her sense of design, her never-failing animal-like absorption in the instant—that spiral of inner activity which is rare and devastating to watch—the precious calculation of her appearance and the fact that she has an innate courtesy to her audience which makes her wear her costumes for their pleasure—

These are only a few things she gave me and which I shall treasure—I am not a judge of voice but hers was exciting for me—

Thank you, dear Francis, for a great experience—

The Voice at Its Best: The Great Recordings

by David A. Lowe

The Callas discography is extensive and still growing. Heartbreaking gaps remain (the Chicago *Trovatore* with Bjoerling, for instance), but all in all, the Callas admirer has much for which to be grateful. For those whose admiration has crossed over into fanaticism—and their numbers are legion—there can hardly be such a thing as an uninteresting Callas performance. More dispassionate judges, however, would argue that beginning as early as the studio recordings of *La Forza del Destino* and *Manon Lescaut* Callas left documents that do not particularly invite rehearing. The uninitiated, if exposed initially to the "wrong" recordings, may rightfully wonder what all the shouting and swooning was and is about. After all, some of the mementos of Callas's career feature quite hideous sounds. One can develop a tolerance and perhaps even an affection for Callas at less than her best, but the taste is definitely an acquired one. To appreciate Callas in her prime, however, one need only be capable of responding to superb operatic singing.

The notes that follow are in no way intended as a comprehensive commentary on the Callas discography. John Ardoin has already provided that service, and in a masterly way. The focus here, rather, is on those recorded performances that capture all of Callas's strengths and few or none of her weaknesses. These are the recordings that one may offer up without trepidation to the most demanding of vocal connoisseurs, the performances in which Callas scales the heights of dramatic and vocal grandeur, the performances on which her claim to immortality must ultimately be based. Many of Callas's advocates will feel that the listing is far too short and omits some of their very favorite Callas recordings. Few would dispute the claim, however, that Callas never sounded consistently better or worked greater miracles than in the recordings mentioned below. Moreover, an attempt has been made to isolate those performances that exist in acceptable sound and in which Callas is surrounded by worthy colleagues. In short, if one were building a Callas collection, one could hardly go wrong by starting with the selections outlined here. Incidentally, most of them are not studio recordings, because with rare exceptions Callas "live" was even more glorious than Callas in the studio.

In the following comments, studio recordings are identified by label, private recordings by place and date of performance.

"Qui la voce" (Cetra, 1949)

"Qui la voce," from Bellini's *I Puritani*, was one of the three arias that Callas sang for her first commercial recording session, with Cetra, in November 1949. So potent is her magic here that had she left to posterity no other documentary evidence of her art, there would still be a Callas cult today and tomorrow. All the hallmarks of Callas in peak form are to be heard in this recording.

Bellini's contribution to the proceedings is not inconsiderable: he provides a cavatina of long-breathed poignance and a cabaletta of daunting brilliance for a text that emphasizes betrayal, desolation, and delirium. To this basic material Callas brings a haunting timbre, uncanny and unerring interpretive instincts, and awesome bel canto technique. The timbre, plangent and doleful in a way reminiscent of a clarinet or an oboe, suggests both crushing melancholy and dazed introspection. Indeed, Callas, as Elvira, creates the paradoxical but dramatically appropriate illusion that she is totally unaware of an audience, that she is singing exclusively to and for her own delirious self. Even the bravura passages in the cabaletta seem to be a part of a half-whispered inner monologue, quite divorced from vocal display. The mood of quiet, bewildered reflection is dispelled only in the final measures of the cabaletta, where the prima donna at last reclaims her rights and sings out in exhibitionistic full voice, ascending to a blazing E-flat in alt.

Callas's musical and dramatic intelligence is everywhere apparent.

In general, she strives for and attains a maximal expressiveness that falls miraculously short of obtrusiveness. Her accents on the words "morir" and "sospir" threaten to spill over into verismo declamation but do not. The portamenti that mark every phrase, if handled any less skillfully, would bespeak sloppy schooling rather than tragic loss. Most amazing is Callas's use of rubato: within an overall framework that is strictly classical in its contours, Callas subtly nudges and retards rhythms so as to underline Elvira's psychic instability. To repeat: in the case of a lesser artist, such reliance on portamento, rubato, and emotionally charged accents would wreak havoc with Bellini's exquisite line, but with Callas, Bellini's long, arching phrases emerge with luminous clarity and overwhelming dramatic force.

The sheer technique that Callas displays in this performance is also noteworthy. The cavatina is a master class in infinitely modulated legato singing, while the cabaletta shows the dazzling effects that can result when a large voice sails through coloratura passages. The tempo for the cabaletta is rather slow, but by singing chromatic descending scales with an instrumental accuracy of intonation and by deliciously pointing two-note turns, Callas delivers vocal thrills that elude singers who sacrifice precision for velocity.

In sum, Callas's first studio recording of "Qui la voce" is an unforgettable performance, a thing of beauty in all respects, and a document that encapsulates the many splendors of bel canto singing at its most evocative. Not bad for a singer only on the threshold of her career.

Tosca (EMI, 1953)

When it comes to operas in the standard repertory, the discophile can usually select from a cornucopia of offerings. Truly definitive recordings remain rarities, however, and the Callas-di Stefano-Gobbi-de Sabata *Tosca* of 1953 is one of them. Once one gets to know this realization of Puccini's score, all other performances, whether in the opera house or on record, seem frustratingly inadequate or even irrelevant.

There is much to admire in de Sabata's brilliantly paced conducting, Gobbi's repellently attractive sensuousness, and di Stefano's easy, full-throated vocalism, but make no mistake: the show belongs to Callas. Her voice, glowing with the smoky warmth of amber, is marvelously secure. In Act II she soars to the treacherous B-flats, B's, and C's with a power and assurance matched in recent years only by Birgit Nilsson. The voice is only the basis, however, for the vivid, compelling portrait of the Roman prima donna that Callas offers.

In the first act, always the most difficult for a soprano as far as characterization is concerned, Callas's singing is marked initially by a restraint that underlines the vulnerability to which Tosca's passion for Cavaradossi has left her open. The restraint is especially noticeable in Callas's avoidance of the chest register, where the dark, baritonal sound could suggest almost anything except vulnerability. Against this background of hushed, seemingly tentative vocal statements, the flashes of lightning that erupt at the recognition of L'Attavanti and in subsequent mention of her stand out in all the greater relief, baring the fierce emotions that lie at the core of Tosca's psyche. The interplay of concealed and revealed sentiments, sketched through purely vocal means, makes for the fascination of Callas's first-act Tosca.

With the second-act confrontation between Scarpia and Tosca, in the persons of Gobbi and Callas, we arrive at drama so intense, so palpable, that it draws us into an unseen theater where we somehow *witness* Scarpia's pursuit of Tosca and his murder at her "sweet" hands. Thanks to Callas's way with words, such clichés of operatic Italian as "Assassino," "Quanto?" "Il prezzo," and even "Sì" are revivified. Perhaps the most remarkable moment in the second act is "Vissi d'arte," which Callas delivers in the phenomenally compact, bottled-up, hyperresonant tones that often characterized her singing in the early 1950s. The timbre itself is redolent of melancholy, and through exquisite modulations in dynamics, particularly in a tapering-off effect at the end of each phrase, Callas etches a wrenching portrait of bewildered despair. The final phrases, with the stifled sob on the downward plunge of an octave, cap the most emotional yet controlled reading of the aria to be heard on records. The very end of the act certainly has its merits, too. "E morto," the tense interval afterward, and "Or gli perdono" provide more drama in a few seconds than many performances muster in an entire evening.

Act III of *Tosca* cannot help but be something of an anticlimax, but Callas still manages to invest its pages with urgency and expectation. She often found dramatic gold where other singers saw only dross, and such is very much the case in Tosca's running commentary on the preparations for Cavaradossi's execution. The voice is drenched in anxiety, and the dangerously high chest tones that Callas summons for "Ecco un artista!" make the phrase unforgettable in its crazed exultation, on the one hand, and in its hideous irony, on the other. The moments that follow—Tosca's agonized discovery that the execution has been genuine, her flight from Scarpia's henchmen, and the savage attack on "O Scarpia, avanti a Dio!"—bring to a devastating close a performance that ranks as one of the loftiest summits of Callas's vocal and dramatic art.

Lucia di Lammermoor (Berlin, 1954)

In a review published in the December 1955 issue of *Opera*, Desmond Shawe-Taylor wrote of Callas's Berlin *Lucia*: "I dare say that she will never sing any better than she does now." He was right. The Berlin *Lucia*, or *Lucia von Lammermoor*, as wags referred to it, is the high-water mark of Callas's vocal art. To judge by recorded performances at any rate, neither before nor after this *Lucia* did the Callas voice per se reveal itself to greater advantage. The limpidity, flexibility, and beauty are stunning. Add to that Callas's interpretive insights and the result is an achievement unparalleled in our time.

Von Karajan provides sumptuous support for Callas and her colleagues, all of whom are in fine form. Callas is the miracle, however. In "Regnava nel silenzio" the voice floats on gossamer wings, as though in defiance of the laws of gravity, and Callas's legato is absolutely seamless. The voice responds to her every wish; the trills and fioriture are impeccable; and the overall mood is one of ecstatic reverie. By virtue of the slow tempo, "Quando rapito" further develops the dream-like atmosphere, and although Callas's interpretation underplays the bravura moments in the cabaletta, the scales and rapid passage-work, tossed off with remarkable lightness and grace, nonetheless dazzle. The D to which Callas ascends at the conclusion of the cabaletta verges on shrillness, but in the context of what has gone before, that is a distinctly minor matter.

The duet with di Stefano is superb in every way. The lilt on "Deh ti placa" again suggests weightlessness. The inflection on the rising phrase "Ah" just preceding "Verrano a te" shows Callas's uncanny ability to imbue even semantic voids with meaning. The opening of "Verrano a te" itself, delivered in an exquisite mezza voce, would make any soprano envious. The audience goes wild after the duet, as well it should.

For all the glory of Callas's singing in Act I, however, it is only in Act II that the performance begins to take on a genuine theatricality. In the first scene Callas, as Lucia, gives her opening phrases a strongly emotional coloration, putting special accent on such key words as "strazio" and "dolor." Her response to the forged letter, "Ah, il core mi balzò," relies on a scaled-down voice and pathetic timbre to depict crushed hopes and the collapse of a soul. In the passage that follows, "Soffriva del pianto," Callas achieves great poignancy by using perfect legato allied with a vocal tone suggestive of weariness and despondency. There is a moment of near-rebellion, when Callas touches very lightly on chest tones for the words "istante di morte," but the mood quickly returns to one of despair, and Callas again scales down the voice to a mere thread of sound. At the conclusion of the scene, as her brother lays out his plot, Callas shows once again her uncanny ability to turn such clichés as "Io tremo" and "Oh, ciel!" into exclamations of an overwhelming dramatic intensity. She then brings the scene to a brilliant close by rising to a secure high D.

The primary interest of the second scene of Act II lies in the great ensembles, and this performance does not let us down. Callas and di Stefano both oversing a bit in the sextet, but the audience does not seem to mind, nor should we. The concluding ensemble builds to a very exciting conclusion, to a large extent because of the bite of Callas's rhythmic accuracy. The final D wobbles slightly but at the same time manages to suggest Lucia's emotional exhaustion.

There are not sufficient superlatives in any language to describe Callas's delivery of the Mad Scene. It is vocal and dramatic art of the most elevated sort, beautiful in all respects. To begin with, Callas actually creates the illusion that Lucia is singing the entire scene in a trance: vocal display seems the farthest thing from Callas's or Lucia's mind. In the long first part of the scene, von Karajan keeps to a rather slow tempo, one which allows Callas to spin legato phrases that seem to go on forever. For the crucial phrases "Del ciel, del ciel clemente" and "Alfin son tua" Callas creates a timbre of special compactness and vibrancy, making these moments unforgettable. The cadenza, with flute accompaniment, is sung impeccably, save for a couple of B-flat staccato attacks that fail to sound in time. Callas ends the cadenza with a downward variant, one that makes eminently good sense dramatically, for there is still another section of the Mad Scene to come. In that section, "Spargi d'amaro pianto," Callas combines drama and bravura. Her trills and scales are effortlessly accurate, and the variations in the reprise include an ascent to an astonishing pianissimo B-flat, followed by a hairpin turn ending on a C-flat. The effect is very much like that achieved by a trapeze artist working without a net. The scene concludes on a rock-solid E-flat in alt that turns a bit sharp but still puts a glorious cap on a Mad Scene the likes of which audiences in this century had not heard before and have not heard since. We are extremely fortunate to have this document of one of Callas's most stupendous evenings in the theater.

Norma (La Scala, 1955)

The December 7, 1955, *Norma* at La Scala finds Callas in superb voice throughout the performance. It is obvious from the opening recitative that the voice is responding well, allowing her to shape and color Norma's lines with a suavity and beauty that Callas never again quite achieved, at least in extant recordings. The "Casta diva" is sung as though in a dream; the long legato phrases are truly worthy of a goddess; and the climactic B-flats do not turn unruly, as they often did for Callas in this demanding aria. The melismas between verses are delicious and accurate, intensifying the otherwordly atmosphere. Callas handles the final cadenza masterfully, with an exquisite diminuendo on the B-flat. The final words, "nel ciel," float effortlessly, with no trace of a wobble, capping the grandest performance of this aria that Callas ever gave. The bravura cabaletta, "Ah bello a me," is sung with absolute security, the rising phrases deliciously pointed, the descending scales impeccable, and the concluding high C solid. The brilliance of execution here is not lost on the Scala audience, which goes properly mad.

In the two first-act duets Callas is paired with Simionato, an excellent and sensitive partner. As usual, Callas makes of "O rimembranza" a special moment, and with the arching phrase "Così trovavo del mio cor la via," so full of reflection and loss, Callas accomplishes another of her miracles of weightlessness. In the section that follows,

"Ah sì, fa core, abbracciami," Callas performs a stunning diminuendo on a high C that elicits audible gasps of admiration from the audience.

Callas proceeds from strength to strength, and in the passage "Ah non tremar" demonstrates the dramatic potential of coloratura. The rapid descending scales and the leaps to high C, which sound like sheer display in the case of certain other sopranos, blaze like streaks of lightning. Thanks to Callas's attacks and full-voiced vocalizing, Norma's venom takes on a genuinely frightening intensity. There is no letup in tension in the trio "Oh, di qual sei tu vittima," where Callas's savage attacks punctuate the proceedings and turn a rather trite melody into a vehicle for the expression of fierce emotions. The real marvel is that Norma's rage, as interpreted by Callas, which is so palpable that one half expects Callas's voice to self-combust, in no way mars the classical beauty and lines of the trio. The finale rises to an almost unbearable pitch of excitement as Callas unleashes a perfectly placed dazzling high D.

The primary interest in the first scene of Act II lies in Norma's scene with her children and the duet with Adalgisa. Callas etches the line "Teneri figli" with rare pathos, the mezza voce and legato combining to produce remarkable beauty. For "Mira, o Norma" Simionato and Callas are perfectly attuned to each other, and although the blend of their voices does not erase memories of Ponselle and Telva or Sutherland and Horne, this is still singing of a very high order.

Callas completely dominates the opera's last scene, summoning unearthly breath control and pianissimi for phrases like "Come del primo amor" and "Ah, padre! un prego ancor," and massive fortissimi for "Sangue romano—scorgeran torrenti." In the duet with Pollione, "In mia man alfin tu sei," Callas again demonstrates that bravura passage work can be delivered with ferocity, that trills can frighten. The most sublime moment in this performance, however, comes with Norma's confession, "Son io," a line which in Callas's interpretation acquires such shattering poignance that the audience erupts in a collective moan. The tragic nobility of Callas's "Deh! Non volerli vittime," rendered in a molten legato and in burnished tones, climaxes a performance by which all future Normas, no doubt to their considerable dismay, must be measured. With *Norma* Callas once again shows that beautiful singing and high drama can be one and the same thing, but the amalgam she achieves here demands a goodly portion of magic.

La Sonnambula (Cologne, 1957)

The Cologne *Sonnambula* is one of Callas's last recorded performances in which everything goes right, and the results, predictably, are heavenly. True, there is perhaps a slight premonition of the vocal crisis that was not too far away: Callas shies away from applying much pressure on notes in the area of high C and above. As a consequence, however, the performance and interpretation are all the more winning. In earlier portrayals of Amina, both in the studio and on stage, Callas's voice sometimes acquires a steely quality very much at odds with Amina's personality. In the Cologne performance, however, Callas approaches many of the high-lying passages softly and almost cooingly. The fioriture thus seem more like fine embroidery than prima-donna razzle-dazzle.

Callas's singing of the opening recitative in the first act is marked by restraint and lovely half-tones. The aria itself, "Come per me sereno," demonstrates masterly phrasing and a wonderful sense of lift in its arching phrases. Throughout the piece Callas sprinkles lingering diminuendos that underline both her vocal security and Amina's fragility. Callas then etches the cabaletta, "Sovra il sen la man mi posa," with ineffable grace, touching lightly on the staccato passages and darting through incredibly complicated passage-work. She crowns her entrance with a ringing E-flat in alt.

In the subsequent duets with Elvino, "Caro, dal dì che univa" and "Son geloso," Callas is an admirable partner, scaling her voice down to match Monti's thinnish tenor. The various diminuendi and trills are impeccable, and the overall effect one of extraordinary elegance. At the conclusion of the duet the audience erupts in a well-deserved ovation.

In the second scene of the first act Amina has a mini-mad scene as she sleepwalks her way into the Count's bedroom. Callas sings the lines in an ecstatic fil di voce that truly suggests a trance. Her singing in the ensuing ensemble, "D'un pensiero," combines nobility and pathos and features the pulsating, fluttering legato that is the hallmark of Callas in her prime. For the climax of the scene Callas launches another E-flat in alt, and most successfully.

Amina's role in the first scene of the second act is limited to a number of recitatives. Callas, with her gift for characterization and dramatic accent, infuses these passages with more emotion than most singers can summon from a long aria. "Reggimi, o buona madre," beginning high and softly, flutters to earth in a way reminiscent of an innocent bird that has been shot down. For "Il mio anello! Oh madre" Callas relies on the reedy timbre of hers that in itself suggests melancholy incarnate.

The two great moments in the last scene are the aria "Ah, non credea mirarti" and the cabaletta "Ah! non giunge!" "Ah, non credea mirarti" is one of the most beautiful melodies that Bellini ever penned, and its successful delivery depends exclusively on the singer's artistry, because the orchestral support is minimal, leaving the voice quite exposed except for a few passages with string obbligato. Callas achieves the ultimate in expressivity here, playing with rubato, lingering over diminuendos, and producing a timbre and legato that reveal bel canto singing of the highest order.

In Luchino Visconti's staging of *Sonnambula* "Ah! non giunge!" occasioned a sudden shift in theatrical orientation. Throughout the performance Callas had been the fragile Amina, singing with restraint and one might almost say caution. For the bravura finale, however, all the house lights went on and Callas emerged as the prima donna of legend—not the legendary Callas, however, but a reincarnation of the nineteenth-century image of the prima donna. In this recording Callas at this point finally pulls out all the stops and for the only time in the entire performance plunges from time to time into her chest register. The phrase just before the reprise, in which Callas ascends to an E-flat in full voice and then makes a diminuendo on it, can almost frighten the unprepared listener because of the size, control, and power of Callas's voice. In the reprise itself Callas tosses off embellishments with a delicacy that she did not achieve in any other recorded performance of *Sonnambula*, and the high-lying soft fioriture seem death-defying. Callas's overall achievement in this performance is twofold. The singing itself is out-and-out stupendous. Equally importantly, however, Callas makes of Amina, one of the most ludicrous figures in the nineteenth-century Italian repertory, a creature of charm and pathos. Singers before and after Callas have sung the role as well as she, if we are speaking purely of technique, but no one else has made of Amina considerably more than a wind-up coloratura doll.

Un Ballo in Maschera (La Scala, 1957)

Listening to the Scala *Ballo in Maschera* makes one aware of the extent to which Callas consciously scaled down her voice and lightened its color for such roles as Lucia, Amina, and even Norma. *Un Ballo in Maschera* requires a hefty, dramatic voice, and Callas provides it. In her first bit of singing, the trio in the second scene of Act I, she sends forth tidal waves of broad, genuinely Verdian sound: the arching phrases suggest flying buttresses, and the ebony chest voice increases the impression of solidity and might.

Callas's grandest singing comes in the second act. Her reading of "Ecco l'orrido campo" is the most satisfying one ever captured on a recording. The opening recitative is deeply dramatic, delivered with incisive, insinuating accents that all but generate sparks. The lyrical portion of the aria is etched in broad lines that perfectly mirror Amelia's anxiety without distorting Verdi's musical design. In the passage beginning "Mezzanotte," Amelia's terror is palpable and riveting. For the final prayer, with its high-lying phrases, Callas summons a massive sound and ascends to top C with utter security. The cadenza, with its air of desperation and helplessness, is a miracle of emotionally colored, beautiful vocalism. The subsequent duet with Riccardo (di Stefano) is altogether admirable, with Callas portraying through her voice every twist and turn in Amelia's tormented reactions. This is singing on a grand scale, and when Callas and di Stefano finish their duet on a blazing high C the audience loses no time in unleashing its fervent appreciation.

The end of the act features two ensembles. In the first, with Riccardo and Renato, Callas generates considerable excitement through the precision of her singing and the bite of her attack: rarely does one hear such a large voice sail through Amelia's intricate intervals with such accuracy and velocity. For the final ensemble, to the accompaniment of Sam and Tom's ghoulish laughter, Callas offers buoyant, floating phrases, including a lovely ascent to and diminuendo on high B-flat.

In Act III Callas's major moment comes with the aria "Morrò, ma prima in grazia," the recitative to which, with its descent to the chest register, perfectly establishes the necessary mood of fatalistic pleading. The aria itself is sculpted in vibrant, dark tones, and the conclusion is overwhelming in its impact: the sheer size of the voice is amazing, and the emotions spilling forth through it are frighteningly intense. In the vengeance ensemble Callas's voice lashes out, riding the crest of Verdi's fortes with ease. In the final ensemble Callas not only shows the Oscar (Eugenia Ratti) what real trills are but additionally highlights the drama by singing them in very expressive, somber tones.

In Act IV Callas makes the most of the brief interchange with Riccardo, turning the few lines allotted her into an intensely dramatic cameo. She continues strongly in the final ensemble, easily dominating and shaping it. All in all, this *Ballo in Maschera* is the most rewarding performance of the opera on record. Ratti is shrill in the upper register, but the rest of Callas's colleagues outdo themselves, as does Callas. A night to remember and to cherish.

The Callas Discography

EDITOR'S NOTE: *The discography was originally assembled by Dominique Ravier under the supervision of Sergio Segalini. The editor has expanded it but also eliminated label references for recordings not originally issued by Cetra, Mercury, or EMI/Angel. The so-called "pirated" recordings, many of them now apparently legal, exist on a bewildering array of labels, most of them private and often ephemeral. The status and availability of such recordings fluctuate practically from day to day, thus ruling out any definitive catalog.*

Complete Recordings

1949
Verdi, *Nabucco*. With Amalia Pini (Fenena), Gino Bechi (Nabucco), Luciano Neroni (Zaccaria), Gino Sinimberghi (Ismaele). Vittorio Gui conducting. Performance of December 20, Teatro San Carlo, Naples.

1950
Bellini, *Norma*. With Giulietta Simionato (Adalgisa), Kurt Baum (Pollione), Nicola Moscona (Oroveso). Guido Picco conducting. Performance of May 23, Palacio de Bellas Artes, Mexico City.

Verdi, *Aida*. With Giulietta Simionato (Amneris), Kurt Baum (Radames), Nicola Moscona (Ramfis). Guido Picco conducting. Performance of May 30, Palacio de Bellas Artes, Mexico City.

Puccini, *Tosca*. With Mario Filippeschi (Cavaradossi), Robert Weede (Scarpia). Umberto Mugnai conducting. Performance of June 8, Palacio de Bellas Artes, Mexico City.

Verdi, *Il Trovatore*. With Giulietta Simionato (Azucena), Kurt Baum (Manrico), Leonard Warren (Count di Luna), Nicola Moscona (Ferrando). Guido Picco conducting. Performance of June 20, Palacio de Bellas Artes, Mexico City.

Wagner, *Parsifal*. With Africo Baldelli (Parsifal), Boris Christoff (Gurnemanz), Rolando Panerai (Amfortas). Vittorio Gui conducting. Concert performance of November 20–21, RAI, Rome.

1951

Verdi, *Il Trovatore*. With Cloe Elmo (Azucena), Giacomo Lauri-Volpi (Manrico), Paolo Silveri (Count di Luna), Italo Tajo (Ferrando). Tullio Serafin conducting. Performance of January 27, Teatro San Carlo, Naples.

Verdi, *I Vespri Siciliani*. With Giorgio Kokolios-Bardi (Arrigo), Enzo Mascherini (Monforte), Boris Christoff (Procida). Erich Kleiber conducting. Performance of May 26, Teatro Comunale, Florence.

Verdi, *Aida*. With Oralia Dominguez (Amneris), Mario del Monaco (Radames), Giuseppe Taddei (Amonasro). Oliviero de Fabritiis conducting. Performance of July 3, Palacio de Bellas Artes, Mexico City.

Verdi, *La Traviata*. With Cesare Valletti (Alfredo), Giuseppe Taddei (Germont). Oliviero de Fabritiis conducting. Performance of July 17, Palacio de Bellas Artes, Mexico City.

1952

Rossini, *Armida*. With Francesco Albanese (Rinaldo), Gianni Raimondi (Carlo), Alessandro Ziliani (Goffredo), Antonio Salvarezza (Eustazio). Tullio Serafin conducting. Performance of April 26, Teatro Comunale, Florence.

Bellini, *I Puritani*. With Giuseppe di Stefano (Arturo), Roberto Silva (Giorgio), Piero Campolonghi (Riccardo). Guido Picco conducting. Performance of May 29, Palacio de Bellas Artes, Mexico City.

Verdi, *La Traviata*. With Giuseppe di Stefano (Alfredo), Piero Campolonghi (Germont). Umberto Mugnai conducting. Performance of June 3, Palacio de Bellas Artes, Mexico City.

Donizetti, *Lucia di Lammermoor*. With Giuseppe di Stefano (Edgardo), Piero Campolonghi (Enrico). Guido Picco conducting. Performance of June 10, Palacio de Bellas Artes, Mexico City.

Verdi, *Rigoletto*. With María Teresa García (Maddalena), Giuseppe di Stefano (Duke), Piero Campolonghi (Rigoletto), Ignacio Ruffino (Sparafucile). Umberto Mugnai conducting. Performance of June 17, Palacio de Bellas Artes, Mexico City.

Puccini, *Tosca*. With Giuseppe di Stefano (Cavaradossi), Piero Campolonghi (Scarpia). Guido Picco conducting. Performance of June 28, Palacio de Bellas Artes, Mexico City.

Ponchielli, *La Gioconda*. With Fedora Barbieri (Laura), Maria Amadini (La Cieca), Gianni Poggi (Enzo), Paolo Silveri (Barnaba), Giulio Neri (Alvise). Antonino Votto conducting. With the orchestra and chorus of RAI, Turin. Recorded September. [Cetra]

Bellini, *Norma*. With Ebe Stignani (Adalgisa), Joan Sutherland (Clotilde), Mirto Picchi (Pollione), Giacomo Vaghi (Oroveso). Vittorio Gui conducting. Performance of November 18, Covent Garden, London.

Verdi, *Macbeth*. With Enzo Mascherini (Macbeth), Italo Tajo (Banco), Gino Penno (Macduff). Vittorio de Sabata conducting. Performance of December 7, La Scala, Milan.

1953

Donizetti, *Lucia di Lammermoor*. With Giuseppe di Stefano (Edgardo), Tito Gobbi (Enrico), Raffaele Arie (Raimondo). Tullio Serafin conducting the orchestra and chorus of the Maggio Musicale Fiorentino. Recorded February. [EMI]

Verdi, *Il Trovatore*. With Ebe Stignani (Azucena), Gino Penno (Manrico), Carlo Tagliabue (Count di Luna), Giuseppe Modesti (Ferrando). Antonino Votto conducting. Performance of February 28, La Scala, Milan.

Bellini, *I Puritani*. With Giuseppe di Stefano (Arturo), Nicola Rossi-Lemeni (Giorgio), Rolando Panerai (Riccardo). Tullio Serafin conducting the orchestra and chorus of La Scala. Recorded March 24–30. [EMI]

Cherubini, *Medea*. With Carlo Guichandut (Jason), Gabriella Tucci

(Glauce), Mario Petri (Creon), Fedora Barbieri (Neris). Vittorio Gui conducting. Performance of May 7, Teatro Comunale, Florence.

Mascagni, *Cavalleria Rusticana*. With Giuseppe di Stefano (Turiddu), Rolando Panerai (Alfio). Tullio Serafin conducting the chorus and orchestra of La Scala. Recorded July–August. [EMI]

Puccini, *Tosca*. With Giuseppe di Stefano (Cavaradossi), Tito Gobbi (Scarpia). Vittorio de Sabata conducting the chorus and orchestra of La Scala. Recorded August 10–21. [EMI]

Verdi, *La Traviata*. With Francesco Albanese (Alfredo), Ugo Savarese (Giorgio). Gabriele Santini conducting the orchestra and chorus of RAI, Turin. Recorded September. [Cetra]

Bellini, *Norma*. With Elena Nicolai (Adalgisa), Franco Corelli (Pollione), Boris Christoff (Oroveso). Antonino Votto conducting. Performance of November 19, Teatro Giuseppe Verdi, Trieste.

Cherubini, *Medea*. With Fedora Barbieri (Neris), Gino Penno (Jason), Giuseppe Modesti (Creon). Leonard Bernstein conducting. Performance of December 10, La Scala, Milan.

1954

Gluck, *Alceste*. With Renato Gavarini (Admete), Paolo Silveri (High Priest), Rolando Panerai (Apollo), Nicola Zaccaria (Oracle). Carlo Maria Giulini conducting. Performance of April 4, La Scala, Milan.

Bellini, *Norma*. With Ebe Stignani (Adalgisa), Mario Filippeschi (Pollione), Nicola Rossi-Lemeni (Oroveso). Tullio Serafin conducting the chorus and orchestra of La Scala. Recorded April 23–May 3. [EMI]

Leoncavallo, *Pagliacci*. With Giuseppe di Stefano (Canio), Tito Gobbi (Tonio), Rolando Panerai (Silvio), Nicola Monti (Beppe). Tullio Serafin conducting the orchestra and chorus of La Scala. Recorded May 27–June 17. [EMI]

Verdi, *La Forza del Destino*. With Elena Nicolai (Preziosilla), Richard Tucker (Alvaro), Carlo Tagliabue (Don Carlo), Nicola Rossi-Lemeni (Padre Guardiano). Tullio Serafin conducting the chorus and orchestra of La Scala. Recorded August 17–27. [EMI]

Rossini, *Il Turco in Italia*. With Iolanda Gardino (Zaida), Nicola Rossi-Lemeni (Selim), Franco Calabrese (Geronio), Nicolai Gedda (Narciso), Mariano Stabile (Poet). Gianandrea Gavazzeni conducting the orchestra and chorus of La Scala. Recorded August 31–September 8. [EMI]

Spontini, *La Vestale*. With Ebe Stignani (High Priestess), Franco Corelli (Licinio), Nicola Rossi-Lemeni (Pontifex Maximus), Enzo Sordello (Cinna). Antonino Votto conducting. Performance of December 7. La Scala, Milan.

1955

Giordano, *Andrea Chénier*. With Mario del Monaco (Andrea), Aldo Protti (Gerard). Antonino Votto conducting. Performance of January 8, La Scala, Milan.

Bellini, *La Sonnambula*. With Eugenia Ratti (Lisa), Cesare Valletti (Elvino), Giuseppe Modesti (Rodolfo). Leonard Bernstein conducting. Performance of March 5, La Scala, Milan.

Verdi, *La Traviata*. With Giuseppe di Stefano (Alfredo), Ettore Bastianini (Giorgio). Carlo Maria Giulini conducting. Performance of May 28, La Scala, Milan.

Bellini, *Norma*. With Ebe Stignani (Adalgisa), Mario del Monaco (Pollione), Giuseppe Modesti (Oroveso). Tullio Serafin conducting. Concert performance of June 29, RAI, Rome.

Puccini, *Madama Butterfly*. With Lucia Danieli (Suzuki), Nicolai Gedda (Pinkerton), Mario Borriello (Sharpless). Herbert von Karajan conducting the orchestra and chorus of La Scala. Recorded August 1–6. [EMI]

Verdi, *Aida*. With Fedora Barbieri (Amneris), Richard Tucker (Radames), Tito Gobbi (Amonasro). Tullio Serafin conducting the orchestra and chorus of La Scala. Recorded August 10–24. [EMI]

Verdi, *Rigoletto*. With Giuseppe di Stefano (Duke), Tito Gobbi (Rigoletto), Nicola Zaccaria (Sparafucile). Tullio Serafin conducting the orchestra and chorus of La Scala. Recorded September 3–16. [EMI]

Donizetti, *Lucia di Lammermoor*. With Giuseppe di Stefano (Edgardo), Rolando Panerai (Enrico), Nicola Zaccaria (Raimondo). Herbert von Karajan conducting. Performance of September 29, La Scala at the Berlin Staatsoper.

Bellini, *Norma*. With Giulietta Simionato (Adalgisa), Mario del Monaco (Pollione), Nicola Zaccaria (Oroveso). Antonino Votto conducting. Performance of December 7, La Scala, Milan.

1956

Verdi, *La Traviata.* With Gianni Raimondi (Alfredo), Ettore Bastianini (Giorgio). Carlo Maria Giulini conducting. Performance of January 19, La Scala, Milan.

Rossini, *Il Barbiere di Siviglia.* With Tito Gobbi (Figaro), Luigi Alva (Almaviva), Melchiore Luise (Bartolo), Nicola Rossi-Lemeni (Basilio). Carlo Maria Giulini conducting. Performance of February 15, La Scala, Milan.

Donizetti, *Lucia di Lammermoor.* With Gianni Raimondi (Edgardo), Rolando Panerai (Enrico), Antonio Zerbini (Raimondo). Franceso Molinari-Pradelli conducting. Performance of March 22, Teatro San Carlo, Naples

Verdi, *Il Trovatore.* With Fedora Barbieri (Azucena), Giuseppe di Stefano (Manrico), Rolando Panerai (di Luna), Nicola Zaccaria (Ferrando). Herbert von Karajan conducting the orchestra and chorus of La Scala. Recorded August 3–9. [EMI]

Puccini, *La Bohème.* With Anna Moffo (Musetta), Giuseppe di Stefano (Rodolfo), Rolando Panerai (Marcello). Antonino Votto conducting the orchestra and chorus of La Scala. Recorded August 20–25, September 3–4. [EMI]

Verdi, *Un Ballo in Maschera.* With Fedora Barbieri (Ulrica), Eugenia Ratti (Oscar), Giuseppe di Stefano (Riccardo), Tito Gobbi (Renato.) Antonino Votto conducting the orchestra and chorus of La Scala. Recorded September 4–12. [EMI]

Donizetti, *Lucia di Lammermoor.* With Giuseppe Campora (Edgardo), Enzo Sordello (Enrico), Nicola Moscona (Raimondo). Fausto Cleva conducting. Performance of December 8, Metropolitan Opera, New York.

1957

Rossini, *Il Barbiere de Siviglia.* With Tito Gobbi (Figaro), Luigi Alva (Almaviva). Alceo Galliera conducting the Philharmonia Orchestra and Chorus. Recorded February 7–14. [EMI]

Bellini, *La Sonnambula.* With Fiorenza Cossotto (Teresa), Eugenia Ratti (Lisa), Nicola Monti (Elvino), Nicola Zaccaria (Rodolfo). Antonino Votto conducting the chorus and orchestra of La Scala. Recorded March 3–9. [EMI]

Donizetti, *Anna Bolena.* With Giulietta Simionato (Jane Seymour),

Gianni Raimondi (Percy), Nicola Rossi-Lemeni (Henry VIII).
Gianandrea Gavazenni conducting. Performance of May 14, La
Scala, Milan.

Gluck, *Ifigenia in Tauride*. With Dino Dondi (Orest), Francesco Albanese (Pylade), Anselmo Colzani (Thoas). Nino Sanzogno conducting. Performance of June 1, La Scala, Milan.

Donizetti, *Lucia di Lammermoor*. With Eugenio Fernandi (Edgardo),
Rolando Panerai (Enrico), Giuseppe Modesti (Raimondo). Tullio
Serafin conducting. Concert performance of June 29, RAI, Rome.

Bellini, *La Sonnambula*. With Carlo Monto (Elvino), Nicola Zaccaria
(Rodolfo), Fiorenza Cossotto (Teresa). Antonino Votto conducting. Performance of La Scala at Cologne Opera House, July 4.

Puccini, *Turandot*. With Elisabeth Schwarzkopf (Liù), Eugenio Fernandi
(Calaf), Nicola Zaccaria (Timur). Tullio Serafin conducting the
orchestra and chorus of La Scala. Recorded July 9–15. [EMI]

Puccini, *Manon Lescaut*. With Giuseppe di Stefano (Des Grieux), Giulio
Fioravanti (Lescaut). Tullio Serafin conducting the orchestra and
chorus of La Scala. Recorded July 18–27. [EMI]

Bellini, *La Sonnambula*. With Fiorenza Cossotto (Teresa), Nicola Monti
(Elvino), Nicola Zaccaria (Rodolfo). Antonino Votto conducting.
Performance of La Scala at King's Theater, Edinburgh, August 21.

Cherubini, *Medea*. With Miriam Pirazzini (Neris), Renata Scotto
(Glauce), Mirto Picchi (Jason), Giuseppe Modesti (Creon). Tullio
Serafin conducting the orchestra and chorus of La Scala. Recorded
September 12–19. [Mercury]

Verdi, *Un Ballo in Maschera*. With Giulietta Simionato (Ulrica), Eugenia Ratti (Oscar), Giuseppe di Stefano (Riccardo), Ettore Bastianini (Renato). Gianandrea Gavazzeni conducting. Performance
of December 7, La Scala, Milan.

1958

Verdi, *La Traviata*. With Alfredo Kraus (Alfredo), Mario Sereni (Giorgio). Franco Ghione conducting. Performance of March 27, Teatro
Nacional de São Carlos, Lisbon. [EMI]

Verdi, *La Traviata*. With Cesare Valletti (Alfredo), Mario Zanassi
(Giorgio). Nicola Rescigno conducting. Performance of June 20,
Covent Garden, London.

Cherubini, *Medea*. With Teresa Berganza (Neris), Jon Vickers (Jason),

Nicola Zaccaria (Creon). Nicola Rescigno conducting. Perform-ance of November 6, Civic Opera, Dallas.

1959

Bellini, *Il Pirata*. With Pier Miranda Ferraro (Gualtiero), Constantino Ego (Ernesto). Nicola Rescigno conducting. Concert Performance of January 27, American Opera Society, New York.

Donizetti, *Lucia di Lammermoor*. With Ferrucio Tagliavini (Edgardo), Piero Cappuccilli (Enrico), Bernard Ladysz (Raimondo). Tullio Serafin conducting the Philharmonia Orchestra and Chorus. Re-corded March 16–21. [EMI]

Cherubini, *Medea*. With Fiorenza Cossotto (Neris), Jon Vickers (Jason), Nicola Zaccaria (Creon). Nicola Rescigno conducting. Perform-ance of June 30, Covent Garden, London.

Ponchielli, *La Gioconda*. With Pier Miranda Ferraro (Enzo), Fiorenza Cossotto (Laura), Piero Cappuccilli (Barnaba), Ivo Vinco (Al-vise). Antonino Votto conducting the orchestra and chorus of La Scala. Recorded September 5–10. [EMI]

1960

Bellini, *Norma*. With Christa Ludwig (Adalgisa), Franco Corelli (Pol-lione), Nicola Zaccaria (Oroveso). Tullio Serafin conducting the orchestra and chorus of La Scala. Recorded September 5–12, 1960. [EMI]

Donizetti, *Poliuto*. With Franco Corelli (Poliuto), Ettore Bastianini (Severo), Nicola Zaccaria (Callistene). Antonino Votto conduct-ing. Performance of December 7, La Scala, Milan.

1961

Cherubini, *Medea*. With Giulietta Simionato (Neris), Jon Vickers (Ja-son), Nicolai Ghiaurov (Creon). Thomas Schippers conducting. Performance of December 11, La Scala, Milan.

1964

Puccini, *Tosca*. With Renato Cioni (Cavaradossi), Tito Gobbi (Scar-pia). Carlo Felice Cillario conducting. Performance of January 24, Covent Garden, London.

Bizet, *Carmen*. With Andréa Guiot (Micaëla), Nicolai Gedda (José),

Robert Massard (Escamillo). Georges Prêtre conducting the Choeurs René Duclos and Orchestre du Théâtre de l'Opéra. Recorded July 6–20. [EMI]

Puccini, *Tosca*. With Carlo Bergonzi (Cavaradossi), Tito Gobbi (Scarpia). Georges Prêtre conducting the chorus of the Théâtre National de l'Opéra de Paris and the orchestra of the Société des Concerts du Conservatoire. Recorded December 3–14. [EMI]

1965

Puccini, *Tosca*. With Franco Corelli (Cavaradossi), Tito Gobbi (Scarpia). Fausto Cleva conducting. Performance of March 19, Metropolitan Opera, New York.

Puccini, *Tosca*. With Richard Tucker (Cavaradossi), Tito Gobbi (Scarpia). Fausto Cleva conducting. Performance of March 25, Metropolitan Opera, New York.

Puccini, *Tosca*. With Renato Cioni (Cavaradossi), Tito Gobbi (Scarpia). Georges Prêtre conducting. Performance of July 5, Covent Garden, London.

Excerpts and Recitals

1949

Concert: "Liebestod" (in Italian), *Tristan und Isolde*; "Qui la voce," *I Puritani*; "Casta diva," *Norma*; "O patria mia," *Aida*. Francesco Molinari-Pradelli conducting the Turin RAI. Performance of March 7.

Puccini, *Turandot*. With Mario del Monaco (Calaf). Tullio Serafin conducting. Performance of May 20, Teatro Colón, Buenos Aires.

Bellini, *Norma*. With Fedora Barbieri (Adalgisa). Tullio Serafin conducting. Performance of June 17, Teatro Colón, Buenos Aires.

Recital: "Liebestod" (in Italian), *Tristan und Isolde*; "Casta diva," *Norma*; "Qui la voce," *I Puritani*. Arturo Basile conducting. Recorded November 8–10, Turin.

1950

Verdi, *Aida*. With Giulietta Simionato (Amneris), Kurt Baum (Radames), Robert Weede (Amonasro). Guido Picco conducting. Performance of June 3, Palacio de Bellas Artes, Mexico City.

Verdi, *Aida.* With Ebe Stignani (Amneris), Mirto Picchi (Radames), Giulio Neri (Ramfis). Vincenzo Bellezza conducting. Performance of October 2. Rome Opera.

1951

Concert: "Ecco l'orrido campo," *Un Ballo in Maschera;* "Io son Titanìa," *Mignon;* Proch's "Variations." Manno Wolf-Ferrari conducting. Broadcast of March 12, 1951, RAI, Turin.

Puccini, *Tosca.* With Gianni Poggi (Cavaradossi), Paolo Silveri (Scarpia). Antonino Votto conducting. Performance of September 24, Teatro Municipal, Rio de Janeiro.

1952

Concert, "Vieni t'affretta," *Macbeth;* "Ardon gli incensi," *Lucia di Lammermoor;* "Ben io t'invenni," *Nabucco;* "Dov'è l'indiana bruna," *Lakmé.* Oliviero de Fabritiis conducting. Broadcast of February 18, RAI, Rome.

Donizetti, *Lucia di Lammermoor.* Guido Picco, conducting. Performance of June 14, Palacio de Bellas Artes, Mexico City.

Recording session: "Non mi dir," *Don Giovanni.* Tullio Serafin conducting the orchestra of the Maggio Musicale Fiorentino, August. [EMI]

1953

Verdi, *Aida.* With Giulietta Simionato (Adalgisa), Kurt Baum (Radames), Jess Walters (Amonasro). Sir John Barbirolli conducting. Performance of June 4, Covent Garden, London.

1954

Donizetti, *Lucia di Lammermoor.* With Giuseppe di Stefano (Edgardo), Rolando Panerai (Enrico), Giuseppe Modesti (Raimondo). Herbert von Karajan conducting. Performance of January 18, La Scala, Milan.

Recital albums: (1) *Puccini Heroines:* "In quelle trine morbide," "Sola, perduta, abbandonata," *Manon Lescaut;* "Sì, mi chiamano Mimì," "Donde lieta uscì," *La Bohème;* "Un bel dì," "Tu, tu piccolo iddio," *Madama Butterfly;* "Senza mamma," *Suor Angelica;* "O mio babbino caro," *Gianni Schicchi;* "In questa reggia," "Tu che di gel sei cinta,"

Turandot [EMI]. (2) *Lyric/Coloratura*: "Io son l'umile ancella," "Poveri fiori," *Adriana Lecouvreur*; "Ebben? n'andrò lontano," *La Wally*; "La mamma morta," *Andrea Chénier*; "L'altra notte," *Mefistofele*; "Una voce poco fa," *Il Barbiere di Siviglia*; "Ombre légère," *Dinorah*; "Dov'è l'indiana bruna," *Lakmé*; "Mercè, dilette amiche," *I Vespri Siciliani*. Tullio Serafin conducting the Philharmonia Orchestra. Recorded September 15–21. [EMI]

Concert: "Tutte le torture," *Die Entführung aus dem Serail*; "Ombra leggera," *Dinorah*; "Depuis le jour," *Louise*; "D'amor al dolce impero," *Armida*. Alfredo Simonetto conducting. Concert of December 26, RAI, San Remo.

1955

Album recording: *Callas at La Scala*: "Dei tuoi figli, *Medea*; "Tu che invoco," "O Nume tutelar," "Caro oggetto," *La Vestale*; "Come per me," "Ah non credia," *La Sonnambula*. Tullio Serafin conducting the orchestra of La Scala. Recorded June 12. [EMI]

1956

Concert: "Tu che invoco," *La Vestale*; "Bel raggio," *Semiramide*; "Ai vostri giocchi," *Hamlet*; "Vieni al tempio," *I Puritani*. Alfredo Simonetto conducting. Concert of September 27, RAI, Milan.

Puccini, *Tosca* (excerpts from Act II). With George London. Dimitri Mitropoulos conducting the orchestra of the Metropolitan Opera, New York. The Ed Sullivan Show, New York, November 25, 1956.

1957

Concert: "D'amor sull'ali rosee," *Il Trovatore*; "Pace, pace," *La Forza del Destino*; "Liebestod," (in Italian), *Tristan und Isolde*; "Ai vostri giocchi," *Hamlet*; "Regnava nel silenzio," *Lucia di Lammermoor*. Antonino Votto conducting the Athens Festival Orchestra. Concert of August 5, Herodes Atticus, Athens.

Concert Rehearsal: "Tutte le torture," *Die Entführung aus dem Serail*; "Qui la voce," *I Puritani*; "Vieni t'affretta," *Macbeth*; "Ah, fors'è lui," *La Traviata*; "Al dolce guidami," *Anna Bolena*. Nicola Rescigno conducting the Dallas Symphony. Rehearsal of November 20, State Fair Music Hall, Dallas.

1958

Bellini, *Norma* (Act I). With Miriam Pirazzini (Adalgisa), Franco Corelli (Pollione). Gabriele Santini conducting. Performance of January 2, Rome Opera.

Recital: "Vissi d'arte," *Tosca*; "Una voce poco fa," *Il Barbiere di Siviglia*. John Pritchard conducting. Concert of June 17, BBC Television, London.

Recital: "Un bel dì," *Madama Butterfly*; "Casta diva," *Norma*. John Pritchard conducting. Concert of September 23, BBC Television, London.

Recital album: *Verdi Heroines I:* "Vieni t'affretta," "La luce langue," "Una macchia," *Macbeth*; "Ben io t'invenni," *Nabucco*; "Ernani involami," *Ernani*; "Tu che le vanità," *Don Carlo*. Nicola Rescigno conducting the Philharmonia Orchestra. Recorded September 19–24. [EMI]

Recital album: *Mad Scenes:* "Piangete voi," "Al dolce guidami," *Anna Bolena*; "A vos jeux, mes amis," *Hamlet*; "Col sorriso," *Il Pirata*. Nicola Rescigno conducting the Philharmonia Orchestra and Chorus. Recorded September 24–25. [EMI]

Concert: "Casta diva," *Norma*; "D'amor sull'ali rosee," "Miserere" (with Albert Lance), *Il Trovatore*; "Una voce poco fa," *Il Barbiere di Siviglia*; *Tosca*, Act II, with Albert Lance (Cavaradossi), Tito Gobbi (Scarpia). Georges Sebastian conducting the orchestra of the Théâtre National de l'Opéra. Performance of December 19, Opéra, Paris.

1959

Concerts: "Tu che invoco," *La Vestale*; "Vieni t'affretta," *Macbeth*; "Una voce poco fa," *Il Barbiere di Siviglia*; "Tu che le vanità," *Don Carlo*; "Col sorriso," *Il Pirata*. Nicola Rescigno conducting. Concerts of May 15, Musikhalle, Hamburg, and May 19, Liederhalle, Stuttgart.

Concert: "Tu che invoco," *La Vestale*; "Ernani involami," *Ernani*; "Tu che le vanità," *Don Carlo*; "Col sorriso," *Il Pirata*. Nicola Rescigno conducting. Concert of July 11, Concertgebouw, Amsterdam.

Concert: "Col sorriso," *Il Pirata*; "Una macchia," *Macbeth*. Nicola Rescigno conducting. Concert of September 23, Royal Festival Hall, London.

Concert: "Sì, mi chiamano Mimì," *La Bohème*; "L'altra notte," *Mefistofele.* Sir Malcolm Sargent conducting. Broadcast of October 3,
BBC Television, London.

1960

Studio recital: "Bel raggio," *Semiramide*; "D'amor al dolce impero,"
Armida; "Arrigo! ah parli a un core," *I Vespri Siciliani.* Antonio
Tonini conducting the Philharmonia Orchestra. Recorded July.
[EMI unpublished.]

1961

Album recital: *Callas in Paris (I):* "J'ai perdu mon Eurydice," *Orphée*;
"Divinités du Styx," *Alceste*; "Habanera," "Séguedille," *Carmen*;
"Printemps qui commence," "Amour viens aider," "Mon cœur
s'ouvre à ta voix," *Samson and Delilah*; "Je veux vivre," *Romeo and
Juliet*; "Je suis Titania," *Mignon*; "Pleurez mes yeux," *Le Cid*; "De-
puis le jour," *Louise.* Georges Prêtre conducting the Radiodiffusion
Française Orchestra. Recorded March 28–31, April 4–5. [EMI]
Studio recital: "Sorgete," *Il Pirata*; "Com'è bello," *Lucrezia Borgia*; "Nac-
qui all'affanno," *Cenerentola*; "Selva opaca," *William Tell*; "Legger
potessi in me," *Anna Bolena*; "Bel raggio," *Semiramide.* Antonio
Tonini conducting the Philharmonia Orchestra. Recorded November. [EMI. All unpublished except *Pirata*]

1962

Concert: "Ocean! thou mighty monster," *Oberon*; "La luce langue,"
Macbeth; "Nacqui all'affanno," *Cenerentola*; "Pleurez mes yeux,"
Le Cid; "Al dolce guidami," *Anna Bolena.* Georges Prêtre con-
ducting. Concert at Royal Festival Hall, London, February 27.
Concert: "O don fatale," *Don Carlo*; "Pleurez mes yeux," *Le Cid*; "Nac-
qui all'affanno," *Cenerentola*; "Habanera," "Séguedille," *Carmen*;
"Ernani involami," *Ernani.* Georges Prêtre conducting. Concert of
March 16. Musikhalle, Hamburg.
Studio recital: "Nacqui all'affanno," *Cenerentola*; "O don fatale," *Don
Carlo*; "Ocean! thou mighty monster," *Oberon.* Antonio Tonini
conducting the Philharmonia Orchestra. Recorded April. [EMI
unpublished.]

Concert: "Habanera," "Séguedille," *Carmen*. Charles Wilson, pianist. May 19, Madison Square Garden, New York.

Concert: "Tu che le vanità," *Don Carlo*; "Habanera," "Séguedille," *Carmen*. Georges Prêtre conducting. Concert of November 4, Covent Garden, London.

1963

Album recital: *Callas in Paris (II)*: "Malheureuse Iphigénie," *Iphigénie en Tauride*; "D'amour l'ardente flamme," *La Damnation de Faust*; "Comme autrefois," *Les Pêcheurs de Perles*; "Adieu notre petite table," "Je marche sur tous les chemins," *Manon*; "Air des lettres," *Werther*; "Il était un roi de Thulé," "Ah! je ris," *Faust*. Georges Prêtre conducting the orchestra of the Société des Concerts du Conservatoire. Recorded May 3–8. [EMI]

Concert: "Quando m'en vo," *La Bohème*. Georges Prêtre conducting. Concert of May 17, Deutsche Oper, Berlin.

Concert: "Bel raggio," *Semiramide*; "Quando m'en vo," *La Bohème*; "Casta diva," *Norma*; "Ben io t'invenni," *Nabucco*; "Tu, tu piccolo iddio," *Madama Butterfly*. Georges Prêtre conducting. Concert of May 23, Liederhalle, Stuttgart.

Concert: "Bel raggio," *Semiramide*. Georges Prêtre conducting. Concert of May 31, Royal Festival Hall, London.

Concert: "Bel raggio," *Semiramide*; "Nacqui all'affanno," *Cenerentola*; "Air des lettres," *Werther*; "Adieu notre petite table," *Manon*; "Ben io t'invenni," *Nabucco*; "Quando m'en vo," *La Bohème*; "Tu, tu piccolo iddio," *Madama Butterfly*; "O mio babbino caro," *Gianni Schicchi*. Georges Prêtre conducting the orchestra of the Société des Concerts du Conservatoire. Concert of June 5, Théâtre des Champs-Elysées, Paris.

Album recital: "Ah! Perfido!" Beethoven; "Ocean! thou mighty monster," *Oberon*; "Or sai che l'onore," "Non mi dir," "Mi tradì," *Don Giovanni*; "Porgi, amor," *Marriage of Figaro*. Nicola Rescigno conducting the orchestra of the Société des Concerts du Conservatoire. Recorded December 6–23, 1963, and January 8, 1964. [EMI]

Album recital: *Verdi Heroines II*: "Salce, salce," "Ave Maria," *Otello*; "Ah! degli scanni," "Ciel, ch'io respiri," *Aroldo*; "O don fatale," "Non pianger, mia compagna," *Don Carlo*. Nicola Rescigno conducting the orchestra of the Société des Concerts du Conservatoire.

Recorded December 17–27, 1963, and February 20, 21, 1964. [EMI]

Album recital: "Nacqui all'affanno," *Cenerentola*; "Selva opaca," *William Tell*; "Bel raggio," *Semiramide*; "Convien partir," *La Fille du Régiment*; "Com'è bello," *Lucrezia Borgia*; "Prendi, per me," *L'Elisir d'Amore*. Nicola Rescigno conducting the orchestra of the Société des Concerts du Conservatoire. Recorded December 4–23, 1963, and April 13–24, 1964. [EMI]

1964

Album recital: "Liberamente or piangi," *Attila*; "Se vano è il pregare," "Te vergine," *I Lombardi*; "Ritorna vincitor," *Aida*; "Tacea la notte," "D'amor sull'ali rosee," *Il Trovatore*; "Ecco l'orrido campo," "Morrò, ma prima in grazia," *Un Ballo in Maschera*; "Arrigo! ah parli a un core," *Vespri Siciliani*. Nicola Rescigno conducting the orchestra of the Société des Concerts du Conservatoire. Recorded February 21 and April 7–22. [EMI. "D'amor sull'ali rosee" and "Te vergine" unpublished.]

Verdi, *Aida* (Nile duet). With Franco Corelli. Georges Prêtre conducting. Recorded June, Paris. [EMI, unpublished.]

1965

Puccini, *Tosca* (excerpts). With Renato Cioni (Cavaradossi), Tito Gobbi (Scarpia). Georges Prêtre conducting. Performances of March 1 and March 3, Paris Opéra.

Bellini, *Norma* (excerpts). With Gianfranco Cecchele (Pollione), Giulietta Simionato/Fiorenza Cossotto (Adalgisa), Ivo Vinco (Oroveso). Georges Prêtre conducting. Performances of May 14, 17, 21, 29, 1965, Paris Opéra.

1969

Album recital: "Non so le tetre immagini," "Vola talor," *Il Corsaro*; "Liberamente or piangi," *Attila*; "Arrigo! ah parli a un core," *I Vespri Siciliani*; "Te vergine," *I Lombardi*. Nicola Rescigno conducting the orchestra of the Société des Concerts du Conservatoire. Recorded February and March. [EMI, unpublished, except *Corsaro*.]

1972

Duets: "Io vengo a domandar," *Don Carlo*; "Già nella notte densa," *Otello*; "Qual prode," *I Vespri Siciliani*; "Ah! per sempre," *La Forza del Destino*; "Pur ti riveggo," *Aida*. With Giuseppe di Stefano. Antonio de Almeida conducting the London Symphony. Recorded November 30–December, 1972, and Spring, 1973. [Philips, unpublished.]

1973

Concerts: "Io vengo a domandar," *Don Carlo*; "Qual prode," *I Vespri Siciliani*; "Final Duet," *Carmen*; "Garden Duet," *Faust*; "Suicidio," *La Gioconda*; "Tu qui Santuzza," "Voi lo sapete," *Cavalleria Rusticana*; "O mio babbino caro," *Gianni Schicchi*. With Giuseppe di Stefano. Ivor Newton, piano. Concerts of October 25 (Hamburg), October 29 (Berlin), November 2 (Düsseldorf), November 6 (Munich), November 9 (Frankfurt), November 26 and December 2 (London).

1974

Concerts: Excerpts from 1974 concerts.

Concert: "Habanera" and "Final Duet," *Carmen*; "Voi lo sapete" and "Tu qui Santuzza," *Cavalleria Rusticana*; "O mio babbino caro," *Gianni Schicchi*; "Una parola, Adina," *L'Elisir d'Amore*. With Giuseppe di Stefano. Robert Sutherland, piano. Concert of October 24, Fukuoka, Japan.

Selected Annotated Bibliography

Ardoin, John. *The Callas Legacy.* New York: Charles Scribner's Sons, 1982. An admirably objective study of Callas's art as revealed in her recordings.

Ardoin, John, and Gerald Fitzgerald. *Callas.* New York: Holt, Rinehart and Winston, 1974. A splendid pictorial biography, with the quality of the text matching that of the photographs.

Callas, Evangelia. *My Daughter, Maria Callas.* New York: Fleet, 1960. Memoirs that portray Callas as a wretched ingrate but in no way illuminate her career or art.

Callas, Maria, and Anita Pensotti. "Memoirs," *Oggi,* January and February 1957. Callas recounts her life up to 1956, with great emphasis on what she perceives as her ordeals.

Galatopoulos, Stelios. *Callas: La Divina.* London: J. M. Dent and Sons, 1966. A sympathetic but barely literate account of Callas's career.

Goise, Denis. *Maria Callas, la diva, scandale.* Paris: G. Authier, 1978. A breathless, gossipy retelling of Callas's life, with the major focus on the last years. Trashy beyond words.

Jellinek, George. *Callas: Portrait of a Prima Donna.* New York: Arno Press, 1978. A reissue of the 1960 edition. The quality of the photographs has suffered in the reprinting, but the text remains first-class. Jellinek admires Callas's art and writes of it with clarity and enthusiasm.

Linakis, Steven. *Diva: The Life and Death of Maria Callas.* Englewood Cliffs, N.J., Prentice-Hall, 1980. In what often seems a parody of the style associated with hard-boiled detective-narrators, Linakis writes of the cousin he hardly knew.

The results are not flattering to Callas or Onassis, but they do even less credit to the author. These memoirs are best read for their unconscious hilarity.

Lorcey, Jacques. *Maria Callas: D'art et d'amour*. Paris: Éditions PAC, 1983. A huge volume (615 pages) with excellent photographs. The text represents a largely uncredited synthesis of existing materials and tries the reader's patience with plot synopses of every opera in which Callas appeared. All in all, a well-intentioned work that would have benefited from the firm hand of an exacting editor.

Maria Callas. Moscow: Progress, 1978. A collection of translated articles and interviews assembled as a labor of love by a number of Callas's Moscow admirers. Of primary interest are the photographs of Callas in Moscow, where she served as a judge for the Tchaikovsky Competition.

Marchand, Polyvios, ed., *Maria Callas*. Athens: Gnosi Publications, 1983. An invaluable collection of documents related to Callas's career in Greece. (In Greek.)

Meneghini, Giovanni Battista. *My Wife Maria Callas*. Translated, with an introduction, by Henry Wisneski. New York: Farrar, Straus & Giroux, 1982. A sad book that unwittingly skewers both Meneghini and Callas. Callas's letters as well as the section on the negotiations with the Met are revelatory in a disheartening way.

Picchetti, María Teresa, and Marta Teglia. *El arte de Maria Callas como metalenguaje*. Buenos Aires: Editorial Bocarte, 1969. A ludicrous attempt to bring structuralism to bear on Callas's art. All the dichotomies and polarities turn out to revolve around Callas and Tebaldi. The book is funny until it becomes irritating.

Rémy, Pierre-Jean. *Maria Callas: A Tribute*. Translated by Catherine Atthill. New York: St. Martin's Press, 1978. A well-written, sensitive biography and appreciation that draws a clear distinction between fact and lore, i.e., gossip.

Segalini, Sergio. *Callas: Les images d'une voix*. Paris: F. Van de Velde, 1979. The most substantial pictorial biography yet to appear. Many rare photographs. A beautiful book.

Stassinopoulos, Arianna. *Maria Callas: The Woman behind the Legend*. New York: Simon & Schuster, 1981. Stassinopoulos apparently has no genuine interest in Callas's artistry. The result is a popular biography that is somehow obscene in its very conception. One reads the book with fascination and then rushes to shower afterward.

Wisneski, Henry. *Maria Callas: The Art behind the Legend*. Garden City, N.Y.: Doubleday, 1975. A pioneering biography in pictures, the text for which does them all justice.

Guide to Works and Composers

Adriana Lecouvreur—Cilea
Aida—Verdi
Alceste—Gluck
Andrea Chénier—Giordano
Anna Bolena—Donizetti
Armida—Rossini
Aroldo—Verdi
Atalanta—Handel
Attila—Verdi
Il Barbiere di Siviglia—Rossini
Der Bettelstudent—Millöcker
Boccaccio—von Suppé
La Bohème—Puccini
Carmen—Bizet
Cavalleria Rusticana—Mascagni
La Cenerentola—Rossini
Le Cid—Massenet
Les Contes d'Hoffmann—Offenbach
Il Corsaro—Verdi
La Damnation de Faust—Berlioz
Dido and Aeneas—Purcell
Dinorah—Meyerbeer
Don Carlo—Verdi
Don Giovanni—Mozart
L'Elisir d'Amore—Donizetti
Die Entführung aus dem Serail—Mozart

Faust—Gounod
Fedora—Giordano
Fidelio—Beethoven
La Forza del Destino—Verdi
Der Freischütz—Weber
Gianni Schicchi—Puccini
La Gioconda—Ponchielli
Guillaume Tell—Rossini
Hamlet—Thomas
Iphigénie en Tauride—Gluck
Lakmé—Delibes
I Lombardi—Verdi
Louise—Charpentier
Lucia di Lammermoor—Donizetti
Lucrezia Borgia—Donizetti
Macbeth—Verdi
Madama Butterfly—Puccini
Manon—Massenet
Manon Lescaut—Puccini
Medea—Cherubini
Mefistofele—Boito
Mignon—Thomas
Nabucco—Verdi
Norma—Bellini
Le Nozze di Figaro—Mozart
Oberon—Weber

Orfeo ed Euridice—Haydn

Orphée—Gluck

Otello—Rossini

Otello—Verdi

Pagliacci—Leoncavallo

Parsifal—Wagner

Les Pêcheurs de Perles—Bizet

Il Pirata—Bellini

Poliuto—Donizetti

Ho Protomastoras—Kalomiras

La Reine de Saba—Gounod

Rigoletto—Verdi

Roméo et Juliette—Gounod

Samson et Dalila—Saint-Saëns

Semiramide—Rossini

La Sonnambula—Bellini

Suor Angelica—Puccini

Thaïs—Massenet

Tiefland—d'Albert

Tosca—Puccini

La Traviata—Verdi

Tristan und Isolde—Wagner

Il Trovatore—Verdi

Turandot—Puccini

Il Turco in Italia—Rossini

I Vespri Siciliani—Verdi

La Vestale—Spontini

Die Walküre—Wagner

La Wally—Catalani

Werther—Massenet